Study Guide

Human Development
A Life-Span View

SIXTH EDITION

Robert V. Kail
Purdue University

John C. Cavanaugh
Pennsylvania State System of Higher Education

Prepared by

Dea K. DeWolff

Terri A. Tarr
Indiana University
Purdue University Indianapolis

WADSWORTH
CENGAGE Learning

Australia • Brazil • Japan • Korea • Mexico • Singapore • Spain • United Kingdom • United States

For product information and technology assistance, contact us at **Cengage Learning Customer & Sales Support, 1-800-354-9706**

For permission to use material from this text or product, submit all requests online at **www.cengage.com/permissions** Further permissions questions can be emailed to **permissionrequest@cengage.com**

ISBN-13: 978-1-111-83617-7
ISBN-10: 1-111-83617-5

Wadsworth
20 Davis Drive
Belmont, CA 94002-3098
USA

Cengage Learning is a leading provider of customized learning solutions with office locations around the globe, including Singapore, the United Kingdom, Australia, Mexico, Brazil, and Japan. Locate your local office at: **www.cengage.com/global**

Cengage Learning products are represented in Canada by Nelson Education, Ltd.

To learn more about Wadsworth, visit **www.cengage.com/wadsworth**

Purchase any of our products at your local college store or at our preferred online store **www.cengagebrain.com**

Printed in the United States of America
1 2 3 4 5 6 7 16 15 14 13 12

TABLE OF CONTENTS

How to Use This Book

- Skim the text, paying attention to chapter outlines and outline headings.
- Before reading each section in the textbook, read the **Learning Objectives** at the beginning of the section.
- After reading each section, try to answer the **Test Yourself** questions at the end of each section in the textbook.

In the *Study Guide*:

- Read **To Master the Learning Objectives** for each section and try to answer each question on a separate piece of paper.
- Complete each section of the study guide. On **Know the Terms** sections, try to figure out the answers before looking at your choices.
- At the end of each chapter, integrate the chapter information by completing the **Summary**.
- Test yourself using the **Multiple-Choice** and **Essay** questions.
- Check your answers and re-read the pages that are associated with each question that you could not answer correctly.

THE STUDY OF HUMAN DEVELOPMENT

1.1   Thinking about Development

1.2   Developmental Theories

1.3   Doing Developmental Research

This chapter includes a discussion of developmental theories and research, a look at common influences and issues in development, and the methods that developmentalists use to make discoveries.

1.1 THINKING ABOUT DEVELOPMENT

TO MASTER THE LEARNING OBJECTIVES:

What fundamental issues of development have scholars addressed throughout history?

- Explain how one's genes (nature) and one's environment (nurture) interact with each other to influence development.

- Explain the difference between continuous and discontinuous development, and be able to give examples of both types of development.

- Explain the difference between context-specific and universal development.

What are the basic forces in the biopsychosocial framework? How does the timing of these forces make a difference in their impact?

- Define the biopsychosocial framework. Give examples of biological, psychological, sociocultural, and life-cycle forces in development, and know how they interact to shape development.

How does neuroscience enhance our understanding of human development?

- Define neuroscience and explain what issues it can help us understand.

1.1 KNOW THE TERMS

Biological forces	Nature-nurture
Biopsychosocial framework	Neuroscience
Continuity-discontinuity	Psychological forces
Human development	Sociocultural
Life-cycle forces	Universal versus context-specific

1. _____ is the multidisciplinary study of how people change and how they remain the same over time.

2. The _____ issue addresses the degree to which genetic influences and environmental influences determine the type of person you are.

3. The _____ issue is concerned with whether a particular developmental phenomenon follows a smooth progression throughout the life-span or whether it follows a series of abrupt shifts.

4. The issue of whether there is one path of development or several is addressed by the _____ issue.

5. The _____ on development include all genetic and health-related factors that affect development.

6. The _____ on development include all internal perceptual, cognitive, emotional, and personality factors that affect development.

7. Interpersonal, societal, cultural, and ethnic factors are the _____ forces that influence development.

8. Differences in how the same event may affect people of different ages are called _____.

9. The _____ is used to organize biological, psychological, and sociocultural influences on development.

10. _____ is the study of the brain and nervous system, especially in terms of brain-behavior relationships.

1.1 KNOW THE DETAILS OF THINKING ABOUT DEVELOPMENT

1. Any one particular feature of development is caused exclusively by either a genetic or an environmental influence.

   TRUE or FALSE

2. Nurture refers to genetic or hereditary influences that influence development.

   TRUE or FALSE

3. The continuity-discontinuity issue addresses the question of whether development occurs in a smooth progression throughout the life-span or in a series of abrupt shifts.

   TRUE or FALSE

4. A developmentalist who takes a universal view of development would say that development occurs in fundamentally different ways depending on the context.

   TRUE or FALSE

5. Biological forces in development include all genetic and health-related factors that affect development.

   TRUE or FALSE

6. Cognitive, emotional, personality, and perceptual factors are psychological forces that can affect development.

   TRUE or FALSE

7. Life-cycle forces cause the same event to have different effects on people depending on their age.

   TRUE or FALSE

8. The biopsychosocial framework emphasizes that forces work alone to explain human development.

   TRUE or FALSE

9. Puberty and menopause are examples of sociocultural forces.

   TRUE or FALSE

10. All biological forces are determined by our genetic codes.

    TRUE or FALSE

11. Parents, friends, institutions, and society are all sociocultural forces.

    TRUE or FALSE

12. Neuroscientific approaches can be used to show interactions between biological, psychological, sociocultural, and life-cycle forces.
TRUE or FALSE

1.2 DEVELOPMENTAL THEORIES

TO MASTER THE LEARNING OBJECTIVES:

What is a developmental theory?

- Define developmental theory.

How do psychodynamic theories account for development?

- Describe how one moves through Erikson's stages of psychosocial development.

- Define epigenetic principle.

What is the focus of learning theories of development?

- Explain the operant conditioning principles of reinforcement and punishment.

- Explain how imitation (or observational learning) and self-efficacy influence behavior.

How do cognitive-developmental theories explain changes in thinking?

- Describe how Piaget would explain the process of development.

- Describe how information processing theory explains development.

- Describe Vygotsky's theory and the importance of social context to development.

What are the main points in the ecological and systems approach?

- Explain the roles of the microsystem, mesosystem, exosystem, and macrosystem in development according to Bronfenbrenner's ecological theory.

- Describe the competence-environmental press theory.

What are the major tenets of life-span and life-course theories?

- Describe the life-span perspective, including multidirectionality, plasticity, historical context, multiple causation, and selective optimization with compensation.

- Describe the life-course perspective, including timing of life events, synchronization of individual and familial transitions, and impact of earlier life events.

1.2 KNOW THE TERMS

Competence	Microsystems
Ecological theory	Observational
Environmental "press"	Operant conditioning
Epigenetic principle	Punishment
Exosystems	Psychodynamic
Information-processing theory	Psychosocial
Life-course perspective	Reinforcement
Life-span perspective	Selective optimization with compensation
Macrosystems	Self-efficacy
Mesosystems	Theory

1.   In human development, a _____ is an organized set of ideas that is designed to explain development.

2.   _____ theories propose that development is determined by how well people resolve conflicts they face at different ages.

3.   Erikson's _____ theory proposes that personality development is the result of the interaction of an internal maturational plan and external societal demands.

4.   The _____ of Erikson's theory means that each psychosocial strength has its own special period of particular importance.

5.   According to B.F. Skinner, in _____, the consequences of a behavior determine whether a behavior is repeated in the future.

6.   A _____ is a consequence that increases the future likelihood of the behavior that if follows.

7.   A _____ is a consequence that decreases the future likelihood of the behavior that it follows. This could include spanking and withdrawal of privileges.

8.   Learning by simply watching other people is called imitation or _____ learning.

9.   Peoples' beliefs about their own abilities and talents are called _____. These beliefs may determine when people will imitate others.

10. The _____ proposes that human cognition consists of mental hardware and software.

11. According to _____, human development cannot be separated from the environmental contexts in which a person develops (see figure).

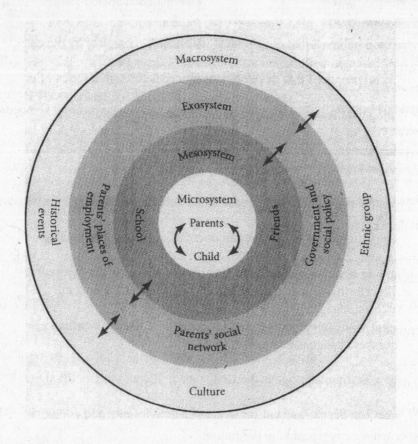

12. According to Bronfenbrenner, one's _____ includes the people, such as parents, and objects in one's immediate environment.

13. Bronfenbrenner's_____ include the interrelations between one's microsystems.

14. Bronfenbrenner's _____ are social settings that influence one's development even though one does not experience them first hand.

15. According to Bronfenbrenner, the _____ includes the cultures and subcultures in which the microsystems, mesosystems, and exosystems are embedded.

16. According to the competence-environmental press theory, people adapt the best when there is a good match between their abilities, or _____, and the demands of the environment.

17. According to the competence-environmental press theory, the demands of one's environment are known as _____.

18. The _____ is the view that development is determined by many forces and cannot be understood within a single framework.

19. The basic assumption of the _____ model is that the processes of selection, compensation, and optimization form a system that generates and regulates development and aging.

20. The _____ describes the ways different generations experience biological, psychological, and sociocultural forces in their various historical contexts.

1.2 KNOW THE DETAILS OF DEVELOPMENTAL THEORIES

1. Psychodynamic theories focus on how learning shapes behavior.
   TRUE or FALSE

2. Conflicts play a major role in development according to psychodynamic theories.
   TRUE or FALSE

3. Bandura, Erikson, and Piaget all proposed psychodynamic theories of development.
   TRUE or FALSE

4. Erikson proposed that development proceeds through a series of eight stages.
   TRUE or FALSE

5. Ecological theories are based on the epigenetic principle.
   TRUE or FALSE

6. John Watson, a proponent of behaviorism, believed that genes have a stronger influence on development than experience.
   TRUE or FALSE

7. According to operant conditioning theory, the consequences of a behavior determine whether the behavior is repeated in the future.
   TRUE or FALSE

8. Negative reinforcement increases the likelihood that a behavior will occur in the future.
   TRUE or FALSE

9. Observational learning is a component of operant conditioning.
   TRUE or FALSE

10. Bandura believes that self-efficacy plays a major role in determining whether someone will attempt a task.
    TRUE or FALSE

11. Cognitive-developmental theorists focus on the ways in which people think and how these processes change over time.

    TRUE or FALSE

12. The sensorimotor stage is the first stage in Piaget's theory of cognitive development.

    TRUE or FALSE

13. According to Piaget, human cognition consists of mental hardware and mental software.

    TRUE or FALSE

14. Vygotsky views development as an apprenticeship.

    TRUE or FALSE

15. According to ecological theory, human development is inseparable from the environmental contexts in which a person develops.

    TRUE or FALSE

16. In Bronfenbrenner's theory, the mesosystem refers to the broadest environmental context, such as the culture, in which an individual develops.

    TRUE or FALSE

17. The exosystem refers to social settings that a person may not experience firsthand but that still influence development.

    TRUE or FALSE

18. The competence-environmental press theory postulates that how well people adapt is a function of the match between a person's abilities and the demands put on them by the environment.

    TRUE or FALSE

19. According to the life-span perspective, human development is determined primarily by biological forces.

    TRUE or FALSE

20. Multidirectionality, plasticity, historical context, and multiple causation are key features of the life span perspective.

    TRUE or FALSE

21. Elective selection, loss-based selection, and compensation are three processes featured in the information-processing approach.

    TRUE or FALSE

22. The life-course perspective describes how biological, psychological, and sociocultural forces of development affect generations differently within their own historical contexts.

    TRUE or FALSE

1.3 DOING DEVELOPMENTAL RESEARCH

TO MASTER THE LEARNING OBJECTIVES:

How do scientists measure topics of interest in studying human development?

- Define systematic observation, structured observation, naturalistic observation, sampling behavior with tasks, self-reports, reliability, validity, populations, and samples.

What research designs are used to study human development?

- Know the differences between correlational and experimental studies.
- Explain what positive correlations, negative correlations, and the strength of a correlation coefficient mean.
- Explain the difference between independent and dependent variables.
- Describe qualitative research.
- Describe the advantages and disadvantages of cross-sectional, longitudinal, and sequential research designs.

How do researchers integrate results from multiple studies?

- Describe meta-analysis.

What ethical procedures must researchers follow?

- Know the ethical procedures that researchers should follow.

How do investigators communicate results from research studies?

- Know what information is contained in journal citations.

How does research affect public policy?

- Give examples of how research has affected public policy.

1.3 KNOW THE TERMS

Cohort effects   Population

Correlational study   Qualitative research

Correlation coefficient   Reliability

Cross-sectional   Sample

Dependent variable   Self-reports

Experiment   Sequential

Independent variable   Structured observations

Longitudinal   Systematic observation

Meta-analysis   Validity

Naturalistic observation

1. _____ involves watching people and carefully recording what they do or say.

2. In _____, people are observed as they behave spontaneously in some real-life situation.

3. In _____, a researcher creates a setting that is particularly likely to elicit the behavior of interest.

4. _____ are people's answers to questions about the topic of interest.

5. The _____ of a measure is the extent to which it provides a consistent index of a characteristic.

6. The _____ of a measure refers to whether or not it really measures what researchers think it measures.

7. A _____ is a broad group of people who are of interest to researchers.

8. A subset of the population of interest is called a _____.

9. In a _____, investigators look at relations between variables as they exist naturally in the world.

10. A _____ expresses the strength and direction of a relation between two variables.

11. An _____ is a systematic way of manipulating key factors that a researcher thinks causes a particular behavior.

12. The factor that is manipulated by the researcher in an experiment is called the _____.

13. The behavior that is observed after other variables are manipulated is called the _____.

14. The _____ research method involves gaining an in-depth understanding of human behavior and what governs it.

15. _____research designs involve testing or observing the same people at different points in their lives.

16. A _____ research design involves testing people of different ages in a study to determine developmental differences.

17. _____are differences between age groups (cohorts) that are the result of environmental events.

18. _____studies are complex research designs that are based on cross-sectional and longitudinal approaches to research.

19. _____is a tool that allows researchers to synthesize the results of many studies to estimate the relations between variables.

1.3 KNOW THE DETAILS OF DOING DEVELOPMENTAL RESEARCH

1. Systematic observation involves watching people and carefully recording what they say or do.
   TRUE or FALSE

2. In naturalistic observations, the researcher creates a setting that is particularly likely to elicit the behavior of interest.
   TRUE or FALSE

3. A limitation of self-reports is that they may be invalid because of response bias.
   TRUE or FALSE

4. A weakness of physiological measures is that they are not specific in what they measure.
   TRUE or FALSE

5. The reliability of a measure depends on whether it really measures what researchers think it measures.
   TRUE or FALSE

6. Validity indicates the extent to which a measure provides a consistent index of a characteristic.
   TRUE or FALSE

7. A correlational study involves looking at relations between variables as they exist naturally in the world.
   TRUE or FALSE

8. When a correlation is less than 0, two variables are completely unrelated.
   TRUE or FALSE

9. A strength of correlational studies is that they can be used to determine cause and effect.
   TRUE or FALSE

10. In a correlational study, investigators systematically manipulate the key factors that they think cause a particular behavior.
    TRUE or FALSE

11. The factor that is manipulated in an experimental design is called the independent variable.
    TRUE or FALSE

12. Qualitative research involves gaining in-depth understanding of human behavior and what governs it.
    TRUE or FALSE

13. Researchers interested in the stability of a behavior should use a longitudinal design rather than a cross-sectional design.
    TRUE or FALSE

14. A cross-sectional study involves studying the same individuals repeatedly at different points in their lives.
    TRUE or FALSE

15. Cohort effects affect cross-sectional studies.
    TRUE or FALSE

16. Sequential designs are simpler and less expensive than either cross-sectional or longitudinal designs.
    TRUE or FALSE

17. Meta-analysis involves comparing the results of many studies.
    TRUE or FALSE

18. To conduct research ethically, investigators must submit their research proposals to review panels after they collect their data but before they submit their report to a scientific journal.
    TRUE or FALSE

SUMMARY

1.1 THINKING ABOUT HUMAN DEVELOPMENT

1. **What fundamental issues of development have scholars addressed throughout history?**

    Three main issues are prominent in the study of human development. The _____ issue involves the degree to which genetics and the environment influence human development. In general, theorists and researchers view nature and nurture as mutually _____ influences, meaning development is always shaped by both. The continuity-discontinuity issue focuses on whether the _____ explanations (continuity) or _____ explanations (discontinuity) must be used to explain changes in people over time. Continuity approaches emphasize _____ change and discontinuity approaches emphasize _____ change. In the issue of universal versus context-specific development, the question is whether development follows the _____ general path in all people or is fundamentally dependent on the sociocultural context.

2. **What are the basic forces in the biopsychosocial framework? How does the timing of these forces make a difference in their impact?**

    Development is based on the combined impact of four primary forces. _____ forces include all genetic and health-related factors that affect development. Many of these biological forces are determined by our _____ code.

    _____ forces include all internal perceptual, cognitive emotional, and personality factors that influence development. Collectively, these forces explain the most noticeable differences in people.

    Sociocultural forces include interpersonal, societal, _____, and ethnic factors that affect development. Culture consists of knowledge, attitudes, and _____ associated with a group of people. Overall, sociocultural forces provide the context or backdrop for development.

    _____ forces provide a context for understanding how people perceive their current situation and its effects on them.

    The _____ framework emphasizes that the forces are mutually interactive, and the fact that development cannot be understood by examining forces in isolation. Furthermore, the same event can have different effects depending on when it happens.

3. **How does neuroscience enhance our understanding of human development?**

    Neuroscience is the study of the brain and the nervous system, especially in terms of _____ relationships. Understanding brain activity shows how developmental forces interact.

1.2 DEVELOPMENTAL THEORIES

1. **What is a developmental theory?**

    Developmental theories _____ knowledge in order to provide testable _____ of human behaviors and the ways in which they change over time. Current approaches to developmental theory focus on specific aspects of behavior. At present, there is no single unified theory of human development.

2. **How do psychodynamic theories account for development?**

    Psychodynamic theories propose that behavior is determined by the way people deal with _____ they face at different ages. Erikson proposed a life-span theory of _____ development, consisting of eight universal stages, each characterized by a particular struggle.

3. **What is the focus of learning theories of development?**

    Learning theory focuses on the development of observable behavior. Operant conditioning is based on the notions of environmental control of behavior, _____, which increases the likelihood that a behavior will be repeated, and punishment, which _____ the likelihood that a behavior will be repeated. _____ theory proposes that people learn by observing others.

4. **How do cognitive-developmental theories explain changes in thinking?**

    Cognitive-developmental theory focuses on thought processes. Piaget proposed a four-stage _____ based on the notion that throughout development people create their own _____ to explain how the world works. According to information-processing theory, people deal with information like a _____, and development consists of increased _____ in handling information. Vygotsky emphasized the influence of _____ on development.

5. **What are the main points in the ecological and systems approach?**

    Bronfenbrenner proposed that development occurs in the context of several interconnected systems of increasing complexity. These systems include the _____, the mesosystem, the _____, and the macrosystem. The _____ theory postulates that there is a "best fit" between one's abilities and the demands placed on a person by the _____.

6. **What are the major tenets of the life-span and life-course theories?**

According to the life-span perspective, human development is characterized by multidirectionality, plasticity, historical context, and multiple causation. All four developmental forces are critical. _____ refers to the developmental trends to focus one's efforts and abilities in successively fewer domains as one ages and to acquire ways to compensate for normative losses. The life-course perspective refers to understanding human development within the context of the _____ period in which a generation develops that creates unique sets of experiences.

1.3 DOING DEVELOPMENTAL RESEARCH

1. **How do scientists measure topics of interest in studying human development?**

Research typically begins by determining how to measure the topic of interest. _____ observation involves recording peoples' behavior as it takes place either in a _____ setting (naturalistic observation) or a _____ setting (structured observation). Researchers sometimes create tasks to obtain samples of people's behavior. In _____, people answer questions posed by the experimenter. Physiological measures provide a way to examine body-behavior relationships. Researchers must determine that their measures are _____ and _____; they must also obtain a sample that is _____ of some larger population.

2. **What research designs are used to study human development?**

In correlational studies, investigators examine relations among variables as they occur _____. This relation is often measured by a correlation coefficient, r, which can vary from -1 (strong inverse relation) to 0 (no relation) to $+1$ (strong _____ relation). Correlational studies cannot determine cause and effect, so researchers do experimental studies in which a(n) _____ variable is manipulated, and the impact of this manipulation on a dependent variable is recorded. Experimental studies allow conclusions about cause and effect, but the strict control that is required of other variables often makes the situation artificial. The best approach is to use both experimental and correlational studies to provide converging evidence. Qualitative research permits in-depth analysis of behavior and is often used as a _____ step for, or in conjunction with, quantitative research.

To study development, some researchers use a _____ design in which the same people are observed repeatedly as they grow. This approach provides evidence concerning

15

actual patterns of individual growth but have several shortcomings as well: they are time-consuming, some people _____ of the project, and repeated testing can affect performance.

An alternative, the _____ design, involves testing people of differing ages. This design avoids the problems of the longitudinal design but provides no information about individual _____. Also, what appear to be age differences may be _____ effects. Because neither design is problem-free, the best approach involves using both designs to provide converging evidence. Sequential designs are based on multiple longitudinal and cross-sectional designs.

3. **How do researchers integrate results from multiple studies?**

   Meta-analysis provides a way for researchers to look for trends across _____ studies to estimate the relations among variables.

4. **What ethical procedures must researchers follow?**

   Planning research also involves selecting methods that preserve the rights of research _____. Experimenters must _____ the risks to potential research participants, describe the research so that potential participants can make an informed decision about participating, avoid _____, and keep results anonymous or confidential.

5. **How do investigators communicate results from research studies?**

   Once research data are collected and _____, investigators _____ the results in scientific outlets such as journals and books. Such results form the foundation of knowledge about human development.

6. **How does research affect public policy?**

   Research results are sometimes used to inform and _____ public policy. Controversial topics such as stem cell research also form the basis for public policy in terms of what types of research are _____.

TEST YOURSELF

MULTIPLE-CHOICE QUESTIONS

1. Peyton and his brother Eli are both outstanding athletes. Do they have similar athletic abilities because their parents reared them the same way, or because they both inherited athletic talent from their parents? Developmental theorists refer to this question as the _____ issue.
   a. continuity-discontinuity
   b. nature-nurture
   c. universal versus context-specific development
   d. life-cycle

2. An example of _____ in development occurs when a quiet, shy child becomes a quiet, shy adult.
   a. universality
   b. context-specificity
   c. continuity
   d. discontinuity

3. The universal versus context-specific development issue addresses the question of whether
   a. there is one path of development or several different paths.
   b. genes or environment most influence development.
   c. biopsychosocial forces interact or work independently.
   d. development occurs in a smooth progression or in a series of abrupt shifts.

4. The _____ framework emphasizes that human development involves the interaction of biological, psychological, and sociocultural forces.
   a. universal
   b. discontinuity
   c. life-cycle
   d. biopsychosocial

5. Internal perceptual, cognitive, emotional, and personality factors that affect development are referred to as _____ forces.

    a. sociocultural

    b. biological

    c. life-cycle

    d. psychological

6. A child's school is a _____ force that influences development.

    a. psychological

    b. life-cycle

    c. sociocultural

    d. biological

7. Arturo's age is a _____ factor that might influence the impact his parents' divorce has on his development.

    a. life-cycle

    b. biological

    c. psychological

    d. sociocultural

8. The study of the brain and the nervous system, especially in terms of brain-behavior relationships, is known as

    a. the biopsychosocial framework.

    b. neuroscience.

    c. information-processing theory.

    d. the life-span perspective.

9. _____theorists propose that the way that individuals resolve conflicts they encounter at different ages determines their development.

    a. Cognitive

    b. Learning

    c. Psychodynamic

    d. Ecological

10. The psychodynamic perspective has its roots in

    a. Watson's theory.

    b. Freud's theory.

    c. Bronfenbrenner's view.

    d. Piaget's theory.

11. Erikson's theory is based on the _____ principle, which suggests that each psychosocial issue has a period of time during which it is of most importance.

    a. elective selection

    b. epigenetic

    c. ecological

    d. optimization

12. In his psychosocial theory, Erikson

    a. considers development to be complete by adolescence.

    b. takes a cognitive-developmental approach.

    c. proposes a series of eight stages of development.

    d. emphasizes self-efficacy.

13. According to the principles of _____, the consequences of a behavior determine whether a behavior is repeated in the future.

    a. cognitive-developmental theory

    b. competence-environmental press theory

    c. information-processing theory

    d. operant conditioning

14. _____ is a consequence that decreases the likelihood that a particular behavior will occur in the future.

    a. Punishment

    b. Negative reinforcement

    c. Positive reinforcement

    d. Self-efficacy

15. Observational learning is an important component of

    a. operant conditioning.

    b. information-processing theory.

    c. psychodynamic theory.

    d. social learning theory.

19

16. A person's beliefs about his or her own abilities and talents is known as

    a. observational learning.

    b. the epigenetic principle.

    c. self-efficacy.

    d. operant conditioning.

17. Social-cognitive theory is associated with

    a. Freud.

    b. Skinner.

    c. Piaget.

    d. Bandura.

18. According to _____, children act like little scientists and create theories about the world.

    a. Erikson

    b. Piaget

    c. Bandura

    d. Bronfenbrenner

19. Piaget's theory is associated with which perspective?

    a. Psychodynamic

    b. Learning

    c. Cognitive-developmental

    d. Life-course

20. The computer is used as a metaphor for human thinking in

    a. cognitive-developmental theory.

    b. competence-environmental press theory.

    c. systems theory.

    d. information-processing theory.

21. According to _____ theory, you cannot separate human development from the context in which it occurs.

    a. ecological

    b. cognitive-developmental

    c. information-processing

    d. psychodynamic

22. Hannah lives with her mother, father, and younger sister. Bronfenbrenner would say that Hannah's immediate family is part of her
    a. mesosystem.
    b. exosystem.
    c. macrosystem.
    d. microsystem.

23. The match between a person's abilities and the demands put on them by the environment is of central importance in _____ theory.
    a. psychodynamic
    b. information-processing
    c. competence-environmental press
    d. life-cycle

24. According to the life-span perspective,
    a. development is essentially complete by adolescence.
    b. every period of a person's life can be understood apart from its origins.
    c. human development is multiply determined.
    d. all behavior is consistent across the life-span.

25. The idea that new skills can be learned even in late life is related to the concept of
    a. multidirectionality.
    b. plasticity.
    c. historical context.
    d. multiple causation.

26. Ivory decided to stop working overtime because her children have begun to need her at home nearly every evening, and on weekends to help them with homework and drive them to activities. This is an example of
    a. elective selection.
    b. loss-based selection.
    c. compensation.
    d. optimization.

27. The _____ describes the ways in which various generations experience the biological, psychological, and sociocultural forces of development in their respective historical contexts.

    a. ecological approach

    b. psychodynamic perspective

    c. cognitive-developmental approach

    d. life-course perspective

28. In a _____, people are observed as they behave spontaneously in some real-life situation.

    a. structured observation

    b. naturalistic observation

    c. self-report

    d. sampling of behavior with tasks

29. When scores on a test are very inconsistent from one administration to another, there is reason to be concerned about the test's

    a. correlation coefficient.

    b. cohort effects.

    c. validity.

    d. reliability.

30. Dr. Peters has decided to use class attendance as a measure of student motivation. Her colleague, Dr. Martin, expresses concern that attendance may be due to health rather than motivation. Dr. Martin is questioning the _____ of Dr. Peter's measure of motivation.

    a. reliability

    b. validity

    c. representativeness

    d. artificiality

31. In a life-span development course, a correlation of .90 was found between the amount of time students spent studying for the first exam and their scores on the exam. This means that

    a. students who studied more received lower scores.

    b. students who studied more received higher scores.

    c. students who studied less received 90s.

    d. the amount of time spent studying was not related to scores on the exam.

32. A weakness of correlational designs is that they
    a. are expensive to conduct.
    b. cannot be used to determine cause and effect.
    c. are often laboratory-based, so tend to be artificial.
    d. cannot be used to study the stability of behavior.

33. In a(n) _____ study, key factors are manipulated to determine what causes a particular behavior.
    a. correlational
    b. experimental
    c. sequential
    d. longitudinal

34. An investigator interested in the effect of noise on recall memory randomly assigns college students to either a quiet or a noisy condition and asks them to study a list of words for five minutes. They are tested later to determine the number of words on the list they can recall. In this study, the independent variable is _____, and the dependent variable is _____.
    a. the amount of time they were allowed to study the list; the amount of noise
    b. college students; the number of words recalled
    c. the number of words recalled; the amount of noise
    d. the amount of noise; the number of words recalled

35. Dr. Wong assessed the memory skills of the same group of children when they were 3, 5, 7, and 9 years of age. Dr. Wong conducted a _____ study.
    a. longitudinal
    b. cross-sectional
    c. sequential
    d. confounded

36. A disadvantage of longitudinal studies is
    a. cost.
    b. an inability to answer questions about the stability of behaviors.
    c. only correlational methods can be used.
    d. cohort effects complicate the interpretation of age differences.

37. An investigator studied friendship formation in 5-, 8-, and 11-year-olds by observing students new to a school at the beginning of the 2012-2013 school year. The researcher used a _____ design.
    a. longitudinal
    b. sequential
    c. cross-sectional
    d. confounded

38. When a cross-sectional design study is repeated over regular intervals, the research design is
    a. longitudinal.
    b. sequential.
    c. experimental.
    d. correlational.

39. Dr. Jefferson wants to compare the findings of many studies that measured the relation between parental divorce and academic achievement. What method would be most appropriate for him to use?
    a. Sequential
    b. Meta-analysis
    c. Correlational
    d. Experimental

ESSAY QUESTIONS

1. You are talking to a friend who says, "Development is the result of the genes that you inherit, and those genes put you on a developmental path which stays the same throughout your life. This path is the same for everybody." What can you tell your friend about the issues of nature versus nurture, continuity versus discontinuity, and universal versus context-specific development?

2. Your sister Kumi is having problems with her two-year-old daughter. Your niece, Kayla, has been throwing tantrums to get what she wants. As you watch Kumi and Kayla interact, you see that Kumi will say "no" to Kayla, Kayla will cry and scream, and then Kumi will give in to her. What can you tell Kumi about the principles of operant conditioning that might help her deal with the situation?

3.   A researcher is interested in determining if personality changes or stays the same as a person matures from young adulthood to old age. Should the researcher use a longitudinal or a cross-sectional research design? State the advantages and disadvantages of each type of research design.

ANSWERS WITH PAGE REFERENCES

1.1 KNOW THE TERMS

1. Human development (4)
2. nature-nurture (5)
3. continuity-discontinuity (6)
4. universal versus context-specific (6)
5. biological forces (7)
6. psychological forces (7)
7. sociocultural (7)
8. life-cycle forces (7)
9. bio psychosocial framework (7)
10. Neuroscience (11)

1.1 KNOW THE DETAILS OF THINKING ABOUT DEVELOPMENT

1. F, 5
2. F, 5
3. T, 6
4. F, 6
5. T, 7
6. T, 7
7. T, 7
8. F, 7
9. F, 8
10. F, 8
11. T, 8
12. T, 11

1.2 KNOW THE TERMS

1. theory (12)
2. Psychodynamic (12)
3. psychosocial (12)
4. epigenetic principle (12)
5. operant conditioning (13)
6. reinforcement (13)
7. punishment (13)
8. observational (13)
9. self-efficacy (14)
10. information-processing theory (15)
11. ecological theory (16)
12. microsystem (17)
13. mesosystems (17)
14. exosystems (17)
15. macrosystems (18)
16. competence (18)
17. Environmental "press" (18)
18. life-span perspective (18)
19. selective optimization with compensation (19)
20. life-course perspective (20)

25

1.2 KNOW THE DETAILS OF DEVELOPMENTAL THEORIES

1. F, 12	7. T, 13	13. F, 15	19. F, 18
2. T, 12	8. T, 13	14. T, 16	20. T, 19
3. F, 12	9. F, 13	15. T, 16	21. F, 19
4. T, 12	10. T, 14	16. F, 17	22. T, 20
5. F, 12	11. T, 14	17. T, 17	
6. F, 13	12. T, 15	18. T, 18	

1.3 KNOW THE TERMS

1. Systematic observation (23)
2. naturalistic observation (23)
3. structured observations (23)
4. Self-reports (24)
5. reliability (25)
6. validity (25)
7. population (26)
8. sample (26)
9. correlational study (26)
10. correlation coefficient (26)

11. experiment (27)
12. independent variable (27)
13. dependent variable (27)
14. qualitative research (28)
15. Longitudinal (29)
16. cross-sectional (30)
17. Cohort effects (30)
18. Sequential (30)
19. Meta-analysis (31)

1.3 KNOW THE DETAILS OF DOING DEVELOPMENTAL RESEARCH

1. T, 23	6. F, 25	11. T, 27	16. F, 31
2. F, 23	7. T, 26	12. T, 28	17. T, 31
3. T, 25	8. F, 26	13. T, 29	18. F, 32
4. F, 25	9. F, 26	14. F, 30	
5. F, 25	10. F, 27	15. T, 30	

SUMMARY

1.1 THINKING ABOUT HUMAN DEVELOPMENT

1. nature-nurture (5); interactive (5); same (5); different (6); quantitative (6); qualitative (6); same (6)

2. Biological (8); genetic (8); Psychological (8); cultural (8); behavior (8); Life-cycle (9); biopsychosocial (10)

3. brain-behavior (11)

1.2 DEVELOPMENTAL THEORIES

1. organize (12); explanations (12)

2. conflicts (112; psychosocial (12)

3. Reinforcement (13); decreases (13); Social learning (13)

4. universal (14); theories (14); computer (15); efficiency (16); culture (16)

5. microsystem (17); exosystem (17); competence-environmental press (18); environment (18)

6. Selective optimization with compensation (19); historical time (20)

1.3 DOING DEVELOPMENTAL RESEARCH

1. Systematic (23); natural (23); structured (23); self-reports (24); reliable (25); valid (25); representative (26)

2. naturally (26); positive (27); independent (27); preliminary (28); longitudinal (29); drop out (30); cross-sectional (30); growth (30); cohort (30)

3. multiple (30)

4. participants (32); minimize (32); deception (32)

5. analyzed (33); publish (33)

6. shape (33); permitted (34)

TEST YOURSELF

MULTIPLE-CHOICE QUESTIONS

1. b, 5	11. b, 12	21. a, 16	31.bB, 26
2. c, 6	12. c, 12	22. d, 17	32. b, 27
3. a, 6	13. d, 13	23. c, 18	33. b, 27
4. d, 7	14. a, 13	24. c, 18	34. d, 27
5. d, 8	15. d, 13	25. b, 19	35. a, 29
6. c, 8	16. c, 14	26. a, 19	36. a, 30
7. a, 9	17. d, 14	27. d, 20	37. c, 30
8. a, 11	18. b, 14	28. b, 23	38. b, 30
9. c, 12	19. c, 14	29. d, 25	39. b, 31
10. b, 12	20. d, 15	30. b, 25	

ESSAY QUESTIONS

1. You can tell your friend that both nature and nurture interact with each other to influence development. Virtually no features of development are shaped only by heredity or only by environment. While nature and nurture interact to direct development, both continuous changes and discontinuous changes occur throughout development. Some aspects of development will show a more continuous pattern while others will show discontinuous patterns. Finally, some aspects of development seem to apply to different people across cultures (universal) while other aspects seem to be specific to a particular culture or context. In other words, your friend's statement was incorrect, and perhaps he should take a course in life-span development to learn more about human development. (5-7)

2. You should tell Kumi that reinforcers increase the likelihood that behaviors will be repeated in the future. Reinforcers could include getting a toy, getting to play with something that you want even if your mother said "no," etc. By giving in to Kayla, Kumi is reinforcing her tantrums and increasing the likelihood that Kayla will throw another one. Instead, Kumi should be punishing Kayla's tantrums because punishment decreases the likelihood that a behavior will be repeated. Punishments can include things such as spankings, being sent to one's room, having privileges taken away, or having a toy taken away. Kumi should stop giving in to Kayla because it only reinforces her tantrums. (13)

3. In a longitudinal study a measure of personality might be administered to a group of young adults at one point in time. When this group of adults is middle-aged, the personality measure would be administered again. Finally, when this group of adults reaches old age, the personality measure would be administered again. The main advantage of longitudinal studies is that they allow researchers to observe the stability or instability of behaviors such as personality. One disadvantage of longitudinal studies is the high cost associated with keeping up with a sample of people over a long period of time. A second disadvantage of longitudinal studies is that it is difficult to maintain the constancy of the sample over the course of the study. The people who drop out of the study may be significantly different from those people who stay in the study. This inconsistent sample may influence a researcher's results. A third disadvantage is that subjects in longitudinal studies may become "test-wise." In other words, people may show improvement over time because they become more familiar with the test each time they participate in the study. In a cross-sectional study, a measure of personality would be administered to a group of young adults, a group of middle-aged adults, and a group of older adults. The responses of the three groups would be compared to see if people of different ages show differences in personality. The main advantages of cross-sectional designs are that they avoid the costs of longitudinal designs and they avoid the problems of sample constancy and "test-wise" subjects. The major disadvantage of cross-sectional designs is that cohort effects may be present that make it difficult to draw conclusions about developmental change. Differences in personality between the three age groups may not be the result of age but may be the result of cohort effects. (29-31)

BIOLOGICAL FOUNDATIONS

2.1   In the Beginning: 23 Pairs of Chromosomes

2.2   From Conception to Birth

2.3   Influences on Prenatal Development

2.4   Labor and Delivery

This chapter discusses the role of heredity in shaping development, the stages of prenatal development, the influences on prenatal development, and the process of labor and delivery.

2.1 IN THE BEGINNING: 23 PAIRS OF CHROMOSOMES

TO MASTER THE LEARNING OBJECTIVES:

What are chromosomes and genes? How do they carry hereditary information from one generation to the next?

- Describe what happens to the red blood cells in sickle-cell anemia and why these changes have negative effects.

- Explain the difference between autosomes and sex chromosomes.

- Know the difference between chromosomes, DNA, and genes.

- Know the difference between genotype and phenotype.

- Explain the difference between being homozygous and heterozygous for a particular trait.

- Explain the difference between dominant alleles, recessive alleles, and incomplete dominance.

What are common problems involving chromosomes and what are their consequences?

- Describe how phenylketonuria and Huntington's disease are inherited.

- Describe the disorders associated with extra autosomes or abnormal sex chromosomes.

How is children's heredity influenced by the environment in which they grow up?

- Describe behavioral genetics and polygenic inheritance.

- Describe how twin studies, adoption studies, and the isolation of DNA segments are used to determine the role of heredity and environment.

- Describe the four general properties that describe the relation between genes and environment, including the concepts of heritability coefficient, niche-picking, and non-shared environmental influences.

2.1 KNOW THE TERMS

Alleles	Huntington's disease
Autosomes	Incomplete dominance
Behavioral genetics	Monozygotic
Chromosomes	Niche-picking
Deoxyribonucleic acid (DNA)	Non-shared environmental influences
Dizygotic	Phenotype
Dominant	Phenylketonuria
Gene	Polygenic inheritance
Genotype	Recessive
Heritability coefficient	Sex chromosomes
Heterozygous	Sickle-cell trait
Homozygous	

1. _____ are the threadlike structures in the nuclei of the sperm and egg that contain genetic material.

2. The first 22 pairs of chromosomes are called _____.

3. The 23rd pair of chromosomes that determine the sex of the child are called the _____.

4. Each chromosome consists of one molecule of _____.

5. A _____ consists of compounds that provide a specific set of biochemical instructions.

6. The complete set of genes makes up a person's heredity and is known as the person's _____.

7. One's _____ includes physical, behavioral, and psychological features that are the result of the interaction between one's genes and environmental influences.

8. Different forms of genes are called _____.

9. An individual is _____ if both alleles in a pair of chromosomes are the same.

10. An individual is _____ if the alleles in a pair of chromosomes differ from each other.

11. When an allele is _____, its chemical instructions are followed.

12. When an allele is _____, its chemical instructions are ignored when the allele is combined with a dominant allele.

13. The situation where one allele does not completely dominate another is called _____.

14. _____ occurs in individuals who have one dominant allele for normal blood cells and one recessive sickle-cell allele. These individuals typically only have problems when they are seriously deprived of oxygen, such as when they engage in vigorous exercise or when they are at high altitudes.

15. _____ is an inherited disorder in which babies are born lacking an important liver enzyme.

16. _____ is a fatal disease characterized by the progressive degeneration of the nervous system.

17. The branch of genetics that deals with inheritance of behavioral and psychological traits is called _____.

18. _____ occurs when phenotypes are the result of the combined activity of many separate genes.

19. _____ twins are also called identical twins because they are the result of a single fertilized egg that split in two to form two new individuals.

20. Fraternal twins, or _____ twins, are the result of the fertilization of two separate eggs by two sperm.

21. A _____ is a measure of the extent to which a trait or characteristic is inherited.

22. The process of deliberately seeking environments that are compatible with one's heredity is called _____.

23. _____ are forces within a family that make children different from one another.

2.1 KNOW THE DETAILS OF IN THE BEGINNING: 23 PAIRS OF CHROMOSOMES

1. The first 22 pairs of chromosomes are called autosomes.
    TRUE or FALSE

2. The autosomal chromosomes determine the sex of the child.
    TRUE or FALSE

3. Chromosomes are composed of deoxyribonucleic acid.
    TRUE or FALSE

4. Genotypes, in combination with environmental influences, produce a phenotype, an individual's physical, behavioral, and psychological factors.
    TRUE or FALSE

5. When the alleles in a chromosome pair differ, the pair is heterozygous.
    TRUE or FALSE

6. In a heterozygous chromosome pair, the chemical instructions of the recessive allele are followed and those of the dominant allele are ignored.
    TRUE or FALSE

7. Incomplete dominance occurs in a chromosome pair when the chemical instructions of one allele are followed and those of the other allele are completely ignored.
    TRUE or FALSE

8. Infants born with phenylketonuria are missing an important liver enzyme.
    TRUE or FALSE

9. Most inherited disorders are carried by dominant alleles rather than by recessive alleles.
    TRUE or FALSE

10. Down syndrome is typically caused by a dominant allele that carries the disorder.
    TRUE or FALSE

11. Klinefelter's syndrome and Turner's syndrome are both disorders associated with abnormal sex chromosomes.
    TRUE or FALSE

12. Behavioral genetics is the branch of genetics that deals with the inheritance of behavioral and psychological traits.
    TRUE or FALSE

13. A polygenic pattern of genetic inheritance occurs when many different genes determine a characteristic.

    TRUE or FALSE

14. Monozygotic twins have identical genes.

    TRUE or FALSE

15. Fraternal twins are called dizygotic twins and come from two separate eggs fertilized by two separate sperm.

    TRUE or FALSE

16. The term heritability coefficient refers to the fact that children may deliberately pick environments that fit their heredity.

    TRUE or FALSE

17. Genes sometimes have a role in determining what kind of environment an individual experiences.

    TRUE or FALSE

18. The forces within a family that make children different from one another are referred to as non-shared environmental forces.

    TRUE or FALSE

2.2 FROM CONCEPTION TO BIRTH

TO MASTER THE LEARNING OBJECTIVES:

What happens to a fertilized egg in the first two weeks after conception?

- Describe the timing and the major events associated with the period of the zygote.

- Describe in vitro fertilization and how reproductive technologies are related to eugenics.

When do body structures and internal organs emerge in prenatal development?

- Describe the timing and the major events associated with the period of the embryo.

- Know which layers of the embryo will become which bodily system.

- Know the location and functions of the amnion, amniotic fluid, umbilical cord, and placenta.

- Know the difference between cephalocaudal and proximodistal growth.

When do body systems begin to function well enough to support life?

- Describe the timing and major events associated with the period of the fetus.

- Describe the behavior of the fetus and how it is related to later behavior.

2.2 KNOW THE TERMS

Age of viability	Implantation
Amnion	In vitro fertilization
Amniotic fluid	Mesoderm
Cephalocaudal	Period of the fetus
Cerebral cortex	Placenta
Ectoderm	Prenatal development
Embryo	Proximodistal
Endoderm	Umbilical cord
Eugenics	Vernix
Germ disc	Zygote

1. The many changes that transform the fertilized egg into a newborn human are known as

    _____.

2. The technique of _____ involves fertilizing eggs with sperm in a Petri dish and then

    transferring several of the fertilized eggs to the mother's uterus where they might implant

    in the lining of the wall of the uterus.

3. _____ is the effort to improve the human species by letting only certain people mate

    and pass along their genes.

4. The fertilized egg is called a _____.

5. _____ occurs when the zygote burrows into the uterine wall and establishes

    connections with a woman's blood vessels.

6. The _____ is a small cluster of cells near the center of the zygote that will eventually

    become the baby.

7. Nutrients and wastes are exchanged between mother and the developing organism through

    the _____ (see #1 on figure).

8. Once the zygote is completely embedded in the uterine wall it is called an _____.

9. The outer layer of the embryo which will become the hair, outer layer of skin, and the

    nervous system is called the _____.

10. The middle layer of the embryo which will become the muscles, bone, and circulatory

    system is called the _____.

11. The inner layer of the embryo, which will become the lungs and the digestive system, is called the _____.

12. The embryo will rest in a sac called the _____ (see #4 on figure).

13. The amnion is filled with _____, which cushions the embryo and maintains a constant temperature (see #3 on figure).

14. The _____ houses blood vessels that join the embryo to the placenta (see #2 on figure).

15. The _____ principle states that growth proceeds from the head to the base of the spine.

16. The _____ principle states that growth occurs in body parts near the center of the body before it occurs in parts that are more distant.

17. The _____ is the longest period of prenatal development and begins at the 9th week after conception and lasts until birth.

18. The thick, greasy substance that protects the fetus is called _____.

19. The _____ is the wrinkled surface of the brain that regulates many important human behaviors.

20. A 22- to 28-week old fetus is at the _____ because most of its bodily systems will be functioning well enough that it is likely to survive.

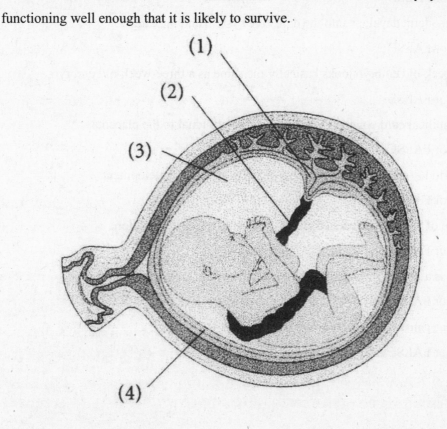

2.2 KNOW THE DETAILS OF FROM CONCEPTION TO BIRTH

1. Human prenatal development typically occurs over a period of 38 weeks.
    TRUE or FALSE

2. After one sperm has penetrated the cellular wall of an egg, no other sperm are able to do so.
    TRUE or FALSE

3. In vitro fertilization involves injecting sperm into the fallopian tubes.
    TRUE or FALSE

4. The period of the zygote ends when the zygote becomes embedded in the uterine wall.
    TRUE or FALSE

5. The germ disc eventually becomes the placenta.
    TRUE or FALSE

6. Once the zygote is completely embedded into the uterine wall, it is called a fetus.
    TRUE or FALSE

7. The ectoderm becomes hair, the outer layer of skin, and the nervous system.
    TRUE or FALSE

8. The mesoderm develops into the digestive system and the lungs.
    TRUE or FALSE

9. An 8-week-old embryo looks basically the same as a three-week-old embryo.
    TRUE or FALSE

10. The umbilical cord connects the developing individual to the placenta.
    TRUE or FALSE

11. The period of the fetus is the longest phase of prenatal development.
    TRUE or FALSE

12. The age of viability is reached at about 12 weeks after conception.
    TRUE or FALSE

13. Vernix is a greasy substance that protects the fetus while in amniotic fluid.
    TRUE or FALSE

14. The fetus can detect sounds and flavors.
    TRUE or FALSE

2.3 INFLUENCES ON PRENATAL DEVELOPMENT

TO MASTER THE LEARNING OBJECTIVES:

How is prenatal development influenced by a pregnant woman's age, her nutrition, and the stress that she experiences while pregnant?

- Describe how maternal nutrition is related to prenatal development.
- Explain how maternal stress affects prenatal development.
- Explain how maternal age can affect prenatal development.

How do disease, drugs, and environmental hazards sometimes affect prenatal development?

- Describe the effects of thalidomide on prenatal development.
- Describe the effects of cigarette smoking on prenatal development.
- Explain the effects associated with alcohol consumption by the mother during pregnancy.
- Know the effects associated with the consumption of aspirin, caffeine, cocaine, heroin, marijuana, and nicotine by the mother during pregnancy.
- Know the effects associated with contracting AIDS, Chlamydia, cytomegalovirus, genital herpes, rubella, syphilis, and toxoplasmosis during pregnancy.
- Know the effects of exposure to lead, mercury, and X-rays during pregnancy.
- Describe how ingesting PCBs affects development.

What general principles affect the ways prenatal development can be harmed?

- List the four general principles concerning the effects of teratogens on prenatal development.

How can prenatal development be monitored? Can abnormal prenatal development be corrected?

- Describe how genetic counseling can help prevent some inherited disorders.
- Describe the procedures used in ultrasound, amniocentesis, and chorionic villus sampling and the kind of information each provides about prenatal development.
- Describe how various problems of prenatal development can be treated with administration of drugs to the fetus, fetal surgery, and genetic engineering.

2.3 KNOW THE TERMS

Amniocentesis	Spina bifida
Chorionic villus sampling	Stress
Fetal	Teratogen
Fetal alcohol syndrome	Ultrasound

1. Consuming inadequate amounts of folic acid during pregnancy can result in _____ , a disorder in which the embryo's neural tube does not close properly during prenatal development.

2. A person's physical and psychological responses to threatening or challenging situations are known as _____.

3. An agent that causes abnormal prenatal development is called a _____.

4. _____ often occurs in babies whose mothers consumed large amounts of alcohol while they were pregnant with them.

5. The prenatal diagnostic technique called _____ uses sound waves to generate a picture of the fetus.

6. _____ is a prenatal diagnostic technique that involves withdrawing a sample of amniotic fluid through the abdomen, using a syringe.

7. _____ is a prenatal diagnostic technique that involves taking a sample of tissue from part of the placenta.

8. The field of medicine that is concerned with treating prenatal problems before birth is called _____ medicine.

2.3 KNOW THE DETAILS OF INFLUENCES ON PRENATAL DEVELOPMENT

1. Insufficient folic acid during pregnancy is associated with increased risk of spina bifida in the baby.
   TRUE or FALSE

2. Poor maternal nutrition during pregnancy is associated with an increased risk of prematurity, low birth weight, and problems with nervous system development.
   TRUE or FALSE

3. Stress during pregnancy has not been found to have any negative consequences on the developing baby.
   TRUE or FALSE

4. Women in their 40s are just as likely as women in their 20s to have healthy babies.
   TRUE or FALSE

5. A teratogen is any supplement that pregnant women should take to improve their chances of having a healthy baby.
   TRUE or FALSE

6. Thalidomide, alcohol, aspirin, caffeine, and nicotine are all known teratogens.
   TRUE or FALSE

7. Exposure to second-hand smoke during pregnancy is associated with having smaller babies.
   TRUE or FALSE

8. Pregnant women who consume large quantities of alcoholic beverages often give birth to babies with Down syndrome.
   TRUE or FALSE

9. AIDS can be passed from the mother to an embryo or fetus through the placenta or as the baby passes through the birth canal.
   TRUE or FALSE

10. Prenatal exposure to polychlorinated biphenyls (PCBs) harms children's cognitive skills and reading achievement.
    TRUE or FALSE

11. The impact of teratogens on prenatal development is the same for all developing organisms.
    TRUE or FALSE

12. Exposure to teratogens during the period of the embryo is most likely to result in major defects in bodily structure.
    TRUE or FALSE

13. Damage from teratogens is always evident at birth.
    TRUE or FALSE

14. The prenatal diagnostic procedure called chorionic villus sampling involves inserting a needle through the mother's abdomen to obtain a sample of the fluid surrounding the fetus.
    TRUE or FALSE

15. Amniocentesis and chorionic villus sampling increase the risk of miscarriage.
    TRUE or FALSE

41

2.4 LABOR AND DELIVERY

TO MASTER THE LEARNING OBJECTIVES:

What are the different phases of labor and delivery?

- List and describe the events associated with the three stages of labor.

What are "natural" ways of coping with the pain of childbirth? Is childbirth at home safe?

- List some of the benefits associated with prepared childbirth classes.

- Know the circumstances under which home delivery is safe.

What adjustments do parents face after a baby's birth?

- **Describe the physical and psychological adjustments parents make after their child is born.**

- **Define "baby blues."**

- **Describe how maternal postpartum depression affects babies.**

What are some complications that can occur during birth?

- Describe the problems associated with hypoxia, prematurity, and low birth weight.

- Describe cephalopelvic disproportion, irregular position, preeclampsia, and prolapsed umbilical cord.

- Know the causes of and possible preventions of the high infant mortality rate in the United States.

What contributes to infant mortality in developed and less developed countries?

- Know which countries have the highest and the lowest infant mortality rates.

- Describe the factors that influence infant mortality.

2.4 KNOW THE TERMS

Cesarean section	Infant mortality
Crowning	Low birth weight
Extremely low birth weight	Preterm
Hypoxia	Very low birth weight

1. The appearance of the top of the baby's head during labor is known as _____.

2. Lack of oxygen during delivery is called _____. This situation may occur if the umbilical cord becomes pinched or tangled during delivery.

3.   Making an incision in the abdomen to remove a baby from the mother's uterus is called
     _____.

4.   Babies born before the 36th week after conception are _____.

5.   _____ newborns weigh less than 2,500 grams (5.5 pounds) at birth.

6.   Babies who weigh less than 1,500 grams (3 pounds) are considered to be _____.

7.   Babies who weigh less than 1,000 grams (2.2 pounds) are considered to be _____.

8.   _____ is the number of infants out of 1,000 births who die before their first birthday.

2.4 KNOW THE DETAILS OF LABOR AND DELIVERY

1.   Contractions enlarge the cervix during stage 1 of labor.

     TRUE or FALSE

2.   The placenta is expelled during stage 2 of labor.

     TRUE or FALSE

3.   Stage 3 is usually the longest stage of labor.

     TRUE or FALSE

4.   Pain-relieving drugs do not impair the childbirth process or affect the baby.

     TRUE or FALSE

5.   There is no difference between women who do or do not attend childbirth classes in the
     amount of anesthetic used during childbirth.

     TRUE or FALSE

6.   Having a healthcare professional present at every birth and specialized facilities available
     for problems reduces neonatal mortality substantially.

     TRUE or FALSE

7.   High levels of hormones during the later phases of pregnancy increase the risk for
     postpartum depression.

     TRUE or FALSE

8.   Women who breastfeed are less likely to have postpartum depression.

     TRUE or FALSE

9.   Hypoxia during childbirth can cause mental retardation or death.

     TRUE or FALSE

10. Babies born before the 36th week after conception are considered premature.

     TRUE or FALSE

11. Most premature babies are developmentally delayed throughout childhood.

    TRUE or FALSE

12. Babies weighing less than 1,000 grams (2.2 pounds) at birth often do not survive or have developmentally delayed intellectual and motor skills.

    TRUE or FALSE

13. Infant mortality refers to the number of infants out of 1,000 births who die before their first birthday.

    TRUE or FALSE

14. Infant mortality rates in the United States are the lowest in the world.

    TRUE or FALSE

SUMMARY

2.1 IN THE BEGINNING: 23 PAIRS OF CHROMOSOMES

1. **What are chromosomes and genes? How do they carry hereditary information from one generation to the next?**

   At conception, the 23 chromosomes in the sperm merge with the 23 chromosomes in the egg. Each chromosome is one molecule of DNA; a section of DNA that provides specific biochemical instructions is called a _____. All of a person's genes make up a _____; the _____ refers to the physical, behavioral, and psychological characteristics that develop when the genotype is exposed to a specific environment.

   Different forms of the same gene are called _____. A person who inherits the same allele on a pair of chromosomes is _____. A person who inherits different alleles on a pair of chromosomes is _____. If an individual is heterozygous, the instructions of the _____ allele are followed whereas those of the recessive allele are ignored.

2. **What are common problems involving chromosomes and what are their consequences?**

   Most inherited disorders are carried by _____ alleles. Examples include sickle-cell disease and _____ in which toxins accumulate and cause mental retardation. Sometimes fertilized eggs do not have 46 chromosomes (44 autosomes and two sex chromosomes). Usually they are aborted spontaneously soon after conception. An exception is _____ syndrome, in which individuals usually have an extra 21st chromosome. Down syndrome individuals have a distinctive appearance and are _____. Disorders of the sex chromosomes are _____ common than autosomal disorders.

3. **How is children's heredity influenced by the environment in which they grow up?**
    Behavioral and psychological phenotypes that reflect an underlying continuum (such as intelligence) often involve _____ inheritance. In polygenic inheritance, the phenotype reflects the activity of many distinct genes. Polygenic inheritance is often examined by studying twins and children, and by identifying DNA markers. The impact of heredity on behavior depends on the environment in which the genetic instructions are carried out, and these heredity-environment interactions occur throughout life. A _____ is a measure of the extent to which a trait is inherited. Niche-picking occurs when individuals actively seek environments related to their genetic makeup. Family environments affect siblings differently (_____); parents provide a unique environment for each child in the family.

2.2 FROM CONCEPTION TO BIRTH

1. **What happens to a fertilized egg in the first two weeks after conception?**
    The first period of prenatal development lasts _____ weeks. It begins when the egg is fertilized by the sperm in the fallopian tube and ends when the fertilized egg has _____ in the lining of the wall of the uterus. By the end of this period, cells have begun to _____.

2. **When do body structures and internal organs emerge in prenatal development?**
    The second period of prenatal development begins two weeks after conception and ends six weeks after that. This is a period of _____ in which most of the major body _____ are created. Growth in this period is cephalocaudal (head develops first) and _____ (parts near the center of the body develop first).

3. **When do body systems begin to function well enough to support life?**
    The third period of prenatal development begins nine weeks after conception and lasts until birth. The highlights of this period are a remarkable increase in the _____ of the fetus and changes in body systems that are necessary for life. By _____, most body systems function well enough to support life. This is known as the age of viability.

2.3 INFLUENCES ON PRENATAL DEVELOPMENT

1. **How is prenatal development influenced by a pregnant woman's age, her nutrition, and the stress she experiences while pregnant?**

    Parents' age can affect prenatal development. _____ often have problem pregnancies mainly because they rarely receive adequate prenatal care. After age 35, pregnant women are more likely to _____ or give birth to a child with mental retardation. Prenatal development can also be harmed if a pregnant mother has inadequate _____, or experiences considerable stress.

2. **How do diseases, drugs, and environmental hazards sometimes affect prenatal development?**

    Teratogens are agents that cause _____ prenatal development. Many drugs that adults take are teratogens. For most drugs, scientists have not established amounts that can be consumed safely by pregnant women. Several diseases are teratogens. Only by avoiding these diseases entirely can a pregnant woman escape their harmful consequences.

    _____ teratogens are particularly dangerous because a pregnant woman may not know that these substances are present in the environment.

3. **What general principles affect the ways that prenatal development can be harmed?**

    The impact of teratogens depends upon the _____ of the organism, the period of prenatal development when the organism is exposed to the teratogen, and the _____ of exposure. Sometimes the impact of a teratogen is not evident until later in life.

4. **How can prenatal development be monitored? Can abnormal development be corrected?**

    Many techniques are used to track the progress of prenatal development. A common component of prenatal care is _____, which uses sound waves to generate a picture of the fetus. This picture can be used to determine the _____ of the fetus, its sex, and whether there are any gross physical deformities. When genetic disorders are suspected, _____ and chorionic villus sampling are used to determine the genotype of the fetus. Fetal medicine is a new field in which problems of prenatal development are corrected medically, with _____ or using genetic engineering.

2.4 LABOR AND DELIVERY

1. **What are the different stages of labor and delivery?**

    Labor consists of three stages. In stage 1, the muscles of the uterus _____. The contractions, which are weak at first and gradually become stronger, causing the opening of the cervix to enlarge. In stage 2, the baby moves through the _____. In stage 3, the _____ is delivered.

2. **What are "natural" ways of coping with the pain of childbirth? Is childbirth at home safe?**

    Natural or prepared childbirth is based on the assumption that parents should understand what takes place during pregnancy and birth. In natural childbirth, pain-relieving medications are avoided because this medication prevents women from _____ during labor and because they affect the fetus. Instead women learn to cope with pain through _____, imagery, and the help of a supportive coach. Most American babies are born in hospitals, but many European babies are born at home. Home delivery is safe when the mother is _____, pregnancy and birth are trouble-free, and a healthcare professional is present to deliver the baby.

3. **What adjustments do parents face after a baby's birth?**

    Following the birth of a child, a woman's body undergoes several changes: her breasts become filled with milk, her uterus becomes smaller, and hormone levels _____. Both parents adjust psychologically and sometimes fathers feel _____. After giving birth, some women experience postpartum depression: they are have a poor appetite and disturbed _____ and are apathetic.

4. **What are some complications that can occur during birth?**

    During labor and delivery, the flow of blood to the fetus can be disrupted, because the _____ is squeezed shut. This causes a lack of oxygen to the fetus that is called _____. Some babies are born prematurely and others are "small for date." Premature babies develop more _____ at first but catch up by two or three years of age. Small-for-date babies often do not fare well, particularly if they weigh less than 1,500 grams and if their _____ is stressful.

5. **What contributes to infant mortality in developed and less developed countries?**

    Infant mortality is relatively _____ in many countries around the world, primarily because of inadequate care _____ and disease and inadequate _____ after birth.

TEST YOURSELF

MULTIPLE-CHOICE QUESTIONS

1. Egg and sperm cells each contain _____ chromosomes.

    a. 23

    b. 26

    c. 43

    d. 46

2. Which sex chromosome pair would produce a male?

    a. XX

    b. YY

    c. XY

    d. YO

3. Physical, behavioral, and psychological features are referred to as a person's

    a. chromosomes.

    b. autosomes.

    c. phenotype.

    d. genotype.

4. When the alleles in a gene pair are the same, the pair is

    a. heterozygous.

    b. homozygous.

    c. a phenotype.

    d. a genotype.

5. Inheritance of cheek dimples operates on the dominant-recessive principle. The gene for dimples (D) is dominant, and the gene for no dimples (d) is recessive. Who would not have cheek dimples?

    a. Julia, who is Dd

    b. Jon, who is DD

    c. Sara, who is dd

    d. Neither Julia nor Sara would have cheek dimples

6. Which of the following disorders is carried by dominant alleles?

    a. Huntington's disease

    b. Phenylketonuria

    c. Sickle-cell disease

    d. Down syndrome

7. Seth was born with extra chromosomes. He

    a. will not survive long past birth.

    b. is likely to develop more rapidly than average.

    c. is likely to have normal development.

    d. may survive but is likely to have disturbed development.

8. Sasha was born with an extra 21st chromosome, so she is likely to have

    a. phenylketonuria.

    b. Huntington's disease.

    c. sickle-cell disease.

    d. Down syndrome.

9. Intelligence is determined by a number of different genes. Therefore, intelligence follows a

    _____ pattern of inheritance.

    a. dominant-recessive

    b. sex-linked

    c. polygenic

    d. incomplete dominance

10. Barry and Larry are twins that came from a single fertilized egg that split in two. They are

    _____ twins.

    a. monozygotic

    b. dizygotic

    c. codominant

    d. polygenic

11. If a trait is strongly influenced by genetic factors, one would expect to find that, with respect to that trait,

    a. dizygotic twins are more alike than monozygotic twins.

    b. dizygotic twins are more alike than siblings.

    c. adopted children resemble their adoptive parents more than their biological parents.

    d. adopted children resemble their biological parents more than their adoptive parents.

12. Etta, who inherited musical ability from her father, often seeks out opportunities to exercise her singing talent. Etta's behavior is a good example of

    a. a reaction range.

    b. incomplete dominance.

    c. polygenic inheritance.

    d. niche-picking.

13. The forces within a family that make children different from each other are called

    a. non-shared environmental influences.

    b. niche-picking.

    c. polygenic inheritance.

    d. a reaction range.

14. Which of the following shows the periods of prenatal development in their correct sequence from first to last?

    a. Zygote, embryo, fetus

    b. Fetus, embryo, zygote

    c. Zygote, fetus, embryo

    d. Embryo, zygote, fetus

15. _____ is being performed when a human egg is fertilized by sperm while both are in a Petri dish.

    a. Artificial insemination

    b. In vitro fertilization

    c. Implantation

    d. Eugenics

16. Attempting to improve the human species by allowing only certain select people to reproduce is called

    a. eugenics.

    b. viability.

    c. niche-picking.

    d. implantation.

17. A fertilized egg is first known as a(n)

    a. embryo.

    b. zygote.

    c. germ disc.

    d. fetus.

18. When the zygote has burrowed into the uterine wall and established connections with a woman's blood vessels, _____ has just occurred.

    a. in vitro fertilization

    b. ovulation

    c. fertilization

    d. implantation

19. Nutrients and waste are exchanged between the mother and the fetus through the

    a. placenta.

    b. endoderm.

    c. ectoderm.

    d. mesoderm.

20. Implantation is complete

    a. when fertilization occurs.

    b. at the end of the period of the embryo.

    c. at the end of the period of the zygote.

    d. at the end of the period of the fetus.

21. In prenatal development, most body structures and internal organs are formed during the period of the

    a. fetus.

    b. embryo.

    c. zygote.

    d. germ disc.

22. The muscles, bones, and circulatory system are formed from the

    a. ectoderm.

    b. endoderm.

    c. mesoderm.

    d. amnion.

23. The embryo rests in a sac called the

    a. placenta.

    b. germ disc.

    c. umbilical cord.

    d. amnion.

24. The thick, greasy substance that protects the fetus' skin is called

    a. vernix.

    b. amniotic fluid.

    c. cortex.

    d. cartilage.

25. The age of viability is reached _____ weeks after conception.

    a. 8 to 10

    b. 12 to 15

    c. 22 to 28

    d. 32 to 38

26. Maternal stress during pregnancy is associated with _____ in babies.

    a. central nervous system damage

    b. chromosomal abnormalities

    c. increased vulnerability to illness

    d. premature birth and low birth weight

27. Which of the following women is most likely to have a child whose development was harmed prenatally?

    a. Mindy, who had the flu while she was pregnant

    b. Suzanne, who had a cold while she was pregnant

    c. Carol, who drank alcohol heavily throughout her pregnancy

    d. Jasmine, whose diet included food from each of the five major food groups

28. When a developing organism is exposed to a teratogen during the period of the zygote, the usual result is

    a. major defects in bodily structure.

    b. minor defects in bodily structure.

    c. improperly functioning bodily systems.

    d. spontaneous abortion.

29. Katie is seven weeks pregnant with her fourth child and is gaining weight much more quickly than she did during her first three pregnancies. She suspects she might be carrying twins. Which of the following procedures could determine whether she is pregnant with twins the earliest with the least risk of causing a miscarriage?

    a. A blood test

    b. Ultrasound

    c. Amniocentesis

    d. Chorionic villus sampling

30. _____ is a prenatal diagnostic procedure in which tissue is obtained from the placenta.

    a. Ultrasound

    b. Amniocentesis

    c. Fetal medicine

    d. Chorionic villus sampling

31. Crowning occurs during stage _____ of labor.

    a. 1

    b. 2

    c. 3

    d. 4

32. Which of the following events occurs during stage 3 of labor?

    a. The cervix enlarges to 10 centimeters.

    b. Crowning occurs.

    c. The placenta is expelled.

    d. The baby is delivered.

33. Which of the following strategies would you least expect to find as part of prepared childbirth?

    a. Teaching pregnant women ways to relax during labor

    b. Encouraging pregnant women to maximize the use of pain-relieving drugs during birth

    c. Informing pregnant women about basic facts of pregnancy and childbirth

    d. Having pregnant women bring a supportive "coach" with them to class

34. A pregnant woman with high blood pressure, protein in her urine, and swelling in her extremities has symptoms of

    a. a prolapsed umbilical cord.

    b. a baby in an irregular position.

    c. cephalopelvic disproportion.

    d. preeclampsia.

35. Premature babies are those who arrive before the _____ week of gestation.

    a. 38th

    b. 36th

    c. 30th

    d. 25th

36. Hannah gave birth to a baby who weighed 3 pounds. Her baby would be classified as

    a. normal weight.

    b. low birth weight.

    c. very low birth weight.

    d. extremely low birth weight.

37. Which of the following countries has the highest rate of infant mortality?

    a. United States

    b. Japan

    c. Canada

    d. Sweden

ESSAY QUESTIONS

1. Your friends Fred and Wilma are expecting their first child. Both Fred and Wilma have dark, curly hair, but they hope that their baby will have straight, blond hair because they have always hated their dark, unruly curls. Using the table in your text on page XX, what can you tell Fred and Wilma about genetic inheritance and the likelihood that they will get their wish?

2. Your friend Lafon is pregnant, and she told you that she knows the three stages of prenatal development—the first trimester, the second trimester, and the third trimester—but she wasn't exactly sure about what happens during each of the stages. What can you tell Lafon about the three stages of prenatal development and the major events that occur during each of the stages?

3. Lafon also is concerned that her baby will be okay when it is born, and she is wondering if there is anything that she can do to help ensure that she has a healthy baby. What can you tell her about the effects of teratogens that can help her make some informed decisions during her pregnancy?

4. Your pregnant friend Lafon is in her 6th month of pregnancy, and she isn't sure if she should take the prepared childbirth classes that are being offered at the local hospital. The class meets for three hours every Monday night for six weeks, and that looks like a big commitment of time to Lafon. What can you tell Lafon about the benefits of prepared childbirth classes?

5. Lafon had her baby two weeks ago, and she is worried that she isn't a good mother. Right after her son was born, she was thrilled and excited, but now she finds her son's crying irritating, she resents the fact that she barely has time for simple things like taking a shower, and she frequently bursts into tears. What can you tell Lafon about adjusting to parenthood and postpartum depression that might help her?

6. Recently one of your friends told you that prenatal care is a waste of time for a mother who is young and healthy. What can you tell your friend about prenatal care in teenage mothers and about infant mortality in the United States that would contradict his statement?

ANSWERS WITH PAGE REFERENCES

2.1 KNOW THE TERMS

1. Chromosomes (42)
2. autosomes (43)
3. sex chromosomes (43)
4. deoxyribonucleic acid (DNA) (43)
5. gene (43)
6. genotype (44)
7. phenotype (44)
8. alleles (44)
9. homozygous (44)
10. heterozygous (44)
11. dominant (44)
12. recessive (44)
13. incomplete dominance (44)
14. Sickle-cell trait (44)
15. Phenylketonuria (46)
16. Huntington's disease (46)
17. behavioral genetics (47)
18. Polygenic inheritance (48)
19. Monozygotic (49)
20. dizygotic (49)
21. heritability coefficient (50)
22. niche-picking (51)
23. Nonshared environmental influences (52)

2.1 KNOW THE DETAILS

1. T, 43	6. F, 44	11. T, 47	16. F, 51
2. F, 43	7. F, 44	12. T, 47	17. T, 51
3. T, 43	8. T, 46	13. T, 48	18. T, 52
4. T, 44	9. F, 46	14. T, 49	
5. T, 44	10. F, 46	15. T, 49	

2.2 KNOW THE TERMS

1. prenatal development (53)
2. in vitro fertilization (55)
3. Eugenics (55)
4. zygote (55)
5. Implantation (55)
6. germ disc (55)
7. placenta (55)
8. embryo (55)
9. ectoderm (55)
10. mesoderm (55)
11. endoderm (55)
12. amnion (57)
13. amniotic fluid (57)
14. umbilical cord (57)
15. cephalocaudal (57)
16. proximodistal (57)
17. period of the fetus (57)
18. vernix (57)
19. cerebral cortex (57)
20. age of viability (57)

2.2 KNOW THE DETAILS OF PRENATAL DEVELOPMENT

1. T, 53	5. F, 55	9. F, 55	13. T, 57
2. T, 54	6. F, 55	10. T, 56	14. T, 58
3. F, 54	7. T, 55	11. T, 56	
4. T, 54	8. F, 55	12. F, 57	

2.3 KNOW THE TERMS

1. spina bifida (59)

2. stress (60)

3. teratogen (61)

4. Fetal alcohol syndrome (62)

5. ultrasound (67)

6. Amniocentesis (67)

7. Chorionic villus sampling (68)

8. fetal (68)

2.3 KNOW THE DETAILS OF INFLUENCES ON PRENATAL DEVELOPMENT

1. T, 59	5. F, 61	9. T, 63	13. F, 66
2. T, 60	6. T, 62	10. T, 64	14. F, 67
3. F, 60	7. T, 62	11. F, 65	15. T, 68
4. F, 61	8. F, 62	12. T, 65	

2.4 KNOW THE TERMS

1. crowning (70)

2. hypoxia (73)

3. cesarean section (73)

4. preterm (74)

5. Low birth weight (74)

6. very low birth weight (74)

7. extremely low birth weight (74)

8. Infant mortality (76)

2.4 KNOW THE DETAILS OF LABOR AND DELIVERY

1. T, 70	5. F, 71	9. T, 73	12. T, 74
2. F, 71	6. T, 72	10. T, 74	13. T, 76
3. F, 71	7. T, 72	11. F, 74	14. F, 76
4. F, 71	8. T, 73		

SUMMARY

2.1 IN THE BEGINNING: 23 PAIRS OF CHROMOSOMES

1. gene (43); genotype (44); phenotype (44); alleles (44); homozygous (44); heterozygous (44); dominant (44)

2. recessive (46); Phenylketonuria (46); Down (46); mentally retarded (46); more (47)

3. polygenic (48); heritability coefficient (50); Nonshared environmental influence (52)

2.2 FROM CONCEPTION TO BIRTH

1. two (53); implanted (55);differentiate (55)

2. rapid growth (56); structures (56); proximodistal (56)

3. size (56); 22-28 weeks (57)

2.3 INFLUENCES ON PRENATAL DEVELOPMENT

1. Teenagers (61); miscarry (61); nutrition (59)

2. abnormal (61); Environmental (63)

3. genotype (65); amount (66)

4. ultrasound (67); position (67); amniocentesis (67); surgery (69)

2.4 LABOR AND DELIVERY

1. contract (70); cervix and vagina (70); placenta (71)

2. pushing (71); relaxation (71); healthy (72)

3. drop (77); left out (77); sleep (77),

4. umbilical cord (73); hypoxia (73); slowly (74); environment (75)

5. high (76); before birth (76); nutrition (77)

TEST YOURSELF

MULTIPLE-CHOICE QUESTIONS

1. a, 42	11. d, 49	21. b, 55	31. b, 70
2. c, 43	12. d, 51	22. c, 55	32. c, 71
3. c, 44	13. a, 52	23. d, 56	33. b, 71
4. b, 44	14. a, 53	24. a, 56	34. d, 74
5. c, 44	15. b, 54	25. c, 57	35. b, 74
6. a, 46	16. a, 54	26. d, 60	36. c, 74
7. d, 46	17. b, 54	27. c, 62	37. a, 76
8. d, 46	18. d, 55	28. d, 65	
9. c, 48	19. a, 55	29. b, 67	
10. a, 49	20. c, 55	30. d, 68	

ESSAY QUESTIONS

1. You can tell Fred and Wilma that both dark hair and curly hair are dominant traits. That means that an individual who is heterozygous with one dominant allele and one recessive allele will display the dominant trait. Given that both Fred and Wilma show the dominant traits, they both must have at least one allele for the dominant trait, so it is not likely that their child will NOT inherit the dominant alleles for dark hair and curly hair. (44-45)

2. Tell Lafon that the three stages of prenatal development do not correspond to the trimesters of pregnancy. The first stage of prenatal development is called the period of the zygote, and it lasts from conception until two weeks after conception. During this period, the cells of the new individual are dividing rapidly. This period ends when the zygote (fertilized egg) implants in the lining of the wall of the uterus. The second period of prenatal development is called the period of the embryo, and it lasts from the third week until the eighth week after conception. During this period of prenatal development, most of the organs and systems of the body are formed. The third period of prenatal development, the period of the fetus, lasts from 9 weeks until 38 weeks after conception. During this period the fetus grows from a few ounces to its birth weight of 7 or 8 pounds. Refinement of the structures that were formed during the period of the embryo and their functions also occur during this period. (53-57)

3. You can tell Lafon that there are a number of teratogens that she can try to avoid while she is pregnant. One of the most common is alcohol. Women who drink at least three ounces of alcohol per day while they are pregnant are likely to have babies born with fetal alcohol syndrome. These babies usually have deformed faces, heart problems, retarded growth, and are mentally retarded. Lafon should also avoid diseases such as AIDS, cytomegalovirus, genital herpes, rubella, and syphilis. Common results of exposure to these diseases are blindness, deafness, neurological damage, and mental retardation. Finally, there are environmental hazards that Lafon should avoid. For example, one environmental hazard is PCBs, which can be ingested if one eats fish that come from PCB-contaminated waters. Children whose mothers ate a large amount of PCB-contaminated fish while they were pregnant showed some deficits in verbal skill and memory skill at four years of age. The four-year-olds who showed the greatest deficits had the greatest prenatal exposure to PCBs. (61-64)

4. The purpose of prepared childbirth classes is to teach a pregnant woman and her coach the basic facts about labor and delivery. Women learn relaxation techniques such as deep breathing and visualizing pleasant things. These techniques help them to relax and control the pain during contractions, and the coach learns how to offer support and encouragement to the mother-to-be through labor. Research has shown that mothers who do attend these childbirth classes feel more positive about labor and birth and use less medication during delivery than mothers who do not attend these classes. So, while the classes may be a big time commitment for Lafon, she will probably have a better idea of what to expect during labor and delivery and may be able to relax and control her pain more during labor. (71-72)

5. Lafon should know that her behavior isn't unusual and it does not make her a bad mother. Approximately half of all new mothers feel irritation, resentment, and have crying spells. Caring for a new baby is very time-consuming and stressful. Also, Lafon may be experiencing many physiological and hormonal changes as her body recovers from pregnancy and labor. About 10 to 15 percent of new mothers may experience postpartum depression, which may last for months after the birth of a baby. The feelings of sadness and irritability may be accompanied by feelings of low self-worth, disturbed sleep, poor appetite, and apathy. Postpartum depression is a serious problem that can have harmful effects on the baby and the mother, so if Lafon's "baby blues" last longer than a few weeks, she should seek help. Home visits by healthcare professionals may teach Lafon new ways to cope with her baby. Breast-feeding also may have a positive effect on her mood, perhaps because it causes the release of hormones that are antidepressants (72-73).

6. You can tell your friend that prenatal care is important. Teenage mothers, who often receive inadequate prenatal care, are more likely to have problems during pregnancy, labor, and delivery. Other evidence supporting the importance of prenatal care is the infant mortality rate in the United States. Compared to other industrialized countries, the United States has one of the highest infant mortality rates. Part of the reason for this high infant mortality rate is the high number of low-birth-weight babies born in the United States, which can usually be prevented with good prenatal care. In almost all of the countries with low infant mortality rates, extensive prenatal care is provided to pregnant women at little or no cost. Therefore, good prenatal care contributes to the birth of healthy babies. (61, 76-77)

TOOLS FOR EXPLORING THE WORLD

This chapter describes the newborn, covers physical growth, investigates the development of motor skills, discusses perception in the newborn, and presents information on the developing sense of self.

3.1 THE NEWBORN

TO MASTER THE LEARNING OBJECTIVES:

How do reflexes help newborns interact with the world?

• Know the name and significance of each newborn reflex.

How do we determine if a baby is healthy and adjusting to life outside the uterus?

• List the components of the Apgar scale and describe what the scale tells us about the newborn.

• Describe the information about the newborn that can be learned from the Brazelton Neonatal Behavioral Assessment.

What behavioral states are common among newborns?

- List and describe the four newborn states.

- Describe the three different types of crying found in newborns.

- Describe the techniques that parents use to stop their babies from crying.

- Describe the pattern of REM and non-REM sleep found in the newborn.

- List and describe the factors associated with sudden infant death syndrome.

What are the different features of temperament? Do they change as children grow?

- Describe the dimensions of temperament.

- Describe cross-cultural differences in temperament.

- Explain how temperament is influenced by heredity and environment.

- Explain the stability of temperament across childhood.

3.1 KNOW THE TERMS

Alert inactivity	Reflexes
Basic	REM (irregular)
Crying	Sleeping
Mad	Sudden infant death syndrome (SIDS)
Non-REM (regular)	Temperament
Pain	Waking activity

1. _____ are unlearned responses that are triggered by specific stimulation.

2. When newborns are in the state of _____, their eyes are open, they are attentive, and they seem to be deliberately inspecting the environment.

3. When newborns are in the state of _____, their eyes are open but unfocused, and their arms and legs move in bursts of uncoordinated movements.

4. In the _____ state, newborns cry vigorously and move in an uncoordinated way.

5. In the _____ state, newborns alternate from being still and breathing regularly to moving gently and breathing irregularly.

6. When babies are hungry or tired they often use a _____ cry that starts softly and gradually becomes more intense.

7. A _____ cry is a more intense version of a basic cry.

8. A _____ cry begins with a sudden, long burst of crying followed by a long pause and gasping.

9. During _____ sleep, an infant's eyes will dart rapidly beneath her eyelids, she may move her arms and legs, and she may grimace.

10. During _____ sleep, heart rate, breathing, and brain activity are steady, and newborns lie quietly.

11. In _____, a healthy baby dies suddenly, for no apparent reason.

12. _____ refers to a consistent style or pattern to an infant's behavior.

3.1 KNOW THE DETAILS OF THE NEWBORN

1. Newborn reflexes are learned responses to stimulation in the environment.
TRUE or FALSE

2. Babies who practice the stepping reflex often learn to walk earlier than those who don't practice this reflex.
TRUE or FALSE

3. Reflexes can be used to determine whether the newborn's nervous system is working properly.
TRUE or FALSE

4. The Babinski reflex occurs when a baby throws its arms out then inward in response to a loud noise or when its head falls.
TRUE or FALSE

5. The rooting reflex occurs when a baby responds to its cheek being stroked by turning its head toward the cheek that was stroked and opening its mouth.
TRUE or FALSE

6. The lower the Apgar score, the healthier the newborn is.
TRUE or FALSE

7. The Neonatal Behavioral Assessment Scale is a more comprehensive evaluation of newborn functioning than the Apgar.
TRUE or FALSE

8. A baby with open, unfocused eyes, who is moving its arms in an uncoordinated manner, is in a state of alert inactivity.
TRUE or FALSE

9. Babies cry differently when they're mad than when they're in pain.
TRUE or FALSE

10. Newborns sleep 16 to 18 hours daily.

    TRUE or FALSE

11. The newborn's body is more active during REM sleep than during non-REM sleep.

    TRUE or FALSE

12. REM sleep becomes more frequent as infants grow.

    TRUE or FALSE

13. Most babies who die of SIDS are between two and four months of age.

    TRUE or FALSE

14. The surgency/extroversion dimension of temperament refers to the extent to which a child is angry, fearful, frustrated, shy, and not easily soothed.

    TRUE or FALSE

15. Temperamental characteristics are equally common across cultures.

    TRUE or FALSE

16. Temperament is entirely due to experience.

    TRUE or FALSE

17. Temperament tends to change greatly between infancy and later childhood.

    TRUE or FALSE

3.2 PHYSICAL DEVELOPMENT

TO MASTER THE LEARNING OBJECTIVES:

How do height and weight change from birth to two years of age?

- Describe the pattern of growth that is seen in children from birth to two years of age.

- Know how average size and normal size differ from each other.

What nutrients do young children need? How are they best provided?

- Describe the advantages of bottle-feeding and breast-feeding.

- Describe how children's eating habits change during the first two years of life.

What are the consequences of malnutrition? How can it be treated?

- Describe the effects of malnutrition on growth in young children.

- Explain why it is important to combine changes in diet and parent training when treating malnutrition in children.

What are nerve cells, and how are they organized in the brain?

- List and describe the parts of neurons.

- Describe the structure and various functions of parts of the brain such as the cerebral cortex, hemispheres, the corpus callosum, and the frontal cortex.

How does the brain develop? When does it begin to function?

- Describe the development of the brain throughout prenatal development and the first few years after birth.

- Describe the functions of the left and right hemispheres and the frontal lobe of the brain.

- Describe the various methods that are used to study the functions of the brain.

- Define experience-expectant growth and experience-dependent growth.

3.2 KNOW THE TERMS

Axon	Functional magnetic resonance imaging (fMRI)
Cell body	Hemispheres
Cerebral cortex	Neural plate
Corpus callosum	Neuron
Dendrite	Neurotransmitters
Electroencephalogram (EEG)	Malnourished
Experience-dependent growth	Myelin
Experience-expectant growth	Synaptic pruning
Frontal cortex	Terminal button

1. Being small for one's age may indicate that a child is _____, or receives an inadequate diet.

2. The basic unit of the brain and nervous system that specializes in receiving and transmitting information is called a _____.

3. The _____ is in the center of the neuron, and it keeps the neuron alive (see #1 below).

4. The _____ is the part of the neuron that receives information, and it looks like a tree with many branches (see #2 below).

5. The _____ is a tube-like structure that emerges from the one end of the cell body, and it transmits information to other neurons (see #3 below).

6. The small knob at the end of the axon is called the _____ (see #4 below).

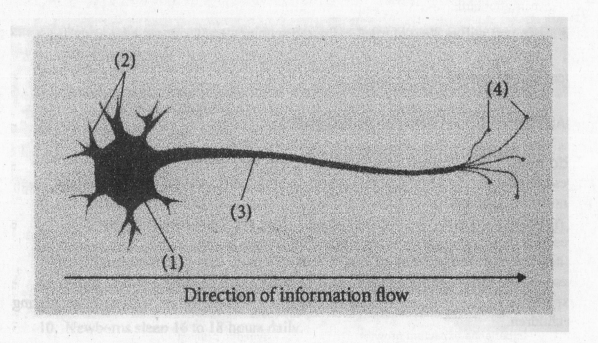

Direction of information flow

7. _____ are the chemical messengers that carry information to nearby neurons.

8. The wrinkled surface of the brain is called the_____.

9. The right and left halves of the cortex are called _____.

10. The _____ connects the two hemispheres with a thick bundle of neurons.

11. Personality and the ability to carry out plans are controlled by the _____.

12. During prenatal development, the flat group of cells that will become the brain and spinal cord is called the _____.

13. The fatty sheath that allows neurons to transmit information more rapidly is called _____.

14. The gradual disappearance of synapses that begins in infancy is called _____.

15. The pattern of brain waves that comes from electrodes that are placed on the scalp is known as an _____.

16. The use of magnetic fields to track the flow of blood in the brain is called _____.

17. _____ is the process by which the wiring of the brain is organized by experiences that are common to most humans.

18. _____ is the process by which the wiring of the brain varies across individuals and cultures based on differing experiences.

3.2 KNOW THE DETAILS OF PHYSICAL DEVELOPMENT

1. Growth is more rapid during infancy than during any other period of life after birth.
   TRUE or FALSE

2. The bodies of infants and children have the same proportions as those of adults.
   TRUE or FALSE

3. Infants require more calories per pound of body weight than adults.
   TRUE or FALSE

4. Bottle-feeding is the best way to make sure babies get the nourishment they need.
   TRUE or FALSE

5. The American Academy of Pediatrics recommends that children be breast-fed for the first year.
   TRUE or FALSE

6. The rate of growth is not affected by malnourishment.
   TRUE or FALSE

7. Children who are malnourished during infancy have been found to have difficulty maintaining attention in school.
   TRUE or FALSE

8. A dendrite looks like a tree with many branches and is the receiving end of the neuron.
   TRUE or FALSE

9. The neurotransmitters are tube-like structures that emerge from the side of the cell body and transmit information to other neurons.
   TRUE or FALSE

10. The wrinkled surface of the brain is the cerebral cortex.
    TRUE or FALSE

11. The corpus callosum is a thick bundle of nerves that links the left and right hemispheres of the brain.
    TRUE or FALSE

12. Personality and the ability to make and carry out plans are largely controlled by areas of the brain at the rear of the cortex.

    TRUE or FALSE

13. The ability to produce and understand language is typically controlled by neurons in the left hemisphere of the brain.

    TRUE or FALSE

14. The neural plate is a group of cells that form a flat structure that is present in the embryo approximately three weeks after conception.

    TRUE or FALSE

15. Myelin is a fatty wrap that reduces the speed at which neurons transmit information.

    TRUE or FALSE

16. Functional magnetic resonance imaging (fMRI) detects the pattern of brain waves.

    TRUE or FALSE

17. Different brain systems specialize at different rates.

    TRUE or FALSE

18. Plasticity of the brain is shown when other neurons take over the functions of damaged neurons.

    TRUE or FALSE

3.3 MOVING AND GRASPING: EARLY MOTOR SKILLS

TO MASTER THE LEARNING OBJECTIVES:

What are the component skills involved in learning to walk? At what age do infants master them?

- Describe some of the important developments that lead to the ability to maintain one's balance and eventually walk.

- Know dynamic systems theory and the difference between differentiation and integration.

- Describe how practice is related to motor development.

- Describe the development of running and hopping.

How do infants learn to coordinate the use of their hands?

- Describe the development of fine motor skills from simple grasping in the newborn to the ability to eat with a spoon in a two-year-old.

- Describe the development of handedness.

3.3 KNOW THE TERMS

Differentiation	**Locomote**
Dynamic systems theory	**Motor skills**
Fine motor skills	**Toddlers**
Integration	**Toddling**

1. Coordinated movements of the muscles and limbs are called _____.

2. To _____ is the ability to move around in the world.

3. _____ are associated with grasping, holding, and manipulating objects.

4. The early, unsteady form of walking is called _____.

5. Young children who are inexperienced walkers are called _____.

6. According to _____, motor development involves many distinct skills that are organized and reorganized over time to meet the demands of specific tasks.

7. The mastery of complex motions involves _____ of individual motions.

8. Mastery of complex motions also involves the _____ of the individual motions into a coherent, coordinated whole.

3.3 KNOW THE DETAILS OF EARLY MOTOR SKILLS

1. Walking is an example of a fine motor skill.
   TRUE or FALSE

2. By about five months of age, most babies will be able to roll over and sit with support.
   TRUE or FALSE

3. Most infants can sit alone by seven months of age.
   TRUE or FALSE

4. By 24 months, most children can climb steps, walk backwards, and kick a ball.
   TRUE or FALSE

5. According to dynamic systems theory, motor development occurs naturally when necessary muscles and neural circuits mature.

    TRUE or FALSE

6. Infants' bodies tend to be bottom-heavy.

    TRUE or FALSE

7. Differentiation refers to the combination of component skills into a coherent, working whole.

    TRUE or FALSE

8. By about 12 to 15 months of age, infants typically master the component skills needed to walk.

    TRUE or FALSE

9. Because of more practice, infants from some traditional African cultures have been found to reach motor milestones later than infants growing up in Europe and North America.

    TRUE or FALSE

10. By two years of age, most children run easily, bending their knees when they run, and can quickly change directions or speed.

    TRUE or FALSE

11. Most infants can successfully reach for objects at about four months of age.

    TRUE or FALSE

12. Most infants begin to use their thumbs to hold objects at about seven or eight months of age.

    TRUE or FALSE

13. Infants are able to coordinate the motions of both hands as soon as they are able to use them.

    TRUE or FALSE

14. Most infants begin to be able to pick up "finger foods" at about one year of age.

    TRUE or FALSE

15. At about one year of age, most infants are ready to begin trying to eat with a spoon.

    TRUE or FALSE

16. A preference for one hand over the other does not typically appear until children enter school.

    TRUE or FALSE

17. Hereditary factors, not sociocultural factors, are the sole determinant of handedness.

    TRUE or FALSE

3.4 COMING TO KNOW THE WORLD: PERCEPTION

TO MASTER THE LEARNING OBJECTIVES:

Are infants able to smell, to taste, and to experience pain?

- Describe the newborn's sense of smell and taste.

- Describe the newborn's sense of touch and pain and how we infer these feelings.

Can infants hear? How do they use sound to locate objects?

- Describe infants' hearing, perception of music, perception of pitch, and differentiation of speech sounds.

How well can infants see? Can they see color and depth?

- Know how infants' visual acuity is assessed.

- Describe the development of color perception.

- Describe the differences in the reactions of non-crawling and crawling infants when they are placed on the "deep" side of the visual cliff.

- Describe the various cues that are used to infer depth (include kinetic cues, visual expansion, motion parallax, retinal disparity, pictorial cues, linear perspective, and texture gradient).

- Describe how infants perceive objects.

- Describe infants' perception of faces.

How do infants coordinate information between different sensory modalities, such as between vision and hearing?

- Explain how researchers can tell if infants can integrate information from vision and touch.

- Know the importance of intersensory redundancy in infants' perception.

71

3.4 KNOW THE TERMS

Cones	Pictorial cues
Kinetic cues	Retinal disparity
Intersensory redundancy	Texture gradient
Linear perspective	Visual acuity
Motion parallax	Visual cliff
Perception	Visual expansion

1. The process by which the brain receives, selects, modifies, and organizes incoming nerve impulses that are the result of physical stimulation is called _____.

2. The smallest pattern that one can distinguish reliably defines visual clarity, or _____.

3. The specialized neurons in the back of the eye along the retina that sense color are called _____.

4. A glass-covered platform that appears to have a "shallow" side and a "deep" side is called a _____.

5. _____ use motion to estimate depth.

6. _____ refers to the fact that as an object moves closer, it fills an ever-greater proportion of the retina.

7. _____ refers to the fact that objects that are near move across our visual fields faster than objects that are in the distance.

8. _____ is one way to infer depth when the retinal images in the left and right eyes differ.

9. Cues for depth that are the same as the cues that artists use to convey depth in drawings and paintings are called _____.

10. _____ occurs when parallel lines come together at a single point in the distance.

11. The cue of depth where the texture of near objects is coarse but distinct and the texture of distant objects is finer and less distinct is called _____.

12. The simultaneous presentation of information to different sensory modes is called _____.

3.4 KNOW THE DETAILS OF PERCEPTION

1. Newborns can recognize familiar odors.

   TRUE or FALSE

2. Infants are not able to differentiate between salty, sour, bitter, and sweet tastes.

   TRUE or FALSE

3. Newborns seem to have a preference for sour tastes.

   TRUE or FALSE

4. The newborn infant's nervous system is not capable of transmitting pain.

   TRUE or FALSE

5. Infants can hear as well as adults.

   TRUE or FALSE

6. Infants can distinguish different musical sounds and melodies.

   TRUE or FALSE

7. Infants prefer looking at patterned stimuli over plain, unpatterned stimuli.

   TRUE or FALSE

8. Newborns' visual acuity is about 20/200 to 20/400.

   TRUE or FALSE

9. Specialized neurons called cones are responsible for depth perception.

   TRUE or FALSE

10. Newborns perceive color in the same way adults do.

    TRUE or FALSE

11. The visual cliff is used to measure infant visual acuity.

    TRUE or FALSE

12. One-and-a-half-month-old infants notice a difference between the deep and shallow sides of a visual cliff.

    TRUE or FALSE

13. Infants do not use retinal disparity as a depth cue.

    TRUE or FALSE

14. By seven or eight months of age, infants process faces similarly to adults.

    TRUE or FALSE

15. Infants are able to integrate information between vision and touch and between vision and hearing.

    TRUE or FALSE

3.5 BECOMING SELF-AWARE

TO MASTER THE LEARNING OBJECTIVES:

When do children begin to realize that they exist?

- Know when self-recognition appears and how it is measured.

- Know how saying "I" and "mine" while playing with toys is related to self-awareness.

What are toddlers' and preschoolers' self-concepts like?

- Describe the characteristics of young children's self-concepts.

When do preschool children begin to acquire a theory of mind?

- Define theory of mind and know the three phases of theory of mind in preschool children.

3.5 KNOW THE DETAILS OF BECOMING SELF-AWARE

1. By nine months of age, infants obviously recognize themselves in a mirror.
    TRUE or FALSE

2. Self-awareness emerges between 18 and 24 months.
    TRUE or FALSE

3. Preschoolers tend to define themselves in terms of their possessions and physical characteristics.
    TRUE or FALSE

4. In the earliest phase of the theory of mind, two-year-olds understand that people have desires and that desires can cause behavior.
    TRUE or FALSE

5. At age three, children are not able to clearly distinguish the mental world from the physical world.
    TRUE or FALSE

6. By age four, children understand that behavior is often based on a person's beliefs about events and situations, even when those beliefs are wrong.
    TRUE or FALSE

7. False belief tasks can be used to assess a child's theory of mind.
    TRUE or FALSE

8. False belief tasks tend to be grasped more slowly by children with autism spectrum disorders.
    TRUE or FALSE

SUMMARY

3.1 THE NEWBORN

1. **How do reflexes help newborns interact with the world?**

    Babies are born with a number of reflexes. Some help them _____ to life outside of the uterus, some help _____ them from danger, and some serve as the basis for later voluntary motor behavior.

2. **How do we determine if a baby is healthy and adjusting to life outside the uterus?**

    The _____ measures five vital signs to determine a newborn baby's physical well-being. The Neonatal Behavioral Assessment provides a comprehensive evaluation of a baby's _____ and physical status.

3. **What behavioral states are common among newborns?**

    Newborns spend their day in one of four states: _____, waking activity, crying, and sleeping. A newborn's crying includes a basic cry, a _____ cry, and a pain cry. The best way to calm a crying baby is by putting it on the shoulder and rocking.

    Newborns spend approximately two-thirds of every day asleep and go through a complete sleep-wake cycle once every four hours. By three or four months, babies sleep through the night. Newborns spend about half of their time asleep in _____ sleep, an active form of sleep that may stimulate growth of the nervous system. Some healthy babies die from sudden infant death syndrome. Factors that contribute to SIDS are prematurity, _____, and parental smoking. Also, babies are vulnerable to SIDS when they sleep on their _____ and when they are overheated. The goal of the Back to Sleep campaign is to prevent SIDS by encouraging parents to have infants sleep on their backs.

4. **What are the different features of temperament? Do they change as children grow?**

    Temperament refers to a consistent style or _____ to an infant's behavior. Modern theories list two to six dimensions of temperament, including, for example, extroversion and _____. Temperament is influenced by both heredity and environment and is a reasonably _____ characteristic of infants and young children.

3.2 PHYSICAL DEVELOPMENT

1. **How do height and weight change from birth to two years of age?**

    Physical growth is particularly _____ during infancy, but babies of the same age differ considerably in their height and weight. Size at maturity is largely determined by _____. Growth follows the _____ principle in which the head and trunk develop before the legs. Consequently, infants and young children have disproportionately large _____ and trunks.

2. **What nutrients do young children need? How are they best provided?**

    Infants must consume a large number of _____ relative to their body weight, primarily because of the energy that is required for growth. Breast-feeding and bottle-feeding both provide babies with adequate nutrition. _____ is a worldwide problem that is particularly harmful during infancy, when growth is so rapid. Treating malnutrition adequately requires improving children's diets and training their parents to provide _____ environments.

3. **What are nerve cells, and how are they organized in the brain?**

    A nerve cell, called a _____, includes a cell body, a dendrite, and an _____. The mature brain consists of billions of neurons organized into nearly identical left and right hemispheres connected by the _____. The cerebral cortex controls most of the functions that we think of as distinctively human. The _____ cortex is associated with personality and goal-directed behavior. The left hemisphere of the cortex is associated with _____, and the right hemisphere is associated with _____ processes such as perceiving music and regulating emotions.

4. **How does the brain develop? When does it begin to function?**

    Brain specialization is evident in _____; further specialization involves more focused brain areas and _____ of stimuli that trigger brain activity. Different systems specialize at different rates. Specialization depends upon _____ from the environment. The relative lack of stimulation in the immature brain makes it better able to _____ from injury.

3.3 MOVING AND GRASPING: EARLY MOTOR SKILLS

1. **What are the component skills involved in learning to walk? At what age do infants master them?**

    Infants acquire a series of motor skills during their first year, culminating in walking a few months after the first birthday. Like most motor skills, learning to walk involves _____ of individual skills, such as maintaining balance and using the legs alternately, and then _____ these skills into a unified, coordinated whole.

2. **How do infants learn to coordinate the use of their hands?**

   Infants first use only one hand at a time, then both hands _____, then both hands in common actions, and, finally, at about five months of age, both hands in different actions with a common purpose. Most people are right handed, a preference that emerges after the _____ and that becomes well-established during the preschool years. Handedness is determined by heredity but can also be influenced by _____.

3.4 COMING TO KNOW THE WORLD: PERCEPTION

1. **Are infants able to smell, to taste, and to experience pain?**

   Newborns are able to _____ and some can recognize their mothers' odors. They also taste, preferring _____ substances and responding negatively to bitter and sour tastes. Infants respond to touch. They probably experience pain, because their _____ to painful stimuli are similar to those of older children.

2. **How well can infants hear?**

   Babies can hear. More importantly, they can distinguish different sounds and can use sound to _____ objects in space.

3. **How well can infants see? Can they see color and depth?**

   A newborn's visual acuity is relatively poor, but on-year-olds can see as well as adults with normal vision. Color vision develops as different sets of _____ begin to function, a process that seems to be complete by three or four months of age. Infants perceive depth, based on kinetic cues, _____, and pictorial cues. They also use motion to recognize objects. Infants are particularly attached to _____ and experience leads infants to form a face template based on faces they see often.

4. **How do infants process and combine information from different sensory modalities, such as between vision and hearing?**

   Infants coordinate information from different senses. They can recognize, by _____, an object that they have felt previously. Infants are often particularly attentive to information presented _____ to multiple senses.

77

3.5 BECOMING SELF-AWARE

1. **When do children begin to realize that they exist?**

   Beginning at about 15 months, infants begin to _____ themselves in the mirror, which is one of the first signs of self-recognition. They also begin to prefer to look at pictures of themselves, begin referring to themselves by name (or use personal pronouns), and sometimes know their age and _____. Evidently, by two years of age most children are self-aware.

2. **What are toddlers' and preschoolers' self-concepts like?**

   Preschoolers often define themselves in terms of observable characteristics, such as possessions, _____ characteristics, preferences, and _____.

3. **When do preschool children begin to acquire a theory of mind?**

   Theory of mind (which refers to a person's ideas about connections between thoughts, _____, intentions, and behavior) develops rapidly during the preschool years. Most two-year-olds know that people have desires and that desires can cause _____. By age three, children distinguish the _____ world from the physical world, but still emphasize desire in explaining others' actions. By age four, however, children understand behavior is based on _____ about the world, even when those beliefs are wrong. Children with autism have a _____ theory of mind.

TEST YOURSELF

MULTIPLE-CHOICE QUESTIONS

1. When a baby throws its arms out and then draws them inward in response to a loud noise or when its head falls, the baby is displaying the _____ reflex.

   a. Babinski

   b. palmar

   c. rooting

   d. Moro

2. Kelly has noticed that whenever she places an object in her newborn son's hand, he grasps it tightly. He is demonstrating the _____ reflex.

   a. Moro

   b. palmar

   c. Babinski

   d. rooting

3. Mariko's newborn baby received an Apgar score of 10. This means that her baby

    a. was stillborn.

    b. has a life-threatening condition.

    c. needs special attention and care.

    d. is in good physical health.

4. The Neonatal Behavioral Assessment Scale (NBAS)

    a. is a prenatal diagnostic procedure.

    b. provides a quick, approximate assessment of the newborn's status.

    c. involves a comprehensive evaluation of a broad range of newborn abilities and behaviors.

    d. assesses the risk an infant has of dying from sudden infant death syndrome.

5. Two-month-old Stephen is calm and his eyes are open and attentive. He seems to be inspecting the room he is in. Stephen is in a(n) _____ state.

    a. alert inactivity

    b. waking activity

    c. crying

    d. sleeping

6. Newborns spend most of their time in which of the following states?

    a. Sleep

    b. Alert inactivity

    c. Waking activity

    d. Crying

7. Most babies sleep five to six hours straight by

    a. 2 or 3 weeks of age.

    b. 3 or 4 months of age.

    c. 5 or 6 months of age.

    d. 7 or 8 months of age.

8. Sudden infant death syndrome (SIDS) is more likely

    a. when infants sleep on their backs than when they sleep on their stomachs.

    b. in the spring or fall than in the winter.

    c. in infants whose parents smoke.

    d. when infants are underdressed and get cold.

9. Hannah is generally happy, active, and vocal. Hannah is high on which temperament dimension?

    a. Surgency/extroversion

    b. Negative affect

    c. Persistence

    d. Effortful control

10. An infant's weight typically _____ between birth and one year of age.

    a. doubles

    b. triples

    c. quadruples

    d. quintuples

11. The correlation between the average of two parents' height and their child's height at two years of age is about

    a. −.9

    b. 0.0

    c. .2

    d. .7

12. Which of the following comparisons of breast-feeding and bottle-feeding is FALSE?

    a. Breast-fed infants are more prone to diarrhea and constipation.

    b. Breast milk contains more antibodies that help to fight disease.

    c. Breast-fed infants are less likely to develop allergies from their milk.

    d. Breast-fed infants make the transition to solid foods more easily.

13. Malnourishment is most harmful during

    a. infancy.

    b. early childhood.

    c. later childhood.

    d. adolescence.

14. Malnourished children

    a. tend to be overly active.

    b. are often listless and lethargic.

    c. are usually very attentive.

    d. need to be in environments with low levels of stimulation.

15. The _____ is the basic unit in the brain and the rest of the nervous system and is a cell that specializes in receiving and transmitting information.

    a. terminal button

    b. dendrite

    c. axon

    d. neuron

16. The _____, located in the center of the neuron, contains the basic biological machinery that keeps the neuron alive.

    a. axon

    b. dendrite

    c. cell body

    d. terminal button

17. _____ are chemical messengers that transmit information to other neurons.

    a. Neurotransmitters

    b. Terminal buttons

    c. Dendrites

    d. Axons

18. Personality and deliberate goal-oriented behavior seem to be controlled in the _____ of the brain.

    a. left hemisphere

    b. right hemisphere

    c. corpus callosum

    d. frontal cortex

19. Language is controlled largely by the _____ of the brain.

    a. left hemisphere

    b. right hemisphere

    c. corpus callosum

    d. frontal cortex

20. The bundle of neurons that connects the right and left hemispheres of the brain is called the

    a. corpus callosum.

    b. frontal cortex.

    c. neural plate.

    d. terminal button.

21. _____ is a fatty wrap that allows neurons to transmit information more rapidly.

    a. The cerebral cortex

    b. Myelin

    c. The neurotransmitter

    d. The terminal button

22. Unnecessary connections between neurons disappear between infancy and adolescence, a process called

    a. neuroplasticity.

    b. synaptic pruning.

    c. neural transmission.

    d. functional magnetic resonance.

23. The extent to which brain organization is flexible is referred to as

    a. synaptic pruning.

    b. functional magnetic resonance.

    c. neural transmission.

    d. plasticity.

24. By what age are most infants able to sit alone?

    a. 3 months

    b. 5 months

    c. 7 months

    d. 12 months

25. Most infants learn to walk alone at about _____ months of age.

    a. 6 to 8

    b. 9 to 10

    c. 12 to 15

    d. 20 to 24

26. Which of the following is NOT an essential skill for locomotion?

    a. The ability to maintain an upright posture

    b. The ability to continuously adjust posture to avoid falling down

    c. The ability to alternately move the legs

    d. The ability to bend legs at the knee when running

27. Taiji has just started being able to coordinate the motions of his hands. He now can hold a toy car in one hand and explore it with his other hand. Taiji is probably about _____ months of age.

    a. 2 to 3

    b. 5 to 6

    c. 8 to 10

    d. 12 to 15

28. Right- or left-hand preference usually starts to emerge

    a. when the child enters school.

    b. during the late preschool years.

    c. by age one year.

    d. at birth.

29. Newborns have

    a. highly developed senses of taste and smell.

    b. a highly developed sense of smell but not taste.

    c. a highly developed sense of taste but not smell.

    d. poorly developed senses of taste and smell.

30. Which of the following statements about infant hearing is true?

    a. Newborns are not sensitive to sound.

    b. Six-month-old infants can hear sounds but cannot distinguish different pitches.

    c. Infants hear better than adults.

    d. Six- to seven-month-old infants are able to distinguish different pitches and differentiate many speech sounds.

31. A typical newborn can see at 20 feet what adults with normal vision can see at _____ feet.

    a. 10

    b. 20

    c. 50 to 100

    d. 200 to 400

32. The ability to see color is

    a. fully developed in newborns.

    b. similar to that of adults by three or four months of age.

    c. similar to that of adults starting at about one year of age.

    d. not fully developed until about three years of age.

33. The ability to perceive color is most closely associated with
    a. cones.
    b. retinal disparity.
    c. visual acuity.
    d. the visual cliff.

34. The visual cliff is used to assess
    a. color perception.
    b. visual acuity.
    c. depth perception.
    d. retinal disparity.

35. By the time infants are able to crawl and their mothers try to coax them across the deep side of a visual cliff, the infants typically will
    a. show fear of the deep side and refuse to cross.
    b. show interest in the deep side and readily cross it.
    c. appear to not detect the difference between the deep and shallow sides of the visual cliff.
    d. experience heart rate deceleration.

36. Retinal disparity is used
    a. as a depth cue.
    b. as a color cue.
    c. to assess visual acuity.
    d. to integrate sight and sound.

37. Infants' sensory systems are attuned to information presented simultaneously to different sensory modes, which is known as
    a. intersensory redundancy.
    b. retinal disparity.
    c. linear perspective.
    d. visual expansion.

38. A mother surreptitiously places a red mark on her one-year-old daughter's nose and then places the infant in front of a mirror. What would you expect the infant to do?
    a. Not notice the red mark on the infant in the mirror
    b. Touch the red mark on the face in the mirror
    c. Reach up and touch her own nose
    d. Cry and turn her face away from the mirror

39. Self-awareness is well-established in most children by the age of

    a. 6 months.

    b. 1 year.

    c. 2 years.

    d. 6 years.

40. According to the theory of mind, two-year-olds

    a. understand that behavior is often based on a person's beliefs about events and situations, even when those beliefs are wrong.

    b. often use "mental verbs" like "think," "believe," "remember," and "forget."

    c. understand that people have desires and that desires can cause behavior.

    d. can clearly distinguish the mental world from the physical world.

41. By about _____ years of age, children begin to understand that behavior is often based on a person's beliefs about events and situations, even when those beliefs are false.

    a. 2

    b. 4

    c. 6

    d. 8

42. Which child is in the highest phase of children's theory of mind?

    a. Jill, who understands that behavior is often based on a person's beliefs even when those beliefs are wrong

    b. Callie, who talks about thoughts and beliefs but emphasizes desires when trying to explain why people act as they do

    c. Sienna, who is aware of desires and often speaks of her wants and likes

    d. Annabelle, who can clearly distinguish the mental world from the physical world

ESSAY QUESTIONS

1. Lafon has just had a baby boy named Anthony. In the hospital and during the first few weeks at home, Lafon noticed that when Anthony cries, he stops as soon as she picks him up. Even when she accidentally poked him with a diaper pin, he stopped crying very quickly after she picked him up. Lafon was wondering if Anthony's behavior is any indication that he will be an easy baby and child. What can you tell Lafon about temperament and the stability of temperament?

2. Your friend, Shayda, just had a baby boy named Kyle who weighed 7 pounds 6 ounces at birth. While you and Shayda are out shopping for clothes for Kyle, you notice that she is filling the cart with lots of 0-3 month size clothes. You ask Shayda if she thinks that it's a good idea to buy so many small-sized clothes given how quickly infants grow. Shayda's response is that Kyle is so small now there's no way that he will outgrow all of these clothes so quickly. What can you tell Shayda about infant growth that may persuade her to put some of the clothes back?

3. You have been hired by a local charitable agency that plans to battle malnutrition in your city. You have been to a few meetings, and you have heard people mention the fact that good nutrition will help these malnourished children so they will do better in school. Based on what you know about battling malnutrition, what other aspect should be added to your program?

4. Your friend Elena has noticed that her seven-month-old daughter, Mariana, has been picking up toys with her left hand and will bat at the objects that are hanging above her in her infant gym. Elena and her husband are both right-handed, and they do not want their daughter to become left-handed because so many items are made for right-handed people (e.g., door handles, desk seats, scissors, etc.). What can you tell Elena about the development of handedness and the role of heredity and environment on the development of handedness?

5. Your friend Cole has noticed that his three-week-old son Nate seems to drink more from his bottle when it contains sugar water than when it contains formula. Cole even thinks that he saw Nate lick his lips when he was given a bottle of sugar water. Cole thinks that he is crazy because he doesn't think that the senses are really functioning in babies who are so young. What can you tell Cole that may help him feel better?

6.   Your friend Sunmi keeps leaving her three-month-old son on the edge of the bed or couch. You told her that you don't think that this is a very safe practice, but she said that three-month-old babies can detect depth and they are afraid of falling, so her son will be okay. What can you tell Sunmi about depth perception and fear (as measured by experiments using a visual cliff) that may change her mind?

ANSWERS WITH PAGE REFERENCES

3.1 KNOW THE TERMS

1. Reflexes (82)
2. alert inactivity (84)
3. waking activity (84)
4. crying (84)
5. sleeping (84)
6. basic (84)
7. mad (84)
8. pain (84)
9. REM (irregular) (85)
10. non-REM (regular) (85)
11. sudden infant death syndrome (SIDS) (86)
12. Temperament (87)

3.1 KNOW THE DETAILS OF THE NEWBORN

1. F, 82
2. T, 82
3. T, 82
4. F, 83
5. T, 83
6. F, 83
7. T, 83
8. F, 84
9. T, 84
10. T, 85
11. T, 85
12. F, 85
13. T, 86
14. F, 87
15. F, 88
16. F, 88
17. F, 88

3.2 KNOW THE TERMS

1. malnourished (92)
2. neuron (93)
3. cell body (93)
4. dendrite (93)
5. axon (94)
6. terminal button (94)
7. Neurotransmitters (94)
8. cerebral cortex (94)
9. hemispheres (94)
10. corpus callosum (94)
11. frontal cortex (94)
12. neural plate (94)
13. myelin (95)
14. synaptic pruning (95)
15. electroencephalogram (96)
16. functional magnetic resonance imaging (fMRI) (96)
17. Experience-expectant growth (97)
18. Experience-dependent growth (97)

3.2 KNOW THE DETAILS OF PHYSICAL DEVELOPMENT

1. T, 89	6. F, 92	11. T, 94	16. F, 96
2. F, 91	7. T, 92	12. F, 94	17. T, 96
3. T, 91	8. T, 93	13. T, 94	18. T, 98
4. F, 91	9. F, 94	14. T, 94	
5. T, 91	10. T, 94	15. F, 95	

3.3 KNOW THE TERMS

1. motor skills (98)	5. toddlers (99)
2. locomote (98)	6. dynamic systems theory (100)
3. Fine motor skills (99)	7. differentiation (101)
4. toddling (99)	8. integration (101)

3.3 KNOW THE DETAILS OF EARLY MOTOR SKILLS

1. F, 99	6. F, 100	10. F, 102	14. F, 103
2. T, 99	7. F, 101	11. T, 102	15. T, 103
3. T, 99	8. T, 101	12. T, 103	16. F, 104
4. T, 100	9. F, 101	13. F, 103	17. F, 104
5. F, 100			

3.4 KNOW THE TERMS

1. perception (105)	7. Motion parallax (108)
2. visual acuity (106)	8. Retinal disparity (108)
3. cones (107)	9. pictorial cues (108)
4. visual cliff (108)	10. Linear perspective (108)
5. Kinetic cues (108)	11. texture gradient (108)
6. Visual expansion (108)	12. intersensory redundancy (113)

3.4 KNOW THE DETAILS OF PERCEPTION

1. T, 105	5. F, 106	9. F, 107	13. F, 108
2. F, 105	6. T, 106	10. F, 107	14. T, 110
3. F, 105	7. T, 106	11. F, 108	15. T, 113
4. F, 105	8. T, 107	12. T, 108	

3.5 KNOW THE DETAILS OF BECOMING SELF-AWARE

1.F, 114	3.T, 115	5.F, 115	7.T, 116
2.T, 114	4.T, 115	6.T, 116	8. T, 118

SUMMARY

3.1 THE NEWBORN

1. adjust (82); protect (82)
2. Apgar (83); behavioral (83)
3. alert inactivity (84); mad (84); REM (85); low birth weight (86); stomach (86)
4. pattern (87); negative affect (87); stable (88)

3.2 PHYSICAL DEVELOPMENT

1. rapid (89); heredity (90); cephalocaudal (91); heads (91)
2. calories (91); Malnutrition (92); stimulating (93)
3. neuron (93); axon (94); corpus callosum (94); frontal (94); language (94); nonverbal (94)
4. infancy (95); narrowing (96); stimulation (97); recover (97)

3.3 MOVING AND GRASPING: EARLY MOTOR SKILLS

1. differentiation (101); integration (101)
2. independently (103); first birthday (103); cultural values (104)

3.4 COMING TO KNOW THE WORLD: PERCEPTION

1. smell (105); sweet (105); responses (105)
2. locate (106)
3. cones (107); retinal disparity (108); faces (110)
4. sight (112); redundantly (113)

3.5 BECOMING SELF-AWARE

1. recognize (114); gender (114)
2. physical (115); competencies (115)
3. beliefs (115); behavior (115); mental (115); beliefs (116); limited (117)

TEST YOURSELF

MULTIPLE-CHOICE QUESTIONS

1. d, 83	12. a, 91	23. d, 97	34. c, 108
2. b, 83	13. a, 92	24. c, 99	35. a, 108
3. d, 83	14. b, 93	25. c, 99	36. a, 108
4. c, 83	15. d, 93	26. d, 100	37. a, 113
5. a, 84	16. c, 93	27. b, 103	38. b, 114
6. a, 85	17. a, 94	28. c, 104	39. c, 114
7. b, 85	18. d, 94	29. a, 105	40. c, 115
8. c, 86	19. a, 94	30. d, 106	41. b, 116
9. a, 87	20. a, 94	31. d, 107	42. a, 116
10. b, 89	21. b, 95	32. b, 107	
11. d, 90	22. b, 95	33. a, 107	

ESSAY QUESTIONS

1. Temperament includes two to six different dimensions, including surgency/extroversion (the extent to which the child is generally happy, active, vocal, and regularly seeks interesting stimulation), negative affect (the extent to which a child is irritable, easily distressed, and prone to anger), and effortful control (the extent to which a child can focus attention, is not easily distracted, and can inhibit responses). Anthony's behavior seems to indicate his low level of negative affect. He doesn't seem to become upset easily, and he is easily soothed. Anthony's behavior may also indicate his ability to inhibit responses. Research on the stability of temperament indicates that temperament is somewhat stable during infancy, childhood, and adolescence. For example, newborns who cry under moderate stress are more likely to cry in stressful situations as five-month-olds, and inhibited toddlers tend to respond more strongly to unfamiliar stimuli as adults. The stability is not perfect though, so while it is likely that Anthony will be a fairly calm, easily soothed child, it isn't possible to perfectly predict his future behavior. (87-88)

2. Shayda should know that growth during infancy is more rapid than at any other time during one's life. In fact, the average infant will double his birth weight by the time he is three months old and will triple his weight by his first birthday. So, Kyle will probably weigh around 15 pounds in just 12 weeks. By the time Kyle is one year old, he will probably weigh about 22 pounds. After presenting these facts to Shayda, you might want to ask her if she thinks that she will get her money's worth out of all of those expensive outfits that Kyle will have outgrown in a few short weeks. Fortunately, this rapid growth does taper off, and Shayda might want to buy more expensive clothes when Kyle is older and not growing as rapidly. (89-91)

3. Malnourished children tend to be listless and inactive. They also tend to be very quiet and uninterested in their environments. This behavior often leads parents to conclude that their children are unresponsive, and the parents may start providing fewer experiences to their children. These missed experiences could be important for stimulating the child, so the child loses because of the direct effects of malnutrition and because of the indirect effects of receiving less stimulation. So, effective programs that treat malnutrition need to include not only dietary supplements but also parental training. Parents need to be encouraged to stimulate their children even though they may think they are unresponsive. Parents also may need to be taught which experiences are appropriate stimulation for their children. Children who are in programs that combine dietary supplements with parent training often catch up with their peers both physically and intellectually. In other words, the children in your program probably won't do much better in school just because they are better nourished, so parental training should be included in your program. (92-93)

4. Most children who are Mariana's age (6-9 months old) will use their left and right hands interchangeably, so it is unlikely that Mariana's use of her left hand is predictive of her later hand preference. It isn't until most children are about one year old that they start to show a preference for one hand over the other. Throughout the toddler and preschool years, preference for one hand becomes stronger and more consistent so that by the time a child enters kindergarten hand preference is well-established and difficult to reverse. Heredity does influence handedness. Identical twins are more likely than fraternal twins to have the same handedness. Given that both Elena and her husband are right-handed, it is likely that Mariana will be right-handed also. However, experience does play a role, too. Evidence of the influence of culture comes from the United States, where teachers used to encourage left-handed children to use their right hands. When this practice stopped, the incidence of left-handedness increased. Given that Mariana has two right-handed parents who are likely to encourage right-handed behavior, she will probably become right-handed, but it is too early to tell. (104)

5. Infants have a highly developed sense of taste. They can easily tell the difference between sweet, salty, bitter, and sour tastes. In fact, infants seem to react to these different tastes in ways that are similar to the reactions of adults. For example, most infants seem to have a sweet tooth because they react to sweet substances by licking their lips, smiling, and sucking on the bottle longer. Infants also show negative reactions to bitter and sour tastes. So, Cole is not going crazy—Nate probably does have a sweet tooth and is reacting positively to the sugar water. (105)

6. When six-week-old infants are placed on the deep side of a visual cliff, their heart rates will drop, indicating that they perceive the depth but only find it interesting, not frightening. However, by the time infants are old enough to crawl (around seven months of age), their heart rates increase when they are placed on the deep side of the visual cliff, indicating that they perceive the depth and are frightened by it. So, Sunmi should know that, yes, her son can detect the drop off the bed or couch, but he probably isn't old enough to be afraid of the drop, and he is likely to fall. (108)

THE EMERGENCE OF THOUGHT AND LANGUAGE

4.1   The Onset of Thinking: Piaget's Account

4.2   Information Processing during Infancy and Early Childhood

4.3   Mind and Culture: Vygotsky's Theory

4.4   Language

This chapter focuses on language development and theories of cognitive development such as Piaget's theory, information-processing theories, and Vygotsky's theory.

4.1 THE ONSET OF THINKING: PIAGET'S ACCOUNT

TO MASTER THE LEARNING OBJECTIVES:

According to Piaget, how do schemes, assimilation, and accommodation provide the foundation for cognitive development throughout the life-span?

- Explain Piaget's concepts of scheme, assimilation, accommodation, and equilibration and how they are related to each other.

93

How does thinking become more advanced as infants progress through the sensorimotor stage?

- Describe the development from reflexive behavior to active experimentation.

- Describe the infant's understanding of objects.

- Explain what "using symbols" means and why it is an important achievement for cognitive development.

What are the distinguishing characteristics of thinking during the preoperational stage?

- Describe how the three-mountains problem demonstrates egocentrism in preoperational children.

- Describe animism in preoperational children.

- Describe how centration is demonstrated in the conservation of liquid quantity task.

- Explain how preoperational children confuse appearance and reality.

What are the strengths and weaknesses of Piaget's theory?

- Describe the implications of Piaget's theory for teaching practices.

- Describe the four criticisms of Piaget's theory.

How have contemporary researchers extended Piaget's theory?

- Explain how Baillargeon's research involving possible events and impossible events conflicts with Piaget's description of the timing of object permanence.

- Describe children's naive theories of physics and biology.

4.1 KNOW THE TERMS

Accommodation	Equilibration
Animism	Essentialism
Assimilation	Object permanence
Centration	Schemes
Core knowledge hypothesis	Sensorimotor
Egocentrism	Teleological explanations

1. According to Piaget, psychological structures that organize experience are called

   _____.

2. _____ occurs when new experiences are readily incorporated into existing schemes.

3. _____ occurs when schemes are modified based on experience.

4. The process of reorganizing one's schemes to return to a state of equilibrium is known as

   _____.

5.   The _____ period is the first of Piaget's four stages of cognitive development. This period lasts from birth to approximately two years.

6.   Piaget's term for understanding that objects exist independently is _____.

7.   The young child's difficulty in seeing the world from another's outlook is called _____.

8.   Crediting inanimate objects with life and life-like properties is called _____.

9.   Narrowly focused thought that characterizes preoperational thought is called _____.

10.   A rudimentary knowledge of the world that is elaborated based on children's experiences is called _____.

11.   Children's beliefs that living things and parts of living things exist for a purpose is called _____.

12.   Children's beliefs that all living things have an essence that can't be seen but that gives an identity is called _____.

4.1 KNOW THE DETAILS OF PIAGET'S ACCOUNT

1.   According to Piaget, thinking changes quantitatively but not qualitatively with age.
TRUE or FALSE

2.   Piaget believed that during infancy, most schemes are based on conceptual categories, not actions.
TRUE or FALSE

3.   Assimilation occurs when a scheme is changed because of a new experience.
TRUE or FALSE

4.   Disequilibrium has occurred when a child spends more time accommodating than assimilating schemes.
TRUE or FALSE

5.   Children can go through Piaget's periods of development in many different sequences.
TRUE or FALSE

6.   Infants are in Piaget's concrete operational period of cognitive development.
TRUE or FALSE

7.   According to Piaget, newborns respond reflexively rather than intentionally.
TRUE or FALSE

8. Piaget proposed that infants lack object permanence in the first six months of life.
   TRUE or FALSE

9. According to Piaget, infants are able to use symbols by the end of the sensorimotor period.
   TRUE or FALSE

10. Children in Piaget's preoperational period generally believe that other people view the world differently than they do.
    TRUE or FALSE

11. Preoperational thinkers often confuse appearance and reality.
    TRUE or FALSE

12. Piagetian theory suggests that the teacher's role is to create environments where children can discover for themselves how the world works.
    TRUE or FALSE

13. Piagetian theory suggests that teachers can speed up children's cognitive growth by pointing out inconsistencies in children's thinking rather than letting children figure out inconsistencies themselves.
    TRUE or FALSE

14. Piaget has been criticized for overestimating cognitive competence in infants and underestimating cognitive competence in adolescents.
    TRUE or FALSE

15. Piaget's theory has been criticized because children often perform less consistently on Piagetian tasks than Piaget's theory suggests they would.
    TRUE or FALSE

16. One criticism of Piaget's theory is that it overestimates the influence of interactions with family members, peers, and teachers on cognitive development.
    TRUE or FALSE

17. In contrast to Piaget's view that children develop general theories of the world, more recent views of children's cognitive development propose that children develop more specialized theories about narrow areas.
    TRUE or FALSE

18. By the preschool years, children's naive theories of biology include the idea that animals can move themselves, but inanimate objects can only be moved by other objects or by people.
    TRUE or FALSE

4.2 INFORMATION PROCESSING DURING INFANCY AND EARLY CHILDHOOD

TO MASTER THE LEARNING OBJECTIVES:

What is the basis of the information-processing approach?

- Describe the information-processing approach to human thinking. What constitutes a person's hardware and software?

How well do young children pay attention?

- Define attention, orienting response, and habituation.
- Describe what can be done to help children pay attention to relevant information.

What kinds of learning take place during infancy?

- Describe infants' learning in classical conditioning, operant conditioning, and imitation.

Do infants and preschool children remember?

- Describe the three important features of infant's memories that were found by Carolyn Rovee-Collier.
- Describe the improvements in memory as children become toddlers.
- Define autobiographical memory and describe how parents, language skill, and a sense of self contribute to it.
- Describe cultural differences in autobiographical memory.
- Describe preschoolers' eyewitness memory and its relation to source monitoring.
- Describe the three guidelines that should be followed to help improve the reliability of child witnesses

What do infants and preschoolers know about numbers?

- Describe a young infant's ability to distinguish different numbers of objects.
- Describe young children's counting ability, including the three counting principles that most children master by age three.

4.2 KNOW THE TERMS

Attention

Autobiographical memory

Cardinality

Classical conditioning

Habituation

Hardware

One-to-one

Operant conditioning

Orienting response

Software

Stable-order

1. The term mental _____ refers to mental and neural structures that are built in and that allow the mind to operate.

2. The term mental _____ refers to mental programs that are the basis for performing particular tasks.

3. _____ determines which information will be processed further by an individual.

4. An _____ occurs when a person starts, fixes his eyes on a stimulus, and shows changes in heart-rate and brain-wave activity.

5. The diminished response to a stimulus as it becomes more familiar is called _____.

6. _____ occurs when a neutral stimulus elicits a response that was originally produced by another stimulus.

7. _____ focuses on the relation between the consequences of behavior and the likelihood that the behavior will occur.

8. Peoples' memory for the significant events and experiences of their own lives is called _____.

9. The counting principle that states that there must be one and only one number name for each object counted is known as the _____ principle.

10. The counting principle that states that number names must always be counted in the same order is known as the _____ principle.

11. The understanding that the last number name denotes the number of objects one is counting is called the _____ principle.

4.2 KNOW THE DETAILS OF INFORMATION PROCESSING

1. In the information-processing view, human cognition is thought to be based on mental hardware and mental software.
    TRUE or FALSE

2. Information-processing theorists believe that as children develop, their mental software becomes more complex, more powerful, and more efficient.
    TRUE or FALSE

3. An orienting response is the diminished response to a stimulus as it becomes more familiar.
    TRUE or FALSE

4. Young children focus their attention as effectively as adults.
    TRUE or FALSE

5. Infants and toddlers are not capable of learning through classical conditioning.
    TRUE or FALSE

6. Operant conditioning focuses on the relation between the consequences of behavior and the likelihood that the behavior will reoccur.
    TRUE or FALSE

7. Young babies cannot remember events for more than one day.
    TRUE or FALSE

8. Structures in the brain that are responsible for retrieving memories develop much later than those responsible for the initial storage of information.
    TRUE or FALSE

9. Autobiographical memory emerges during infancy.
    TRUE or FALSE

10. Law-enforcement officials and child-protection workers can almost always accurately judge whether children are telling the truth about child abuse.
    TRUE or FALSE

11. Children's testimony is more accurate when they are encouraged to correct the interviewer when they say something that's incorrect.
    TRUE or FALSE

12. Children's testimony is more reliable when they are asked questions that have them evaluate alternative hypotheses rather than questions that ask for a single correct answer.
    TRUE or FALSE

13. Child witnesses are more reliable when they are questioned repeatedly on a single issue.
    TRUE or FALSE

14. By two years of age, children usually know some number words and have begun to count.
    TRUE or FALSE

15. The cardinality principle refers to the principle that there must be one and only one number name for each object that is counted.
    TRUE or FALSE

16. The stable-order principle states that number names must be counted in the same order.
    TRUE or FALSE

4.3 MIND AND CULTURE: VYGOTSKY'S THEORY

TO MASTER THE LEARNING OBJECTIVES:

What is the zone of proximal development? How does it help explain how children accomplish more when they collaborate with others?

- Define intersubjectivity and guided participation.
- Describe Vygotsky's zone of proximal development.

Why is scaffolding a particularly effective way of teaching youngsters new concepts and skills?

- Describe how "teachers" use scaffolding to aid learning.
- How does scaffolding differ in different cultures?

When and why do children talk to themselves as they solve problems?

- Describe the process by which private speech becomes inner speech. What function does private speech serve?

4.3 KNOW THE TERMS

Guided participation	Scaffolding
Intersubjectivity	Zone of proximal development
Private speech	

1. _____ is the mutual, shared understanding among participants in an activity.

2. _____ occurs when children are involved in structured activities with others who are more skilled.

3. The difference between what someone can do with assistance and what she can do by herself is called _____.

4. A teaching style in which teachers gauge the amount of assistance that they offer to the learner's needs is called _____.

5. Comments that are not intended for others but serve the purpose of helping children regulate their behavior are known as _____.

4.3 KNOW THE DETAILS OF VYGOTSKY'S THEORY

1. According to Vygotsky, children progress faster developmentally when they collaborate with more skilled people than when they learn on their own.
   TRUE or FALSE

2. The zone of proximal development is the area between children's capability when working alone and their performance when working with the guidance of a more skilled person.
   TRUE or FALSE

3. Vygotsky proposed that cognition is initially under the child's independent control and then gradually begins functioning in a social setting as well.
   TRUE or FALSE

4. Children require more scaffolding with a familiar task than with a novel task.
   TRUE or FALSE

5. Private speech is an intermediate step toward self-regulation of cognitive skills.
   TRUE or FALSE

6. As children gain greater skill, private speech becomes "inner speech."
   TRUE or FALSE

4.4 LANGUAGE

TO MASTER THE LEARNING OBJECTIVES:

When do infants first hear and make speech sounds?

- Define phonemes.

- Describe how habituation is used to determine if infants can distinguish different speech sounds.

- Describe how an infant's ability to discriminate speech sounds that are not found in her language environments changes as she approaches her first birthday.

- Explain how infants identify words.

- Define infant-directed speech, and describe how the features of this type of speech might aid language development.

When do children start to talk? How do they learn word meanings?

- Define cooing, babbling, and intonation, and describe how each changes during the first year of life.

- Describe some early words that are found in young children's vocabularies.

- Explain why recognizing words as symbols is important for language development.

- Define fast mapping, and describe how joint attention, constraints on word names, sentence cues, and cognitive factors influence word learning.

- Describe developmental changes in word learning.

- Know the difference between overextensions and underextensions.

- Define phonological memory.

- Describe language development in bilingual children.

- Know the difference between referential and expressive word learning styles.

- Describe the importance of the child's language environment.

- Explain how parents and television are related to children's language growth.

- Describe the effectiveness of infant-oriented videos on word learning.

How do young children learn grammar?

- Define telegraphic speech, grammatical morphemes, and overregularization, and explain how they are related to each other.

- Explain behaviorist, linguistic, cognitive, and social-interaction explanations of children's mastery of grammar.

How well do youngsters communicate?

- Explain how turn-taking changes in one- to three-year-olds.

- Describe how preschoolers adjust their messages to listeners' different needs.

- Describe how listening skills change over the preschool years.

4.4 KNOW THE TERMS

Babbling	Overregularization
Cooing	Phonemes
Expressive	Phonological memory
Fast mapping	Referential
Grammatical morphemes	Telegraphic
Infant-directed	Underextension
Overextension	

1. Unique speech sounds that can be used to create words are called _____.

2. Speech that adults use with babies that is slow, loud, and has exaggerated changes in pitch is called _____ speech.

3. Early vowel-like sounds that babies produce are known as _____.

4. Speech-like sounds that consist of a vowel-consonant combination are known as

   _____.

5. The fact that children make connections between new words and referents so quickly that they can't be considering all possible meanings is known as _____.

6. An _____ occurs when children define a word too broadly.

7. An _____ occurs when children define a word too narrowly.

8. The ability to remember speech sounds briefly is called_____.

9. Vocabularies of children who use a(n) _____ language style are dominated by names of objects, people, or actions.

10. Vocabularies of children who use a(n) _____ language style include many social phrases that are used like a single word.

11. Young children often use _____ speech, which contains only the words that are directly relevant to meaning, and nothing more.

12. Words or endings of words that make a sentence grammatical are known as _____.

13. Applying grammatical rules to words that are exceptions to the rules is known as

_____.

4.4 KNOW THE DETAILS OF LANGUAGE

DEVELOPMENT

1. Infants can distinguish speech sounds as early as one month after birth.
   TRUE or FALSE

2. Young infants can discriminate speech sounds that do not occur in their native language, but they later lose this ability.
   TRUE or FALSE

3. When using infant-directed speech, adults speak quickly and in a monotone voice.
   TRUE or FALSE

4. Infants begin to babble before they are able to coo.
   TRUE or FALSE

5. Infants typically understand many words before they can say them.
   TRUE or FALSE

6. Fast mapping refers to the fact that children make connections between new words and referents so rapidly that they cannot be considering all possible meanings for the new word.
   TRUE or FALSE

7. Toddlers are more likely to learn the name of an object when adults look at the object while saying its name instead of looking elsewhere.
   TRUE or FALSE

8. When children are learning new words, they usually follow the rule that if an unfamiliar word is heard in the presence of objects that already have names and those that don't, the word refers to one of the objects that doesn't already have a name.
   TRUE or FALSE

9. Early language learning depends mostly on attentional processes to learn new words, but later on, language and social cues become more important.
   TRUE or FALSE

10. A child's language environment is the single factor that has the most impact on rate of vocabulary growth.

    TRUE or FALSE

11. When children define a word too narrowly, it is referred to as an underextension.

    TRUE or FALSE

12. Children with an expressive language learning style have vocabularies that are dominated by words that are the names of objects, people, and actions.

    TRUE or FALSE

13. Preschool children who often watch *Sesame Street* typically have larger vocabularies in kindergarten than do preschoolers who watch *Sesame Street* less often.

    TRUE or FALSE

14. Phonemes are words or endings of words that make a sentence grammatical.

    TRUE or FALSE

15. Overregularization occurs when children apply rules to words that are exceptions to the rule.

    TRUE or FALSE

16. Behaviorists believe that children are born with a "grammar-learning processor."

    TRUE or FALSE

17. Parents do not usually encourage conversational turn-taking until their children have said their first words.

    TRUE or FALSE

18. By the time they are preschoolers, children have begun to adjust their speech to match the listener and the context.

    TRUE or FALSE

19. Preschoolers are able to recognize when a message is ambiguous and will ask for clarification.

    TRUE or FALSE

SUMMARY

4.1 THE ONSET OF THINKING: PIAGET'S ACCOUNT

1. **According to Piaget, how do schemes, assimilation, and accommodation provide the foundation for cognitive development throughout the life-span?**

   In Piaget's views, children construct their own understanding of the world by creating _____, categories of related events, objects, and knowledge. Infants' schemes are based on _____, but older children's and adolescents' schemes are based on functional, _____, and abstract properties. Schemes change constantly. In _____, experiences are readily incorporated into existing schemes. In _____, experiences cause schemes to be modified. When accommodation becomes more common than assimilation, this is a sign that children's schemes are inadequate, so children reorganize them. This reorganization produces four different phases of mental development from infancy through adulthood.

2. **How does thinking become more advanced as infants progress through the sensorimotor stage?**

   The first two years of life constitute Piaget's sensorimotor period. Over these two years, infants begin to adapt to and explore their environment, understand objects, and begin to use _____.

3. **What are the distinguishing characteristics of thinking during the preoperational stage?**

   From two to seven years of age, children are in Piaget's preoperational stage. Although now capable of using symbols, their thinking is limited by _____, the inability to see the world from another's point of view. Preoperational children also are _____ in their thinking and sometimes confuse appearance with _____.

4. **What are the strengths and weaknesses of Piaget's theory?**

   One important contribution of Piaget's theory is the view that children _____ try to understand their world. Another contribution is specifying conditions for cognitive development. However, the theory has been criticized because it _____ infants' and preschoolers' competence, is vague regarding _____ of change, does not account for variability in performance, and undervalues the influence of the _____ environment.

5. **How have contemporary researchers extended Piaget's theory?**

In contrast to Piaget's idea that children create a comprehensive theory that integrates all knowledge, the modern view is that children are _____, who generate naive theories in particular domains, including physics and biology. Infants understand many properties of objects; they know how objects move, what happens when objects _____, and that objects fall when not supported. Infants understand the difference between animate and inanimate objects. As preschoolers, children know that, unlike inanimate objects, animate objects move themselves, _____, have distinct internal parts, resemble their parents, and repair through healing.

4.2 INFORMATION-PROCESSING DURING INFANCY AND EARLY CHILDHOOD

1. **What is the basis of the information-processing approach?**

According to the information-processing view, cognitive development involves changes in mental _____ and in mental software.

2. **How well do young children pay attention?**

Infants use _____ to filter unimportant stimuli. Compared to older children, preschoolers are less able to pay _____ to task-relevant information. Their attention can be improved by making irrelevant stimuli less noticeable.

3. **What kinds of learning take place during infancy?**

Infants are capable of many different forms of learning, including classical conditioning, operant conditioning, and _____.

4. **Do infants and preschool children remember?**

Infants can remember and can be reminded of events that they seem to have forgotten. _____ emerges in the preschool years, reflecting children's growing language skills and their sense of _____. Preschoolers sometimes testify in cases of child abuse. When they are questioned repeatedly, preschoolers often have difficulty distinguishing what they really _____ from what others may suggest that they have experienced. Inaccuracies of this sort can be minimized by following certain guidelines when interviewing children, such as asking questions that consider _____ explanations of the event.

5. **What do infants know about numbers?**

   Infants are able to distinguish small quantities, such as "twoness" from _____. By three years of age, youngsters can count small sets of objects, and in so doing, adhere to the _____, stable-order, and principles. Learning to count to larger numbers involves learning rules about unit and decade names. This learning is more difficult for English-speaking children compared to children from Asian countries, because names for numbers are _____ in English.

4.3 MIND AND CULTURE: VYGOTSKY'S THEORY

1. **What is the zone of proximal development? How does it help explain how children accomplish more when they collaborate with others?**

   Vygotsky believed that cognition develops first in a _____ setting and only gradually comes under the child's independent control. The difference between what children can do with assistance and what they can do alone constitutes the _____.

2. **Why is scaffolding a particularly effective way of teaching youngsters new concepts and skills?**

   Control of cognitive skills is most readily transferred to the child through scaffolding, a teaching style in which teachers let children take on _____ of a task as they master its different components. Scaffolding is common worldwide, but the specific techniques for scaffolding children's learning _____ from one cultural setting to the next.

3. **When and why do children talk to themselves as they solve problems?**

   Children often talk to themselves, particularly when the task is _____ or after they have made a mistake. Such _____ is one way that children help to regulate their own behavior and represents an intermediate step in the transfer of control of thinking from others to the self.

4.4 LANGUAGE

1. **When do infants hear and make speech sounds?**

   _____ are the basic units of sound from which words are constructed. Infants can hear phonemes soon after birth. They can even hear phonemes that are not used in their native language, but this ability _____ after the first birthday. Infant-directed speech refers to adults' speech to infants that is _____ and that has greater variation in pitch and loudness. Infants prefer infant-directed speech, perhaps because it gives them additional language clues. Newborns' communication is limited to crying, but at about three months of age, babies _____. Babbling soon follows, consisting of a single syllable; over several months, infants' babbling includes longer syllables and _____.

2. **When do children start to talk? How do they learn word meanings?**

After a brief period in which children appear to understand other's speech but do not speak themselves, most infants will begin to speak around the _____. The first use of words is triggered by the realization that words are _____. Soon after, vocabulary expands rapidly.

Most children learn the meanings of words much too rapidly for them to consider all plausible meanings systematically. Instead, children use a number of rules to determine probable meanings of new words. The rules do not always lead to the correct meaning. An _____ is a child's meaning that is narrower than an adult's meaning, and an overextension is a child's meaning that is broader.

Individual children differ in the size of their vocabularies. These differences are attributable to _____ and the quality of the language environment. Bilingual children learn language readily and have a better understanding of the nature of words. Some youngsters use a referential style that emphasizes words as names and that views language as an intellectual tool. Other children use an _____ style that emphasizes phrases and that views language as a social tool.

Children's vocabulary is stimulated by experience. Both parents and television can foster the growth of vocabulary: the key ingredient is actively involving children in language-related activities.

3. **How do young children learn grammar?**

Soon after children speak, they create two-word sentences that are derived from their own experiences. Moving from two-word to more complex sentences involves adding grammatical _____. Children first master grammatical morphemes that express simple relations, then those that denote complex relations. Mastery of grammatical morphemes involves learning rules as well as the _____ to the rules.

Behaviorists proposed that children acquire grammar through _____, but that explanation is incorrect. Today's explanations come from three perspectives: the linguistic perspective emphasizes _____ mechanisms that allow children to infer grammatical rules of their native language, the cognitive perspective emphasizes cognitive processes that allow children to find _____ in the speech they hear, and the social-interaction perspective emphasizes social interactions with _____ in which both parties want improved communication.

4. **How well do young children communicate?**

Parents encourage _____ even before infants talk and, later, demonstrate both the speaker and listener roles for their children. By three years of age, children spontaneously take turns and prompt one another to take their turn. Preschool children adjust their speech in a rudimentary fashion to fit the listener's _____. However, preschoolers are unlikely to identify_____ in another's speech; instead, they are more likely to assume that they knew what the speaker meant.

TEST YOURSELF

MULTIPLE-CHOICE QUESTIONS

1. In Piaget's theory, mental structures that organize information and regulate behavior are called
   a. schemes.
   b. core knowledge hypotheses.
   c. scaffolding.
   d. mental software.

2. According to Piaget, intellectual adaptation occurs through
   a. the processes of accommodation and assimilation.
   b. classical conditioning.
   c. the formation of associations between stimuli and responses.
   d. imitation of others.

3. When new experiences are easily fit into existing schemes, Piaget would say that _____ is taking place.
   a. fast mapping
   b. assimilation
   c. accommodation
   d. overextension

4. Two-year-old Joey played with stuffed animals, picking them up by their ears and dragging them around the house. Joey's parents gave him a live puppy for his birthday. Joey tried to pick her up by her ears and drag her around the house. The puppy wiggled and whimpered. Joey decided he was going to have to change his scheme for playing with animal objects. Piaget would say that this is an example of

    a. overregularization.

    b. assimilation.

    c. accommodation.

    d. habituation.

5. In which of the following is Piaget's periods of cognitive development in proper sequence?

    a. Preoperational, concrete operational, sensorimotor, formal operational

    b. Sensorimotor, preoperational, formal operational, concrete operational

    c. Sensorimotor, preoperational, concrete operational, formal operational

    d. Preoperational, sensorimotor, formal operational, concrete operational

6. The end of the sensorimotor period is marked by

    a. reflexive responding.

    b. the ability to use mental symbols.

    c. the absence of object permanence.

    d. unintentional behavior.

7. Piaget's concept of egocentrism is best illustrated by which of the following?

    a. Five-year-old Katie preening in front of a mirror

    b. Four-year-old Kelly holding a picture in front of the television so Big Bird can see it

    c. Six-year-old Kaitlin calling her friend Kara every day to see if she can play

    d. Three-year-old Kaylie believing that she becomes a princess when she puts on a crown

8. Which of the following statements best demonstrates Piaget's concept of animism?

    a. "Luke hates cats."

    b. "Nick is terribly bull-headed."

    c. "Jake claimed the ball was tired and just didn't want to go in the basket."

    d. "Carson flew like a bird down to the end of the court."

9. Which of the following is NOT a characteristic of preoperational thinking?

    a. Ability to distinguish between appearance and reality

    b. Egocentrism

    c. Animism

    d. Centration

10. Confusion between appearance and reality is a characteristic of

    a. sensorimotor thinking.

    b. concrete operational thinking.

    c. preoperational thinking.

    d. formal operational thinking.

11. Which of the following is NOT a criticism of Piaget's theory of cognitive development?

    a. Piaget's theory overestimates cognitive competence in infants and young children.

    b. Piaget's theory is too vague to test scientifically.

    c. Children's performance across several of Piaget's tasks is less consistent than it should be according to Piaget's theory.

    d. Piaget's theory undervalues the influence of the sociocultural environment on cognitive development.

12. The idea that infants are born with rudimentary knowledge of the world, with the knowledge being elaborated based on the children's experience, is known as

    a. adaptation.

    b. equilibration.

    c. scaffolding.

    d. the core knowledge hypothesis.

13. Preschool children's naive theories of biology include all of the following EXCEPT

    a. thinking that inanimate objects can move by themselves.

    b. understanding that living things have offspring that resemble their parents.

    c. believing that animals get bigger but inanimate objects do not grow.

    d. knowing that the insides of animate objects contain different materials than the insides of inanimate objects.

14. The information-processing view

    a. proposes that cognitive development occurs in a sequence of four stages.

    b. considers adaptation to be the primary mechanism for development.

    c. compares human cognition to computer hardware and software.

    d. is based on behavioral learning theory.

15. Mental programs that are the basis for performing particular tasks are called mental

    a. hardware.

    b. software.

    c. adaptations.

    d. scaffolding.

16. When Chris first saw the shiny red car, he couldn't take his eyes off it. After seeing it several times, he paid less attention to it. His diminished response is due to
    a. attention.
    b. habituation.
    c. an orienting response.
    d. operant conditioning.

17. Gayle wants to teach her four-year-old daughter, Molly, to write her name. However, every time they sit down at the kitchen table to practice, Gayle cannot get Molly to pay attention long enough to write anything. What advice would be most appropriate to give Gayle?
    a. Give up on trying to get Molly to write her name for now. Molly is not yet capable of paying attention for any length of time.
    b. Try to make the work area more interesting and attractive by adding lots of pictures, bright colors, and manipulative objects.
    c. Don't keep telling Molly to practice her name. Let her try it only when she chooses.
    d. Try working in a quieter, less distracting area with fewer people around.

18. Gabby learned that when her mother showed her a bottle, it was an indication that she would soon be fed, therefore she would get excited whenever she saw a bottle. This is best explained through the process called
    a. habituation.
    b. the orienting response.
    c. classical conditioning.
    d. operant conditioning.

19. In infant memory research, three-month-old infants who learned to kick a mobile to make it move
    a. were able to remember to kick to make the mobile move a few days later.
    b. were able to remember to kick to make the mobile move several weeks later only if they were given cues.
    c. were never able to remember to kick to make the mobile move any time after the day they were taught.
    d. never forgot that kicking made the mobile move.

20. Joshua remembers many details about his sixth birthday party. This would be considered

    a. an autobiographical memory.

    b. an orienting response.

    c. habituation.

    d. attention.

21. Which of the following guidelines concerning the reliability of child witnesses is supported by research?

    a. Use questions with a single, correct answer instead of questions that evaluate alternative hypotheses.

    b. Question children repeatedly on a single issue.

    c. Tell children to feel free to say, "I don't know."

    d. Always trust what the child says. In a courtroom situation, children are unlikely to say something happened unless it actually did happen.

22. The cardinality principle states that

    a. there must be one and only one number name for each object that is counted.

    b. number names must be counted in the same order.

    c. the last number name differs from the previous ones in a counting sequence by denoting the number of objects.

    d. numbers can differ in magnitude; some values are greater than others.

23. Sonja understands that number names must be counted in the same order. Sonja has mastered the

    a. one-to-one principle.

    b. cardinality principle.

    c. ordinality principle.

    d. stable-order principle.

24. Vygotsky provided

    a. a complete theory of cognitive development from birth through adolescence.

    b. definitive accounts of cognitive change in specific domains.

    c. a view of development as an apprenticeship.

    d. a perspective of human thinking based on mental hardware and mental software.

25. Five-year-old Winnie was unable to arrange the furniture in her dollhouse by herself. However, she was able to completely arrange the furniture when her mother helped her sort the furniture by room and then suggested that she work on one room at a time. The difference between what Winnie was able to do on her own and what she could do with her mother's help is called

    a. her zone of proximal development.

    b. scaffolding.

    c. equilibration.

    d. habituation.

26. Scaffolding refers to

    a. the difference between what someone can do with and without assistance.

    b. a style in which teachers gauge the amount of assistance that they offer to match a learner's needs.

    c. comments children make that are not intended for others, but, instead, are designed to help them regulate their own behavior.

    d. cognition that is under the child's independent control.

27. Children are more likely to use private speech

    a. after a correct response than after a mistake.

    b. on difficult tasks than on easy tasks.

    c. when they are skilled rather than unskilled at a task.

    d. when their behavior is being regulated by speech from other people.

28. The sound of "p" in the word "put" and the sound of "a" in "cat" are both

    a. morphemes.

    b. phonemes.

    c. underextensions.

    d. overextensions.

29. _____ involves speaking more slowly and with exaggerated changes in pitch and loudness.

    a. An overextension

    b. Babbling

    c. Cooing

    d. Infant-directed speech

30. At two months of age, babies start making vowel-like sounds such as "ooooooo" and "ahhhhhh," which are called

    a. babbling.

    b. intonation.

    c. cooing.

    d. infant-directed speech.

31. Infants' babbling

    a. has the same pattern of intonation regardless of the language spoken by their caregivers.

    b. is influenced by the characteristics of the speech that they hear.

    c. is the same in deaf and hearing infants.

    d. first consists of consonant sounds and then progresses to include vowel sounds.

32. Infants

    a. say their first words at about the same time that they can understand them.

    b. usually understand words before they are able to say them.

    c. usually say words before they understand them.

    d. differ in whether they first understand or say words.

33. A child's ability to make connections between new words and referents so rapidly that they cannot be considering all possible meaning for the new word is referred to as

    a. overregularization.

    b. underextension.

    c. overextension.

    d. fast mapping.

34. Which of the following is a correct statement concerning the rules children use to learn new words?

    a. If an unfamiliar word is heard in the presence of objects that already have names and objects that don't, the word refers to one of the objects that doesn't have a name.

    b. A name refers to a part of an object, not the whole object.

    c. A word name always refers to one particular object, not to all objects of the same type.

    d. If an object already has a name and another name is presented, the new name is incorrect.

35. Eighteen-month-old Shannon saw an older woman with gray hair and called her "Grandma" even though she was not her grandmother. Shannon made a mistake common to young children that is called

    a. telegraphic speech.

    b. overregularization.

    c. an overextension.

    d. an underextension.

36. Children whose vocabularies are dominated by words that are the names of objects, people, or actions have a(n) _____ language learning style.

    a. expressive

    b. overextension

    c. underextension

    d. referential

37. Children whose vocabularies include some names but also many social phrases that are used like a single word have a(n) _____ language learning style.

    a. expressive

    b. referential

    c. overextension

    d. underextension

38. Which of the following should parents do to expand their children's vocabulary?

    a. When reading stories, simply read the story and don't ask children any questions.

    b. Speak to their children infrequently.

    c. Name objects that are the focus of the children's attention.

    d. Do not allow children to watch *Sesame Street* on television.

39. Two-year-old Tyler speaks in sentences such as "Me go" instead of "I want to go," and "She sleep" instead of "She is sleeping." Tyler is using

    a. telegraphic speech.

    b. overregularization.

    c. fast mapping.

    d. grammatical morphemes.

40. Language is learned through imitation and reinforcement according to

    a. linguistic theorists.

    b. cognitive theorists.

    c. social-interaction theorists.

    d. learning theorists.

41. Professor Rubenstein stated that children are born with neural circuits in their brains that allows them to learn language. What viewpoint is Professor Rubenstein conveying?

    a. Social-interaction

    b. Cognitive

    c. Linguistic

    d. Behaviorist

ESSAY QUESTIONS

1. The other day your friend Jamal and his three-year-old daughter, Kia, were at the local shopping mall where they saw an older woman who looked like the witch in *The Wizard of Oz*. Kia pointed at the woman and said, "Look, Dad, there's a witch. She's really mean." Jamal tried to explain to Kia that the woman wasn't a witch and, in fact, she probably is very nice, but Kia insisted that the woman was a witch and that she is very mean. Jamal would like to convince Kia that you "can't judge a book by its cover," but Kia is adamant every time he brings up the subject. What can you tell Jamal about preoperational children's ability to distinguish appearance and reality that might make him feel better?

2. Your seven-month-old son, Matt, loves to play with the remote control for the television. He loves to hear people shout when he changes the channel or turns off the TV in the middle of a show. You remember from your college developmental psychology class that Piaget said that seven-month-olds do not have object permanence—in other words, "out of sight, out of mind." You decide that you will thwart your son and hide the remote control because he doesn't have object permanence. Your spouse, however, has seen new research that suggests that object permanence develops much earlier than Piaget suggested and thinks that Matt will look for the control if you hide it behind a pillow on the couch. Describe the research that demonstrates that object permanence may occur much earlier than Piaget suggested.

3. A teacher at your child's daycare center recently has been accused of child molestation by a three-year-old girl at the daycare. You are talking with one of the other parents and this other parent says, "It must have happened because no child would make up a story like that." What can you tell this other parent about testimony by young children, and what should be done to ensure more reliable testimony from them?

4. Your brother Pretesh is concerned that his two-year-old daughter's counting ability is below average. When she counts, his daughter will say, "one, two, c, door...door balls" when counting the four balls in a picture book. What can you tell Pretesh about the mastery of the principles of counting that will reassure him that his daughter can count perfectly well for someone her age?

5. You have been watching your friend Collum trying to teach his son Sean how to do a puzzle. Sean has done this puzzle many times, and he usually just needs help with the pieces that are in an area that is all black. Collum is trying to help Sean, but his instructions would be appropriate for someone who has never done the puzzle before. What can you tell Collum about Vygotsky's theory in general, and scaffolding in particular, that might help him teach Sean in more effective ways?

6. Your brother and his wife just had a baby, and they are wondering when their baby will begin talking. They hope it is soon, and they have begun saying "mama" and "dada" to their baby. What can you tell them about the course of language development during the first year of life?

7. The other day Superna was in the store with her 13-month-old son, Rahul. As they passed a man in the store, Rahul pointed at the man and said, "Daddy." Superna did not know this man and was very embarrassed, and now she is worried that Rahul does not know who his father is. What can you tell Superna about young children's errors in learning the meanings of words that might make her feel better?

ANSWERS WITH PAGE REFERENCES

4.1 KNOW THE TERMS

1. schemes (124)
2. Assimilation (124)
3. Accommodation (124)
4. equilibration (124)
5. sensorimotor (126)
6. object permanence (127)
7. egocentrism (128)
8. animism (128)
9. centration (129)
10. core knowledge hypothesis (132)
11. teleological explanation (135)
12. essentialism (135)

4.1 KNOW THE DETAILS OF PIAGET'S ACCOUNT

1. F, 124	6. F, 126	11. T, 130	16. F, 132
2. F, 124	7. T, 126	12. T, 131	17. T, 132
3. F, 124	8. T, 127	13. F, 131	18. T, 134
4. T, 125	9. T, 127	14. F, 131	
5. F, 126	10. F, 128	15. T, 132	

4.2 KNOW THE TERMS

1. hardware (137)
2. software (137)
3. Attention (137)
4. orienting response (137)
5. habituation (137)
6. Classical conditioning (138)
7. Operant conditioning (138)
8. autobiographical memory (139)
9. one-to-one (142)
10. stable-order (143)
11. cardinality (143)

4.2 KNOW THE DETAILS OF INFORMATION PROCESSING

1. T, 137	5. F, 137	9. F, 139	13. F, 141
2. T, 137	6. T, 138	10. F, 141	14. T, 142
3. F, 137	7. F, 139	11. T, 141	15. F, 143
4. F, 137	8. T, 139	12. T, 141	16. T, 143

4.3 KNOW THE TERMS

1. Intersubjectivity (144)
2. Guided participation (144)
3. zone of proximal development (145)
4. scaffolding (145)
5. private speech (146)

4.3 KNOW THE DETAILS OF VYGOTSKY'S THEORY

1. T, 144
2. T, 145
3. F, 145
4. F, 145
5. T, 146
6. T, 146

4.4 KNOW THE TERMS

1. phonemes (147)
2. infant-directed (149)
3. cooing (149)
4. babbling (149)
5. fast mapping (151)
6. overextension (154)
7. underextension (154)
8. phonological memory (154)
9. referential (155)
10. expressive (155)
11. telegraphic (157)
12. grammatical morphemes (157)
13. overregularization (158)

4.4 KNOW THE DETAILS OF LANGUAGE

1. T, 147
2. T, 148
3. F, 149
4. F, 150
5. T, 150
6. T, 151
7. T, 152
8. T, 152
9. T, 154
10. T, 154
11. T, 154
12. F, 155
13. T, 156
14. F, 157
15. T, 158
16. F, 158
17. F, 160
18. T, 161
19. F, 161

SUMMARY

4.1 THE ONSET OF THINKING: PIAGET'S ACCOUNT

1. schemes (124); actions (124); conceptual (124); assimilation (124); accommodation (125)

2. symbols (127)

3. egocentrism (128); centered (129); reality (130)

4. actively (131); underestimates (131); processes (131); sociocultural (132)

5. specialists (132); collide (133); grow (134)

4.2 INFORMATION-PROCESSING DURING INFANCY AND EARLY CHILDHOOD

1. hardware (137)

2. habituation (137); attention (137)

3. imitation (138)

4. Autobiographical memory (139); self (140); experienced (146); alternate (146)

5. threeness (142); one-to-one (142); irregular (143)

4.3 MIND AND CULTURE: VYGOTSKY'S THEORY

1. social (144); zone of proximal development (145)

2. more (145); vary (145)

3. difficult (146); private speech (146)

4.4 LANGUAGE

1. Phonemes (147); diminishes (148); slower (149); coo (149); intonation (150)

2. first birthday (151); symbols (151); underextension (154); phonological memory (154);expressive (155)

3. morphemes (157); exceptions (158); imitation (159); inborn (159); recurring patterns (159); adults (159)

4. turn-taking (160); needs (161); ambiguities (161)

TEST YOURSELF

MULTIPLE-CHOICE QUESTIONS

1. a, 124	12. d, 132	23. d, 143	34. a, 152
2. a, 124	13. a, 134	24. c, 144	35. c, 154
3. b, 124	14. c, 137	25. a, 145	36. d, 155
4. c, 125	15. b, 137	26. b, 145	37. a, 155
5. c, 126	16. b, 137	27. b, 146	38. c, 155
6. b, 127	17. d, 137	28. b, 147	39. a, 157
7. b, 128	18. c, 138	29. d, 149	40. d, 158
8. c, 128	19. a, 139	30. c, 149	41. c, 158
9. a, 130	20. a, 139	31. b, 150	
10. c, 130	21. c, 141	32. b, 151	
11. a, 131	22. c, 143	33. d, 151	

ESSAY QUESTIONS

1. Preoperational children cannot distinguish between what something "looks like" and what something "really is." For example, if someone "really is" angry but she "looks like" she is happy, preoperational children will say that she "looks like" she is happy and she "really is" happy. Difficulty in distinguishing appearance and reality is a deep-seated characteristic of preoperational thought. So, Jamal should take some comfort in the fact that Kia is like other children her age, and no matter how much he discusses the issue, he isn't likely to change her mind. (130)

2. Piaget said that object permanence is not fully developed until about 18 months of age. Piaget said that at four or five months, infants would search for hidden objects, but even at nine months infants aren't very effective searchers. Piaget believed that this ineffective searching indicated their poor object permanence. More recent research by Renée Baillargeon indicates that object permanence that does not involve searching is consistently evident in 4 ½-month-olds. Baillargeon showed infants a screen that rotated back and forth. After familiarizing the infants with this display, the infants saw either an impossible event or a possible event. The possible event involved placing a box behind the rotating screen. When the screen touched the box, it stopped. The impossible event again involved placing the box behind the screen, but this time the rotating screen rotated back until it was flat—an impossible event if the box is behind the screen. If a baby does not have object permanence, this event is no different from the rotating screen without the box that he saw at the beginning of the experiment. If a baby does have object permanence, then he should look longer at the impossible event because it defies his expectations. So, Matt should have object permanence but may give up his search for the remote if you hide it well enough. (133-134)

3.   Young children tend to confuse the source of memories and thoughts so that they are unsure if they are remembering an actual event or an event that someone has suggested may have happened. Preschoolers also are more likely to agree with authority figures if they are confused about events. So, the questioning that is part of a child abuse investigation can confuse a child and lead the child into believing that what really happened is the event that the questioning adults think happened. Unfortunately, research has shown that many professionals who become involved in child abuse cases cannot distinguish children who are telling the truth from those who are not. To get the most reliable testimony from preschoolers, they should be interviewed as soon after the event as possible, be allowed to say "I don't know," be allowed to describe the event in their own words avoiding specific questions, be allowed to feel comfortable before moving to questions about the event of interest, and be asked questions that consider alternate explanations of the event. (140-141)

4.   You can reassure your brother that your niece is doing well in the area of counting. Most children begin counting around their second birthday and have mastered the counting principles around five years of age. Your niece has mastered the one-to-one principle in which she assigns one and only one number name to each object to be counted. She also has mastered the stable-order principle in which the same names for numbers are used in a consistent order. Your niece also seems to understand that the last number name denotes the number of items in the set (the cardinality principle). In other words, your niece's mastery of counting principles is more advanced than most two-year-olds. Tell your brother to relax. Your niece has plenty of time to learn the real number names. (142-143)

5.   According to Vygotsky's principle of zone of proximal development, Sean will do better on the puzzle if he is assisted by someone who has more puzzle-building expertise than he does. However, according to the concept of scaffolding, a skilled teacher will gauge his instruction to the learner's needs. In other words, a beginner should get more instruction than someone who is close to mastering a task. Sean is close to mastering this puzzle, and Collum should stop providing so much instruction and should only provide help on the section where Sean needs help. (144-146)

6.　　Your brother and sister-in-law will have a few months to wait because most babies do not say their first words until around their first birthdays. However, during the next year, they should see their baby producing many different sounds. Around three months of age, their baby should start producing vowel-like sounds called cooing. Around four or five months, the baby should start combining these vowel-like sounds with consonants to produce babbling syllables. At first, these syllables will be produced alone (e.g., "ma" or "ba"), and later, these syllables will be repeated (e.g., "mamamama" or "babababa") and combined (e.g., "damaba"). Later, infants' babbling sounds more like speech because they vary the pitch. This intonation will mimic the intonation found in the language that the child hears. Finally, around the first birthday, the baby will say her first word. (149-150)

7.　　When children are learning the meanings of many new words it is not uncommon for them to make errors. Two common errors are underextensions and overextensions. When children underextend word meanings they use a much narrower than accepted meaning of the word. For example, the child might have learned the word "dog" in the context of his parents referring to the family dog. When the child underextends the meaning of "dog," he might not realize that other four-legged, furry, animals that bark are also dogs, but might mistakenly believe that the word "dog" refers only to his dog. Similarly, when children overextend word meanings they use a much broader meaning of the word than is normally accepted. In Rahul's case, he learned that "Daddy" refers to an adult male. Rahul does not realize yet that the word "Daddy" is usually used when referring to one's father. So, when Rahul called the unfamiliar adult male "Daddy," he was only overextending the meaning of the word "Daddy." Superna should realize that even though Rahul's behavior was embarrassing, it was typical of a child his age who overextends the meaning of words. (154)

ENTERING THE SOCIAL WORLD

5.1   Beginnings: Trust and Attachment

5.2   Emerging Emotions

5.3   Interacting with Others

5.4   Gender Roles and Gender Identity

This chapter discusses the development of attachment, the development of emotions, the development of social relationships, and the development of gender roles.

5.1 BEGINNINGS: TRUST AND ATTACHMENT

TO MASTER THE LEARNING OBJECTIVES:

What are Erikson's first three stages of psychosocial development?

- Describe Erikson's trust versus mistrust crisis, and explain why establishing trust is important for later development.

- Describe Erikson's autonomy versus shame and doubt crisis, and explain how the resolution of this crisis is related to the development of will.

- Describe how purpose comes from the resolution of initiative versus guilt.

How do infants form emotional attachments to mother, father, and other significant people in their lives?

- Explain the importance of attachment according to evolutionary psychology.

- Describe the development of attachment, starting with preattachment.

- Describe the differences in how mothers and fathers interact with their infants.

What are the different varieties of attachment relationships, how do they arise, and what are their consequences?

- Explain the differences between secure attachment, avoidant attachment, resistant attachment, and disorganized attachment.

- Describe evidence that supports the view that secure attachment relationships are related to better social relationships later in childhood.

- Describe how parental responsivity and sensitivity are related to the quality of attachment.

- Explain how the temperament of the infant and the personality of the mother are related to the quality of attachment.

Is attachment jeopardized when parents of infants and young children are employed outside of the home?

- Describe the effects of daycare on attachment.

- Describe the factors that one should look for when searching for quality daycare.

5.1 KNOW THE TERMS

Attachment	Internal working model
Avoidant	Purpose
Disorganized	Resistant
Evolutionary psychology	Secure
Hope	Will

1. _____, an openness to new experience tempered by wariness, occurs when trust and mistrust are in balance.

2. _____, the knowledge a young child has that she can act on the world intentionally, occurs when autonomy, shame, and doubt are in balance.

3. A balance between individual initiative and the willingness to cooperate with others is _____.

4.   _____ suggests that many human behaviors represent successful adaptation to the environment.

5.   _____ is an enduring social-emotional relationship between infants and their caregivers.

6.   Infants who have a _____ attachment relationship with their mothers have come to trust and depend on their mothers.

7.   Infants who ignore or turn away from their mothers when they are reunited following a brief separation have _____ attachment relationships.

8.   Infants who want to be held but are difficult to console when they are reunited with their mothers following a brief separation have _____ attachment relationships.

9.   Infants who don't seem to understand what's happening when they are separated and subsequently reunited with their mothers have _____ attachment relationships.

10.   An _____ is an infant's understanding of how responsive and dependable the mother is. This is thought to influence close relationships throughout the child's life.

5.1 KNOW THE DETAILS OF TRUST AND ATTACHMENT

1.   According to Erikson, infants must deal with the crisis of initiative versus guilt during the first year of life.
      TRUE or FALSE

2.   Erikson stated that, with a proper balance of trust and mistrust, infants can acquire hope.
      TRUE or FALSE

3.   During Erikson's second psychosocial stage, children are striving for independence or autonomy from others.
      TRUE or FALSE

4.   At three to five years of age, children face the crisis of initiative versus guilt.
      TRUE or FALSE

5.   John Bowlby's work on attachment is based on psychosocial theory.
      TRUE or FALSE

6.   According to John Bowlby, forming an attachment to an adult makes a child more likely to survive.
      TRUE or FALSE

7.   An infant's first attachment figure is usually the mother.
      TRUE or FALSE

129

8. Infants usually become attached to only one parent.

   TRUE or FALSE

9. Infants usually single out an attachment figure by seven or eight months of age.

   TRUE or FALSE

10. Fathers typically spend more time playing with infants than taking care of them.

   TRUE or FALSE

11. When infants are distressed, they prefer being with their mother to being with their father.

   TRUE or FALSE

12. Babies who are securely attached typically ignore the mother when she returns after a brief separation.

   TRUE or FALSE

13. Babies who are securely attached usually become upset when the mother leaves the room and remain upset or angry when she returns after a brief separation.

   TRUE or FALSE

14. The Strange Situation procedure has been criticized for its emphasis on separation and reunion for measuring attachment because the appropriate response may vary by culture.

   TRUE or FALSE

15. Infants who form secure attachments are more likely to have skilled social interactions later in childhood.

   TRUE or FALSE

16. An internal working model is a set of expectations infants develop about parents' availability and responsivity.

   TRUE or FALSE

17. Insecure attachment is more likely when parents are sensitive and responsive.

   TRUE or FALSE

18. Temperament has not been found to be related to the quality of attachment.

   TRUE or FALSE

19. Early childcare experience does not appear to have an overall effect on mother-infant attachment.

   TRUE or FALSE

5.2 EMERGING EMOTIONS

TO MASTER THE LEARNING OBJECTIVES:

At what ages do children begin to express basic emotions?

- Explain the functional value of emotions.

- Know the basic emotions.

- Describe the development of positive emotions, such as happiness, as well as negative emotions, such as anger and fear.

- Define stranger wariness.

What are complex emotions and when do they develop?

- Explain why complex emotions don't emerge until the very end of infancy.

- Explain how shame and guilt and fear change with development.

- Describe how the cultural setting influences complex emotions.

When do children begin to understand other people's emotions? How do they use this information to guide their own behavior?

- Describe infants' ability to distinguish facial expressions.

- Describe social referencing.

- Describe the development of the ability to regulate one's emotions.

5.2 KNOW THE TERMS

Basic emotions	Social smiles
Social referencing	Stranger wariness

1. The _____ consist of a subjective feeling, a physiological change, and an overt behavior.

2. Around two months of age, infants smile when they see another human face. These smiles are called _____.

3. _____ occurs around six months of age when infants become wary in the presence of an unfamiliar adult.

4. Infants use _____ in an unfamiliar or ambiguous situation by looking at an adult for cues to help them interpret the situation.

131

5.2 KNOW THE DETAILS OF EMERGING EMOTIONS

1. Joy, anger, and fear are all considered to be basic emotions.
    TRUE or FALSE

2. Researchers have used infants' facial expressions to identify infants' underlying emotional states.
    TRUE or FALSE

3. Social smiles usually first appear when infants are about eight months old.
    TRUE or FALSE

4. Anger is usually first seen in infants when they are between four and six months of age.
    TRUE or FALSE

5. Fear is common in newborns.
    TRUE or FALSE

6. Infants tend to be more fearful of strangers in a familiar environment than in an unfamiliar environment.
    TRUE or FALSE

7. Unlike complex emotions, basic emotions require the child to have some self-understanding.
    TRUE or FALSE

8. Guilt, embarrassment, and pride are complex emotions.
    TRUE or FALSE

9. Preschoolers are often afraid of the dark and of imaginary creatures.
    TRUE or FALSE

10. Culture has no influence on emotional expression.
    TRUE or FALSE

11. Social referencing occurs when infants look to their parents to get cues to help them interpret an unfamiliar or ambiguous situation.
    TRUE or FALSE

12. Emotion regulation begins in infancy.
    TRUE or FALSE

5.3 INTERACTING WITH OTHERS

TO MASTER THE LEARNING OBJECTIVES:

When do youngsters first begin to play with each other? How does play change during infancy and the preschool years?

- **De**scribe how peer interactions change during infancy and the preschool years.
- Describe how culture influences make-believe play.
- Describe the benefits of make-believe play.
- Explain how children with imaginary companions differ from those who do not have imaginary companions.
- Know the differences between healthy and unhealthy solitary play.
- Explain how different play styles in boys and girls are related to children choosing same-sex playmates.
- Describe how parents influence children's peer interactions.

What determines whether children help one another?

- Describe how perspective-taking and empathy are related to altruistic behavior.
- **De**scribe how feelings of responsibility, feelings of competence, mood, and costs of altruism are related to altruistic behavior.
- Explain how genes are related to prosocial behavior.
- Explain how parents' disciplinary practices, modeling altruistic behavior, and providing opportunities to behave prosocially are related to children's altruistic behavior.

5.3 KNOW THE TERMS

Altruism	**Enabling**
Constricting	**Parallel play**
Cooperative	**Prosocial**
Empathy	**Simple social play**

1. _____ occurs when children play alone, but they are aware of and are interested in what another child is doing.

2.   Around 15-18 months, toddlers will engage in similar activities and will talk and smile at each other. This is called _____.

3.   Around the second birthday, children's play will be organized around a theme, and each child will take on special roles based on the theme during _____ play.

4.   Girls' interactions with others typically are _____ because their remarks and actions tend to support others and sustain the interaction.

5.   Boys' interactions are often _____ because one boy usually tries to emerge as the victor by threatening, contradicting, or exaggerating.

6.   _____ behavior refers to any behavior that benefits another person.

7.   _____ refers to behavior such as helping and sharing in which the individual does not benefit directly from her behavior.

8.   Actually experiencing another person's feelings is called _____.

5.3 KNOW THE DETAILS OF INTERACTING WITH OTHERS

1.   The first signs of peer interaction usually appear at about two years of age.
     TRUE or FALSE

2.   Parallel play occurs when a distinct theme organizes children's play, and the children take on special roles based on the theme.
     TRUE or FALSE

3.   When children play hide-and-seek, they are engaged in cooperative play.
     TRUE or FALSE

4.   One-year-olds spend most of their time in cooperative play.
     TRUE or FALSE

5.   Children who spend much time in make-believe play tend to be delayed in their cognitive development.
     TRUE or FALSE

6.   Children can learn to overcome some of their fears through the use of make-believe play.
     TRUE or FALSE

7.   Children who have imaginary playmates tend to be less sociable and have fewer friends.
     TRUE or FALSE

8. Wandering aimlessly and hovering are healthy forms of solitary play.
    TRUE or FALSE

9. A preference for playing with same-sex peers usually diminishes at the end of the preschool years.
    TRUE or FALSE

10. Girls have a more enabling play style than do boys.
    TRUE or FALSE

11. Children whose parents often arrange for them to play with other children tend to get along better with their peers.
    TRUE or FALSE

12. Children play more cooperatively and longer when parents are present than when they are not.
    TRUE or FALSE

13. Behavior that is driven by feelings of responsibility toward other people, such as helping and sharing, in which individuals do not benefit directly from their actions, is referred to as prosocial behavior.
    TRUE or FALSE

14. Empathy is positively related to prosocial behavior.
    TRUE or FALSE

15. Parents who use reasoning as a disciplinary style are more likely to have altruistic children.
    TRUE or FALSE

5.4 GENDER ROLES AND GENDER IDENTITY

TO MASTER THE LEARNING OBJECTIVES:

What are our stereotypes about males and females? How well do they correspond to actual differences between boys and girls?

- Define social roles.
- Define gender stereotypes, and describe how children learn them.
- Describe gender-related differences in verbal ability, mathematics, spatial ability, social influence, aggression, and emotional sensitivity.

135

When do young children learn gender roles?

- Describe the ways in which parents treat sons and daughters similarly and differently.

- Explain how peers contribute to gender-typing.

- Define gender identity, and explain how children develop it.

- Explain how the knowledge of gender and gender-typed activities are related to each other.

- Describe the influence of gender schema on behavior and activities.

- Describe the biological influences on gender roles and gender identity.

How are gender roles changing? What further changes might the future hold?

- Describe how different aspects of gender-stereotyping are influenced by parents and society.

5.4 KNOW THE TERMS

Gender constancy	Gender stability
Gender identity	Gender stereotypes
Gender labeling	Relational aggression
Gender-schema theory	Social role

1. A set of cultural guidelines about how one should behave especially with other people is called a _____.

2. _____ are beliefs and images about males and females that may or may not be true.

3. Trying to hurt someone by damaging their relationships with peers is called _____.

4. A sense of oneself as male or female is called _____.

5. Children's understanding that they are either boys or girls and their ability to label themselves accordingly is called _____.

6. Children's understanding that boys become men and girls become women is called _____.

7. The understanding that maleness and femaleness do not change over situations or according to personal wishes is called _____.

8. According to _____, children first decide if an activity is associated with males or females, then use this information to determine if they should learn more about the activity.

5.4 KNOW THE DETAILS OF GENDER ROLES AND GENDER IDENTITY

1. Gender stereotypes are beliefs and images about males and females that may or may not be true.

   TRUE or FALSE

2. Research suggests that males and females often do not differ in the ways specified by cultural stereotypes.

   TRUE or FALSE

3. On average, females have higher verbal abilities than males.

   TRUE or FALSE

4. Boys used to score higher than girls on math achievement tests, but the difference has become negligible in recent years.

   TRUE or FALSE

5. Females tend to have better spatial ability than males.

   TRUE or FALSE

6. Females are typically more compliant and more readily influenced by others than males.

   TRUE or FALSE

7. Males and females typically have similar levels of physical aggression.

   TRUE or FALSE

8. Mothers are more likely than fathers to treat sons and daughters differently.

   TRUE or FALSE

9. Once children learn rules about gender-typical play, they often punish peers who violate those rules.

   TRUE or FALSE

10. Children begin to label themselves as either boys or girls between five and seven years of age.

    TRUE or FALSE

11. Gender constancy refers to the understanding that maleness and femaleness do not change over situations or according to personal wishes.

    TRUE or FALSE

12. In gender-schema theory, children first decide if an object, activity, or behavior is female or male, then use this information to decide whether they should learn more about the object, activity, or behavior.

    TRUE or FALSE

13. Congenital adrenal hyperplasia is a genetic disorder in which adrenal glands secrete large amounts of androgen.

    TRUE or FALSE

SUMMARY

5.1 BEGINNINGS: TRUST AND ATTACHMENT

1. **What are Erikson's first three stages of early psychosocial development?**

   In Erikson's theory of psychosocial development, individuals face various psychosocial crises at different phases in development. The crisis of infancy is to establish a balance between trust and mistrust of the world, producing _____. Between one and three years of age, youngsters must blend autonomy and _____ to produce will. Three- to five-year-olds must balance initiative and guilt to achieve _____.

2. **How do infants form emotional attachments to mother, father, and other significant people in their lives?**

   Attachment is an enduring _____ relationship between infant and parent. For both adults and infants, many of the behaviors that contribute to the formation of attachment are biologically programmed. Bowlby's theory of attachment is rooted in _____ and describes four stages in the development of attachment: _____, attachment in the making, true attachment, and _____.

3. **What are the different varieties of attachment relationships, how do they arise, and what are their consequences?**

   Research with the Strange Situation, in which infant and mother are separated briefly, reveals four primary forms of attachment. Most common is a _____ attachment, in which infants have complete trust in the mother. Less common are three types of attachment relationships in which this trust is lacking. In avoidant relationships, infants deal with this lack of trust by _____ the mother; in resistant relationships, infants often seem angry with the mother; and in disorganized relationships, infants do not _____ the mother's absence. Children who have had secure attachment relationships during infancy often interact with their peers more readily and more _____. Secure attachment is most likely to occur when mothers respond _____ and consistently to their infant's needs. Responsive caregiving results in infants developing an _____ that parents will meet their needs. Secure attachment can be harder to achieve when infants are temperamentally _____.

4. **Is attachment jeopardized when parents of young children are employed outside the home?**

Many U.S. children are cared for at home by a father or other relative, in a daycare provider's home, or in a daycare center. Infants and young children are not harmed by such care as long as the care is _____ and parents remain close to their children.

5.2 EMERGING EMOTIONS

1. **At what age do children begin to express basic emotions?**

Basic emotions, which include _____, anger, and _____, emerge in the first year. Fear first appears in infancy as _____.

2. **What are complex emotions, and when do they develop?**

Complex emotions have an _____ component and include guilt, _____, and pride. They appear between 18 and 24 months and require more sophisticated _____ skills than basic emotions like happiness and fear. Cultures differ in the rules for expressing emotions and the situations that elicit particular emotions.

3. **When do children begin to understand other people's emotions? How do they use this information to guide their own behavior?**

By six months of age, infants have begun to recognize the emotions associated with different _____. They use this information to help evaluate _____ situations. Beyond infancy, children understand the causes of different emotions. Infants use simple strategies to regulate emotions such as fear. As children grow, they become better skilled at regulating their emotions. Children who do not regulate emotions well tend to have problems _____ with others.

5.3 INTERACTING WITH OTHERS

1. **When do youngsters first begin to play with each other? How does play change during infancy and the preschool years?**

Even infants notice and respond to one another, but the first real interactions, at about 12 to 15 months, take the form of _____ play, in which toddlers play alone while watching

139

each other. A few months later, simple social play emerges, in which toddlers engage in similar activities and interact with one another. At about two years of age, _____ play organized around a theme becomes common. Make-believe play is also common and provides one way in which children can examine _____ topics. Most forms of solitary play are harmless.

2. **What determines whether children help one another?**

    Prosocial behaviors, such as _____ or sharing, are more common in children who understand (perspective-taking) and who experience (empathy) another's feelings. Prosocial behavior is more likely when children feel _____ for the person in distress, when they believe that they have the skills needed to help, when they are feeling _____ or successful, and when the perceived costs of helping are _____. Twin studies show that prosocial behavior is influenced by _____, probably through its impact on behavioral control and emotional regulation. Parents can foster prosocial behavior in their children by behaving _____ themselves, by encouraging their children to help at home and elsewhere, and by using _____ to discipline their children.

5.4 GENDER ROLES AND GENDER IDENTITY

1. **What are our stereotypes of males and females? How well do they correspond to actual differences between boys and girls?**

    _____ are beliefs about males and females that are often used to make inferences about a person, simply based on his or her gender; by four years of age, children know these stereotypes well. Studies of gender differences find that girls have greater _____ and boys have greater _____. Differences in math skill are negligible when females have access to education and occupations where math is valuable. Girls are better able to interpret emotions and are more prone to social influence, but boys are more _____. These differences can vary on the basis of a number of factors, including the historical period.

2. **How do young children learn gender roles?**

    Parents treat sons and daughters similarly, except in sex-typed activities. _____ may be particularly important in gender-typing, because they are more likely to treat sons and daughters differently. In Kohlberg's theory, children gradually learn that gender is stable over time and cannot be changed according to personal _____. After children understand gender stability, they begin to learn gender-typical behavior. According to gender-schema theory, children learn about gender by _____ to behaviors of members of their own sex and ignoring behaviors of members of the other sex. Evolutionary developmental psychology reminds us that different roles for males and females caused different traits and _____ to evolve for women and men. The idea that biology influences some aspects of gender roles is also supported by research on females exposed to _____ during prenatal development.

3. **How are gender roles changing? What further changes might the future hold?**

    Gender roles are changing. However, studies of nontraditional families indicate that some components of _____ are more readily changed than others.

TEST YOURSELF

MULTIPLE-CHOICE QUESTIONS

1. Infants under one year of age are in Erikson's first stage of psychosocial development, which involves a crisis of

    a. autonomy versus shame and doubt.

    b. initiative versus guilt.

    c. basic trust versus mistrust.

    d. industry versus inferiority.

2. According to Erikson, a balance between autonomy versus shame and doubt leads to the development of

    a. hope.

    b. purpose.

    c. will.

    d. self.

3. John Bowlby's theory of attachment is based on

    a. psychodynamic theory.

    b. social learning theory.

    c. ecological theory.

    d. evolutionary theory.

4. Most infants develop an attachment to a specific individual by about

    a. 3 to 4 months of age.

    b. 7 to 8 months of age.

    c. 12 to 15 months of age.

    d. 18 to 24 months of age.

5. Which of the following statements concerning infants' relationships with their mothers and fathers is true?

    a. Infants usually form attachments to their mothers and fathers simultaneously.

    b. Fathers usually spend more time taking care of their infants than they do playing with them.

    c. Infants usually become attached only to their mothers.

    d. Infants generally prefer playing with their father over playing with their mother.

6. Mary Ainsworth used _____ to assess the quality of attachment in infants.

    a. the Strange Situation procedure

    b. habituation

    c. interviews with the caregivers

    d. a visual cliff

7. When 15-month-old Marie was reunited with her mother after a three-minute separation, Marie turned away from her mother and ignored her. Marie's behavior suggests that she has a(n) _____ attachment relationship with her mother.

    a. secure

    b. avoidant

    c. resistant

    d. disorganized (disoriented)

8. Eighteen-month-old Eric responded to a brief separation from his mother by holding up his arms to be held when they were reunited and then happily returning to his play activities after a minute or two. Eric behaved as if he had a(n) _____ attachment relationship with his mother.

    a. secure

    b. avoidant

    c. resistant

    d. disorganized (disoriented)

9. The security of an infant's attachment is

    a. unrelated to the quality of future social relationships.

    b. related to the sensitivity and responsivity of the caregiving received.

    c. based purely on biological forces.

    d. stronger when parents typically wait a long time before responding to infant cries.

10. The set of expectations that infants develop about parents' availability and responsivity are referred to as

    a. empathy.

    b. ethology.

    c. social referencing.

    d. an internal working model.

11. Which of the following statements about the impact of daycare on infants or children is most accurate?

    a. Children with extensive experience in daycare are more likely to have behavioral problems.

    b. Children who begin daycare early are more likely than children who begin daycare later to have an insecure attachment.

    c. An insecure attachment is more likely when a child has less sensitive parenting and is in low-quality daycare.

    d. A secure mother-infant attachment is less likely when the childcare arrangements are changed frequently.

12. High-quality childcare has

    a. a high ratio of children to caregivers.

    b. high staff turnover.

    c. effective communication between parents and daycare workers.

    d. inexperienced staff.

13. Basic emotions contain each of the following elements EXCEPT

    a. a self-evaluative component.

    b. a subjective feeling.

    c. a physiological change.

    d. an overt behavior.

14. Social smiles first appear at

    a. birth.

    b. 2 months of age.

    c. 6 months of age.

    d. 12 months of age.

15. Seven-month-old Stephen looked away and began to fuss when his aunt, whom he was seeing for the first time, tried to pick him up. Stephen is showing signs of

    a. insecure attachment.

    b. prosocial behavior.

    c. social referencing.

    d. stranger wariness.

16. Who is experiencing a complex emotion?

    a. Nate, who is embarrassed

    b. Pat, who is happy

    c. Gregory, who is surprised

    d. Mark, who is angry

17. When a clown approached Emily at a circus, Emily looked at her mother to see how she was reacting to the clown. After Emily's mother smiled and said hello to the clown, Emily smiled at the clown, too. Emily was showing

    a. a complex emotion.

    b. insecure attachment.

    c. social referencing.

    d. parallel play.

18. When infants look away from something that frightens them, they are using

    a. social referencing.

    b. a complex emotion.

    c. emotion regulation.

    d. stranger wariness.

19. Rachel and Rebecca are coloring pictures in separate coloring books but often look to see what the other is doing. They are engaged in

    a. solitary play.

    b. parallel play.

    c. cooperative play.

    d. make-believe play.

20. One-year-olds spend most of their time in _____ play whereas three-year-olds most often engage in _____ play.

    a. make-believe; parallel

    b. cooperative; make-believe

    c. cooperative; parallel

    d. parallel; cooperative

21. Four-year-old Mitchell has an imaginary friend. Mitchell

    a. is likely to have developmental problems.

    b. is one of very few children his age who has an imaginary companion.

    c. is probably quite sociable and is likely to have more real friends than children without imaginary companions.

    d. is likely to have more difficulty distinguishing between reality and fantasy than do preschoolers without imaginary companions.

22. Which of the following statements concerning gender differences in play is true?

    a. During the elementary school years, children interact primarily with same-sex peers.

    b. Boys' interactions are more likely than girls' to be enabling.

    c. Children segregate by gender only when encouraged to do so by their parents.

    d. Boys and girls do not differ in the ways that they play.

23. Which of the following is the best example of altruistic behavior?

    a. Jennie, who gave some of her prize tokens to a friend who had not won any.

    b. Christine, who said, "Ouch!" when her friend tripped and fell.

    c. Valerie, who gave a friend the apple from her lunch in exchange for the candy bar from the friend's lunch.

    d. Stephanie, who fed her dog every day because that was her assigned chore.

24. When a child actually experiences another child's feelings, the child is displaying

    a. social referencing.

    b. prosocial behavior.

    c. altruism.

    d. empathy.

25. Altruistic behavior is least likely to occur when a child

    a. feels responsible for the person in need.

    b. feels competent to help the person in need.

    c. is happy or feeling successful.

    d. has to make a major sacrifice in order to help the person in need.

26. A _____ is a set of cultural guidelines regarding how a person should behave, particularly with other people.
    a. social role
    b. gender stereotype
    c. gender identity
    d. gender stability

27. Females _____ than males.
    a. tend to be more physically aggressive
    b. have better spatial ability
    c. are less compliant
    d. have stronger verbal abilities

28. As a group, males _____ than females.
    a. have higher verbal ability
    b. have better spatial ability
    c. are more readily influenced by others
    d. are less aggressive

29. Children typically understand that they are either boys or girls, and label themselves accordingly, by age
    a. 1 year.
    b. 2 to 3 years.
    c. 4 years.
    d. 5 to 7 years.

30. When James saw his friend Timmy dress up in a woman's clothing, he pointed at him and said, "Timmy's a girl!" James does not appear to have acquired the concept of
    a. gender constancy.
    b. gender stereotypes.
    c. gender labeling.
    d. gender stability.

31. According to Kohlberg's theory of how gender identity develops,
    a. gender constancy must be acquired before gender roles are learned.
    b. knowledge of gender roles must be acquired before gender stability will be understood.
    c. gender schemas influence interest in activities.
    d. gender schemas have no influence on interest in activities.

32. In _____, children first decide if an object, activity, or behavior is female or male, then use this information to decide whether they should learn more about the object, activity, or behavior.

    a. Kohlberg's theory

    b. social-learning theory

    c. gender-schema theory

    d. the internal working model

ESSAY QUESTIONS

1. You and a friend have just visited some other friends who have an eight-month-old baby. When you get home, your friend comments on how differently the mother and the father interacted with their baby. The father seemed rough with the baby, and your friend wonders if that is normal behavior. What can you tell your friend about the differences in how mothers and fathers interact with their babies?

2. Your friend Marta has a nine-month-old baby, and she said that she isn't concerned about the effects of daycare on attachment because attachment only lasts a few years and doesn't affect other later behavior. What can you tell Marta about the relation between attachment and later social behavior?

3. Your friend Ben has a 12-month-old daughter, Sadie. Recently, Ben and his daughter saw one of Ben's coworkers whom Sadie did not know. When this stranger approached them, Ben thought that Sadie looked at him to gauge his reaction to the stranger and then smiled after she saw Ben smile and greet the stranger in a friendly manner. When Ben told this story to his wife, she laughed and told him that he was giving Sadie more credit than a one-year-old should get. Is Ben or his wife correct? Explain your answer.

4. Your six-year-old niece does not like to play with boys. Your brother thinks that this is okay, but his wife thinks that your niece should play with both boys and girls. What can you tell your sister-in-law about sex differences in interaction styles and how that is related to the selection of same-sex playmates?

5. Your friend Jason told you that he would like his young son, Erik, to grow up and be a nice, helpful person. What can you tell Jason about factors that have been shown to be related to altruistic behavior?

6. Your friend Gretchen is an elementary school teacher. She told you one day that she has noticed that the boys that she has had in class seem to have more language problems than the girls. She's also noticed that fewer of the girls need to go to the reading teacher to get extra help. Gretchen wonders if sex differences in verbal and math ability are substantiated by research or if she has had unusual students. What can you tell Gretchen about sex differences in verbal ability?

ANSWERS WITH PAGE REFERENCES

5.1 KNOW THE TERMS

1. Hope (168)	6. secure (171)
2. Will (169)	7. avoidant (171)
3. purpose (169)	8. resistant (171)
4. Evolutionary psychology (169)	9. disorganized (172)
5. Attachment (170)	10. internal working model (173)

5.1 KNOW THE DETAILS OF TRUST AND ATTACHMENT

1. F, 168	6. T, 170	11. T, 170	16. T, 173
2. T, 168	7. T, 170	12. F, 171	17. F, 174
3. T, 168	8. F, 170	13. F, 171	18. F, 174
4. T, 169	9. T, 170	14. T, 172	19. T, 175
5. F, 169	10. T, 170	15. T, 172	

5.2 KNOW THE TERMS

1. basic emotions (177)	3. Stranger wariness (178)
2. social smiles (177)	4. social referencing (180)

5.2 KNOW THE DETAILS OF EMERGING EMOTIONS

1. T, 172	4. T, 178	7. T, 178	10. F, 179
2. T, 177	5. F, 178	8. T, 178	11. T, 180
3. F, 177	6. F, 178	9. T, 179	12. T, 182

5.3 KNOW THE TERMS

1. Parallel play (183)
2. simple social play (183)
3. cooperative (183)
4. enabling (185)

5. constricting (185)
6. Prosocial (187)
7. Altruism (187)
8. empathy (188)

5.3 KNOW THE DETAILS OF INTERACTING WITH OTHERS

1. F, 183	5. F, 184	9. T, 185	13. F, 187
2. F, 183	6. T, 184	10. T, 185	14. T, 188
3. T, 183	7. F, 184	11. T, 186	15. T, 189
4. F, 183	8. F, 185	12. T, 186	

5.4 KNOW THE TERMS

1. social role (191)
2. Gender stereotypes (191)
3. relational aggression (193)
4. gender identity (196)

5. gender labeling (196)
6. gender stability (196)
7. gender constancy (196)
8. gender-schema theory (197)

5.4 KNOW THE DETAILS OF GENDER ROLES AND GENDER IDENTITY

1. T, 191	5. F, 192	9. T, 196	13. T, 198
2. T, 192	6. T, 192	10. F, 196	
3. T, 192	7. F, 193	11. T, 196	
4. T, 192	8. F, 195	12. T, 197	

SUMMARY

5.1 BEGINNINGS: TRUST AND ATTACHMENT

1. hope (168); shame (168); purpose (169)

2. social-emotional (170); evolutionary psychology (169); preattachment (170); reciprocal relationships (170);

3. secure (171); ignoring (171); understand (172); skillfully (172); sensitively (173); internal working model (173); difficult (174); high quality (174)

5.2 EMERGING EMOTIONS

1. joy (177); fear (177); stranger wariness (178)

2. evaluative (178); embarrassment (178); cognitive (178)

3. facial expressions (180); unfamiliar (180); interacting (181)

5.3 INTERACTING WITH OTHERS

1. parallel (183); cooperative (183); frightening (184)

2. helping (187); responsible (188); happy (188); small (188); heredity (189); altruistically (189); reasoning (189)

5.4 GENDER ROLES AND GENDER IDENTITY

1. Gender stereotypes (191); verbal skill (192); spatial skill (192); aggressive (193)

2. Fathers (195); wishes (196); paying attention (197); behaviors (197); male hormones (198)

3. gender stereotypes (198)

TEST YOURSELF

MULTIPLE-CHOICE QUESTIONS

1. c, 168	11. c, 175	21. c, 184	31. a, 197
2. c, 169	12. c, 177	22. a, 185	32. c, 197
3. d, 169	13. a, 177	23. a, 187	
4. b, 170	14. b, 177	24. d, 188	
5. d, 170	15. d, 178	25. d, 188	
6. a, 171	16. a, 178	26. a, 191	
7. b, 171	17. c, 180	27. d, 192	
8. a, 171	18. c, 182	28. b, 193	
9. b, 173	19. b, 183	29. b, 196	
10. d, 173	20. d, 183	30. a, 196	

ESSAY QUESTIONS

1. You can tell your friend that the differences in the ways that fathers and mothers interact with their children are very different in many cultures. In the United States, mothers do most of the caregiving, and fathers fill the role of "playmate." Mothers are more likely to read and talk to their babies, show their babies toys, and play quiet games like pat-a-cake and peek-a-boo. Fathers are more likely to engage in physical, rough-and-tumble physical activities with their children. Infants are more likely to choose their fathers as playmates and their mothers as a source of comfort when distressed. (170)

2. Attachment does last longer than a few years, and a secure attachment relationship is related to better social relationships later in life. There is much evidence that children who are securely attached have higher-quality friendships and fewer conflicts in their friendships. Children are less likely to have problems such as anxiety, anger, and aggression if they have secure attachment relationships. Secure attachment in infancy even is related to more stable and higher-quality romantic relationships in adolescence. Secure attachment seems to lead infants to trust other people, which leads to more skilled social interactions later. (172-173)

3. You can tell Ben that Sadie was engaging in social referencing, which occurs when infants encounter unfamiliar or ambiguous situations and look to a parent to find cues to interpret the situation. The approach of the stranger would be an ambiguous situation to Sadie, who is old enough to use social referencing. In this ambiguous situation, Sadie looked at Ben to see how he reacted, and when Ben was friendly to the stranger, Sadie smiled. In other words, Ben's ideas about Sadie's behavior are correct. (180-181)

4. Around the world, girls generally play with girls, and boys generally play with boys. Even when parents encourage boys and girls to play together, most children will resist. Part of this resistance seems to come from the fact that girls and boys have very different styles of interacting. Boys tend to prefer more rough-and-tumble play and generally are more competitive and dominating in interactions. Girls seem to find this style of interaction aversive. Girls' interactions tend to be enabling. In other words, girls' remarks and behavior tend to provide support for each other. Boys' interactions tend to be constricting. Boys will try to dominate each other by using intimidation, threats, and exaggeration. When boys and girls interact, girls find that their supportive, compromising style is not very effective with boys. So, your niece is not unusual, and your sister-in-law's efforts to get her to play with boys are not likely to be successful. (185-186)

5. Research has found three factors that are related to altruistic behavior in children. First, parents who are warm and supportive, set guidelines, provide feedback, and use reasoning in their disciplinary style tend to have children who are more altruistic. Second, parents whose children are more altruistic show more warmth and concern for others and model altruistic behavior. Third, children and adolescents are more likely to act prosocially when they are given regular opportunities to help and cooperate with others. Experiences such as participating in community service sensitize children to others' needs. So, Jason can increase the likelihood that Erik will engage in altruistic behavior. (189-190)

6. Research does show that females tend to have better verbal ability than males. For example, females tend to have larger vocabularies and can read, write, and spell better than males. Girls also have fewer reading and other language-related problems than boys. Therefore, you can tell Gretchen that the students that she has seen conform to the patterns found for the average boy and girl. (192)

OFF TO SCHOOL

6.1   Cognitive Development

6.2   Aptitudes for School

6.3   Special Children, Special Needs

6.4   Academic Skills

6.5   Physical Development

This chapter discusses cognitive development in school-age children, intelligence testing and the factors that influence IQ scores, the characteristics and needs of special children, the acquisition of academic skills, and physical development during childhood.

6.1 COGNITIVE DEVELOPMENT

TO MASTER THE LEARNING OBJECTIVES:

What are the distinguishing characteristics of thought during Piaget's concrete-operational and formal-operational stages?

- Describe thought in concrete-operational children.

- Describe thinking in formal-operational children, and describe how their problem-solving approach differs from that of concrete-operational children.

How do children use strategies to improve learning and remembering?

- Describe how working and long-term memory are related.

- Describe when simple memory strategies appear, and describe how memory strategies change with age.

- Define metamemory, metacognitive knowledge, and cognitive self-regulation.

- Explain how monitoring changes with age.

6.1 KNOW THE TERMS

Cognitive self-regulation	Metacognitive knowledge
Deductive reasoning	Metamemory
Elaboration	Organization
Long-term memory	Working memory
Mental operations	

1. Concrete-operational children can reverse _____, which are actions that can be performed on objects or ideas and that consistently yield a result.

2. Formal-operational adolescents can draw conclusions from facts using _____.

3. _____ is the type of memory where a small number of items are held for a brief period of time.

4. _____ is a permanent storehouse of knowledge that has unlimited capacity.

5. _____ is a memory strategy in which related information is placed together.

6. Embellishing to-be-remembered information to make it more memorable is called

_____.

7. _____ is a person's intuitive understanding of memory.

8. Knowledge and awareness of cognitive processes is called _____.

9. Successful students are good at _____, which involves identifying goals, selecting effective strategies, and monitoring accurately.

6.1 KNOW THE DETAILS OF COGNITIVE DEVELOPMENT

1. Children are in Piaget's concrete-operational stage from approximately 7 to 11 years of age.
    TRUE or FALSE

2. Concrete-operational thinkers are egocentric.
    TRUE or FALSE

3. Concrete-operational thinkers are able to reverse their thinking.
    TRUE or FALSE

4. Concrete-operational thinking is limited to the tangible and real.
    TRUE or FALSE

5. The formal-operational period begins at adulthood.
    TRUE or FALSE

6. Formal-operational thinkers are not able to reason abstractly.
    TRUE or FALSE

7. Combinatorial reasoning is characteristic of formal-operational thinking.
    TRUE or FALSE

8. Formal-operational thinkers do not use deductive reasoning.
    TRUE or FALSE

9. One of the shortcomings of Piaget's theory is that he overestimates cognitive competence in adolescence.
    TRUE or FALSE

10. Working memory can store an unlimited amount of information.
    TRUE or FALSE

11. Long-term memory stores information permanently.
    TRUE or FALSE

12. Children begin to use simple strategies for remembering information, such as rehearsal, by the age of seven or eight.
    TRUE or FALSE

13. Younger children are more likely than older children to choose an inappropriate strategy for remembering information.
    TRUE or FALSE

14. The ability to monitor progress toward the goal of a memory task improves with age.
    TRUE or FALSE

15. Cognitive self-regulation is a characteristic of successful students.
    TRUE or FALSE

6.2 APTITUDES FOR SCHOOL

TO MASTER THE LEARNING OBJECTIVES:

What is the nature of intelligence?

- Describe Carroll's hierarchical theory of intelligence.

- Describe Gardner's theory of multiple intelligences and its application in the school setting.

- Define emotional intelligence.

- Describe Sternberg's theory of successful intelligence (include definitions of analytic ability, creative ability, and practical ability).

Why were intelligence tests first developed? What are their features?

- Explain why the first intelligence test was developed by Binet and Simon.

- Explain the concept of mental age.

- Describe what Terman meant by intelligence quotient.

How well do intelligence tests work?

- Describe how well intelligence tests predict success inside and outside of school.

How do heredity and environment influence intelligence?

- Explain how twin studies provide evidence that heredity influences intelligence.

- Describe what studies of adopted children tell us about the impact of heredity on intelligence.

- Describe the aspects of the environment that are related to higher levels of intelligence.

- Describe the effects of intervention programs.

How and why do test scores vary for different racial and ethnic groups?

- Describe the factors that influence racial and ethnic differences in IQ test scores.

- Explain what is meant by culture-fair intelligence tests.

- Explain how test-taking skills and stereotype threat are related to scores on intelligence tests.

6.2 KNOW THE TERMS

Analytic ability	Mental age
Creative ability	Practical ability
Culture-fair	Psychometricians
Emotional intelligence	Stereotype threat
Intelligence quotient	

1. Psychologists who specialize in measuring psychological characteristics such as intelligence and personality are called _____.

2. The ability to use one's own and others' emotions effectively for solving problems and living happily is called _____.

3. _____ involves analyzing problems and generating different solutions.

4. _____ involves dealing adaptively with novel situations and problems.

5. _____ involves knowing what solution or plan will actually work.

6. In intelligence testing, _____ refers to the difficulty of the problems that a child can solve correctly that corresponds to the performance of an average child of a particular chronological age.

7. Scores on the Stanford-Binet were converted into an _____, which was a ratio of mental age to chronological age, multiplied by 100.

8. To avoid cultural bias in intelligence tests, _____ intelligence tests include test items that are based on experiences common to many cultures.

9. _____ occurs when knowledge of stereotypes leads to anxiety and reduced performance consistent with a negative stereotype.

6.2 KNOW THE DETAILS OF APTITUDES FOR SCHOOL

1. Psychometricians are psychologists who specialize in measuring psychological characteristics such as intelligence and personality.
   TRUE or FALSE

2. Hierarchical theories of intelligence include both general and specific components.
   TRUE or FALSE

3. According to Gardner's more recent theory of multiple intelligences, intelligence includes nine distinct components.
   TRUE or FALSE

4. Musical intelligence, spatial intelligence, and intrapersonal intelligence are subtheories of Sternberg's triarchic theory of intelligence.
   TRUE or FALSE

5. Gardner believes that schools should focus on linguistic and logical-mathematical intelligences.
   TRUE or FALSE

6. Sternberg's theory of successful intelligence focuses on analytic, creative, and practical abilities.

   TRUE or FALSE

7. The purpose of the intelligence test developed by Binet and Simon was to identify children who would be unable to learn in school without special instruction.

   TRUE or FALSE

8. Chronological age refers to the difficulty of the problems children can solve correctly.

   TRUE or FALSE

9. On Terman's early version of the Stanford-Binet, intelligence quotients were derived using the formula IQ= CA/MA x 100.

   TRUE or FALSE

10. Today, IQ scores are determined by comparing children's test performance to the average IQ scores of others their age.

    TRUE or FALSE

11. The average IQ score is 120.

    TRUE or FALSE

12. Intelligence tests predict school performance reasonably well.

    TRUE or FALSE

13. Identical twins have been found to have more similar IQs than fraternal twins, suggesting that genes influence intelligence.

    TRUE or FALSE

14. The influence of environment on intelligence has been shown by intervention programs, which have been able to increase children's intelligence test scores by enriching the children's environment.

    TRUE or FALSE

15. On most intelligence tests, there are no ethnic differences in average scores.

    TRUE or FALSE

16. The environment is largely responsible for ethnic group differences in intelligence.

    TRUE or FALSE

17. The Stanford-Binet is an example of a culture-fair intelligence test.

    TRUE or FALSE

6.3 SPECIAL CHILDREN, SPECIAL NEEDS

TO MASTER THE LEARNING OBJECTIVES:

What are the characteristics of gifted and creative children?

- List and describe the prerequisites of exceptional talent in children.

- Define convergent and divergent thinking, and explain the difference between the two.

- Describe the types of home and school environments that nurture creativity in children.

What are the different forms of disability?

- Define intellectual disability.

- Describe biomedical, social, behavioral, and educational factors that put someone at risk for intellectual disability.

- Describe what is meant by learning disability, and describe the three most common types.

What are the distinguishing features of attention-deficit hyperactivity disorder?

- Describe the three symptoms of ADHD, and describe the incidence of ADHD in boys and girls.

- Explain the myths associated with ADHD.

- Describe the treatments for ADHD.

6.3 KNOW THE TERMS

Convergent thinking	**Intellectual disability**
Divergent thinking	**Learning disability**

1. Using information to arrive at a standard, correct answer is called _____.

2. Thinking in novel and unusual directions is called _____.

3. _____ refers to substantial limitations in intellectual ability as well as adapting to an environment, with both emerging before 18 years of age.

4. Someone with normal intelligence who has difficulty mastering at least one academic subject has a _____.

6.3 KNOW THE DETAILS OF SPECIAL CHILDREN, SPECIAL NEEDS

1. The traditional definition of giftedness was a score of 130 or greater on an intelligence test.
    TRUE or FALSE

2. Today's definitions of giftedness include exceptional talent in a variety of areas, such as art, music, creative writing, and dance.
    TRUE or FALSE

3. If a child is exceptionally talented, the talent will grow even in the absence of environmental support and encouragement.
    TRUE or FALSE

4. Gifted children tend to have emotional problems and difficulty getting along with other children.
    TRUE or FALSE

5. Intelligence is associated with divergent thinking; creativity is related to convergent thinking.
    TRUE or FALSE

6. Intellectual disability is defined as a substantial limitation in intellectual ability as well as problems adapting to an environment, with both emerging before 18 years of age.
    TRUE or FALSE

7. Risk factors for intellectual disability include biomedical, social, behavioral, and educational factors.
    TRUE or FALSE

8. Some individuals with an intellectual disability need the constant supervision provided by living in an institution whereas others can go to school, learn academic skills, work, and marry.
    TRUE or FALSE

9. Children classified as learning disabled have below normal intelligence.
    TRUE or FALSE

10. Developmental dyslexia, impaired reading comprehension, and mathematical learning disability are three of the most common types of learning disabilities.
    TRUE or FALSE

11. More boys than girls have an attention-deficit hyperactivity disorder.
    TRUE or FALSE

12. Hyperactivity, inattention, and impulsivity are symptoms of a learning disability.

    TRUE or FALSE

13. Most children with attention-deficit hyperactivity disorder grow out of it in adolescence or young adulthood.

    TRUE or FALSE

14. Research consistently indicates that there is a connection between food allergies and ADHD.

    TRUE or FALSE

15. The MDA study found that a few months of intensive treatment for ADHD had a long-lasting positive impact on ADHD.

    TRUE or FALSE

6.4 ACADEMIC SKILLS

TO MASTER THE LEARNING OBJECTIVES:

What are the components of skilled reading?

- Define word recognition and comprehension.

- Describe the components of reading.

- Describe the cues that aid word recognition.

- Describe the factors that contribute to improved reading comprehension.

As children develop, how does their writing improve?

- Describe the factors that contribute to improved writing in children.

- Define knowledge-telling strategy and knowledge-transforming strategy.

- Explain how improvements in the mechanical requirements of writing affect children's writing.

- Describe children's skill in revising.

How do arithmetic skills change during the elementary-school years? How do U.S. students compare to students from other countries?

- Describe the strategies that children use to add and subtract.

- Compare the math skills of students in the United States to students in other countries and the differences in schools and culture that contribute to the differences.

What are the hallmarks of effective schools and effective teachers?

- Describe the characteristics of schools where students typically succeed.

- Describe the characteristics of effective teachers.

6.4 KNOW THE TERMS

Comprehension	Phonological awareness
Knowledge-telling	Word recognition
Knowledge-transforming	

1. The process of identifying a unique pattern of letters is _____.

2. The process of extracting meaning from a sequence of words is called _____.

3. The ability to distinguish the distinctive sounds in spoken words is called _____.

4. The _____ strategy involves writing down information as it is retrieved from memory.

5. The _____ strategy involves deciding what information to include and how best to organize it for the reader.

6.4 KNOW THE DETAILS OF ACADEMIC SKILLS

1. Word recognition refers to the process of identifying a unique pattern of letters.
   TRUE or FALSE

2. Knowledge of letter and word forms is associated with success in learning to read.
   TRUE or FALSE

3. Phonological awareness has not been found to be related to success in learning to read.
   TRUE or FALSE

4. As children become more experienced readers, they tend to sound out fewer words and retrieve more from memory.
   TRUE or FALSE

5. Reading instruction is most likely to be effective when it addresses a child's weaknesses.
   TRUE or FALSE

6. A knowledge-transforming strategy of writing refers to writing down information on a topic as it is retrieved from memory.
   TRUE or FALSE

7. The POW+TREE strategy gives students a general plan for writing and tells them how to organize their writing in a paragraph.
    TRUE or FALSE

8. Children often count on their fingers as they begin to learn to add.
    TRUE or FALSE

9. In math, the very best students in Asian countries such as Korea and Singapore perform only at the level of average students in the U.S.
    TRUE or FALSE

10. Students in Taiwan and Japan spend more time on homework and value homework more the student in the U.S.
    TRUE or FALSE

11. The safety and nurturance of the school climate is related to whether students are likely to succeed or fail.
    TRUE or FALSE

12. Student success in schools is unrelated to parent involvement in the school.
    TRUE or FALSE

13. Students tend to learn the most when teachers are effective classroom managers.
    TRUE or FALSE

14. Students tend to learn the most when teachers assume that students are responsible for their own learning.
    TRUE or FALSE

15. Peer tutoring is not an effective way for students to learn.
    TRUE or FALSE

6.5 PHYSICAL DEVELOPMENT

TO MASTER THE LEARNING OBJECTIVES:

How much do school-age children grow?

- Describe the growth rate of school-age children.

- Describe ethnic differences in height and weight.

- Describe the nutritional needs of school-age children.

How do motor skills improve during the elementary school years?

- Describe changes in gross and fine motor skills.

- Know the gender differences in motor skills.

Are American children physically fit?

- Describe the rates of physical fitness among children, and explain the factors that contribute to this rate.

What are the consequences of participating in sports?

- Know the benefits of participating in sports.

- Know the characteristics of good and bad coaches.

6.5 KNOW THE DETAILS OF PHYSICAL DEVELOPMENT

1. Boys are more likely than girls to have entered puberty by the end of the elementary school years.

   TRUE or FALSE

2. The average 7- to 10-year-old needs to consume about 2,400 calories per day.

   TRUE or FALSE

3. During elementary school years, children's motor skills improve as they get bigger and stronger.

   TRUE or FALSE

4. During the elementary school years, girls tend to have better handwriting than boys.

   TRUE or FALSE

5. During the elementary school years, girls tend to be stronger than boys but boys tend to be more flexible and have better balance.

   TRUE or FALSE

6. The average school-age child in the United States is physically active.

   TRUE or FALSE

7. Children are most likely to maintain interest in sports when coaches emphasize winning.

   TRUE or FALSE

SUMMARY

6.1 COGNITIVE DEVELOPMENT

1. **What are the distinguishing characteristics of thought during Piaget's concrete-operational and formal-operational stages?**

    In progressing to Piaget's stage of concrete operations, children become less _____, rarely confuse appearances with reality, and are able to _____ their thinking. They now solve conservation and perspective-taking problems correctly. Thinking at this stage is limited to the _____ and the real. With the onset of formal-operational thinking, adolescents can think hypothetically and reason _____. In deductive reasoning, they understand that conclusions are based on _____, not on experience.

2. **How do children use strategies and monitoring to improve learning and remembering?**

    Rehearsal and other memory strategies are used to transfer information from _____ memory, a temporary store of information, to long-term memory, a permanent store of knowledge. Children begin to rehearse at about seven or eight years of age and begin to use other strategies as they get older. Effective use of strategies for learning and remembering begins with an analysis of the _____ of a learning task. It also includes _____ one's performance to determine if the strategy is working. Collectively, these processes define an important group of study skills.

6.2 APTITUDES FOR SCHOOL

1. **Theories of Intelligence**

    Traditional approaches to intelligence include theories that describe intelligence as a general factor as well as theories that include specific factors. _____ theories include both general intelligence as well as various specific skills, such as verbal and spatial ability. Gardner's theory of multiple intelligences proposes nine distinct intelligences. Three are found in psychometric theories (_____, logical-mathematical, spatial), but six are new (_____, bodily-kinesthetic, interpersonal, intrapersonal, naturalistic, and existential intelligence). Gardner's theory has stimulated research on nontraditional forms of intelligence such as emotional intelligence. The theory has implications for education, suggesting, for example, that schools should adjust teaching to each child's unique intellectual strengths.

    According to Robert Sternberg, intelligence is defined using abilities to achieve short-term and long-term goals and depends on three abilities: _____ to analyze problems and generate solutions, creative ability to deal adaptively with novel situations, and _____ to know what solutions will work.

2. **Why were intelligence tests first developed? What are their features?**

Binet created the first intelligence test in order to identify students who would have difficulty in school. Using this work, Terman created the Stanford-Binet in 1916; it remains an important intelligence test. The Stanford-Binet introduced the concept of the _____, which was MA/CA x 100.

3. **How well do intelligence tests work?**

Intelligence tests are reasonably valid measures of achievement in school. They also predict people's performance in the _____.

4. **How do heredity and environment influence intelligence?**

Evidence for the impact of heredity on IQ comes from the finding that (a) siblings' IQ scores become more alike as siblings become more similar genetically, and (b) adopted children's IQ scores are more _____ their biological parents' test scores than their adoptive parents' scores. Evidence for the impact of the environment comes from the finding that children who live in _____ well-organized home environments tend to have higher IQ scores, as do children who participate in intervention programs.

5. **How and why do test scores vary for different racial and ethnic groups?**

There are substantial differences between ethnic groups in their average scores on IQ tests. This difference has been attributed to the great likelihood of Latino-American and African-American youth being _____ and that the tests assesses knowledge based on _____ experiences. Stereotype threat and test-taking skills also contribute to group differences. IQ scores are valid predictors of school success because middle-class experience is often a prerequisite for school success.

6.3 SPECIAL CHILDREN, SPECIAL NEEDS

1. **What are the characteristics of gifted and creative children?**

Traditionally, gifted children have been those with high scores on _____ tests. Modern definitions of giftedness have been broadened to include exceptional talent in the arts. Giftedness must be nurtured by parents and teachers alike. Contrary to folklore, gifted children usually are _____ and emotionally stable. _____ is associated with divergent thinking, in which the aim is to think in novel and unusual directions. Tests of divergent thinking can predict which children are most likely to be creative. Creativity can be fostered by experiences that encourage children to think _____ and to explore alternatives.

2.   **What are the different forms of disability?**

Individuals with intellectual disability have IQ scores of _____ or lower and deficits in adaptive behavior. Biomedical, _____, behavioral, and educational factors place children at risk for intellectual disability.

Children with learning disabilities have _____ intelligence but have difficulty mastering specific academic subjects. The most common is _____, which involves difficulty reading words because children haven't mastered language sounds.

3.   **What are the distinguishing features of attention-deficit hyperactivity disorder?**

Children with ADHD are distinguished by being overactive, _____, and impulsive. According to the Multi-modal Treatment Study of Children with ADHD, treating ADHD with _____ and psychosocial treatment is effective in the short run but does not "cure" children of the disorder.

6.4 ACADEMIC SKILLS

1.   **What are the components of skilled reading?**

Reading includes a number of component skills. Pre-reading skills include knowing letters and the _____ associated with them. _____ is the process of identifying a word. Beginning readers more often accomplish this by sounding out words; advanced readers more often retrieve a word from long-term memory. _____, the act of extracting meaning from text improves with age due to several factors: working memory capacity _____, readers gain more world knowledge, and readers are better able to monitor what they read and to match reading strategies to the goals of the reading task.

2.   **As children develop, how does their writing improve?**

As children develop, their writing improves, reflecting several factors. They know more about the world and so they have more to say; they use more effective ways of _____ their writing; they master the mechanics (e.g., handwriting, spelling) of writing; and they become more skilled at _____ their writing.

3.   **How do arithmetic skills change during elementary-school years? How do U.S. students compare to students in other countries?**

Children first add and subtract by _____, but then use more effective strategies such as retrieving addition facts directly from memory. In mathematics, U.S. students _____ students in most other industrialized nations. This difference can be traced to cultural differences in the time spent in schoolwork and homework, and in parents' _____ toward school, effort, and ability.

4. **What are the hallmarks of effective schools and effective teachers?**

Schools influence students' achievement in many ways. Students are more likely to achieve when their school emphasizes _____, has a safe and nurturing environment, _____ pupils' and teachers' progress, and encourages _____ to be involved. Students achieve at higher levels when their teachers manage classrooms effectively, take _____ for their students' learning, teach _____ of material, pace material well, value tutoring, and show children how to _____ their own learning.

6.5 PHYSICAL DEVELOPMENT

1. **How much do school-age children grow?**

Elementary-school children grow at a steady pace, but more so in their _____ than in the trunk. Boys and girls tend to be about the _____ size for most of these years, but there are large individual and ethnic differences. School-age children need approximately _____ calories daily, preferably drawn from each of the basic food groups. Children need to eat breakfast because this meal should provide about _____ of their daily calories. Without breakfast, they often have trouble concentrating in school.

2. **How do motor skills develop during the elementary-school years?**

Fine and gross motor skills improve substantially over the elementary-school years, reflecting children's greater size and strength. Girls tend to excel at _____ skills that emphasize dexterity as well as gross-motor skills that require flexibility and balance; boys tend to excel in gross-motor skills that emphasize _____. Although some of the differences reflect differences in body make-up, they also reflect differing _____ regarding motor skills for boys and girls.

3. **Are American children physically fit?**

_____ American school children meet today's standards for physical fitness, although childhood _____ is a growing concern.

4. **What are the consequences of participating in sports?**

Many school-age children participate in team sports. Benefits of participation include exercise, enhanced _____, and improved social skills. But participation sometimes leads to _____ behavior, and when adults are involved they sometimes overemphasize _____, which can turn "play" into "work."

TEST YOURSELF

MULTIPLE-CHOICE QUESTIONS

1. During Piaget's concrete-operational stage, children

   a. are more egocentric than they were during the preoperational period.

   b. often confuse appearances with reality.

   c. are unable to reverse their thinking.

   d. are able to perform mental operations.

2. Callie is a concrete-operational thinker whereas Fiona is a formal-operational thinker. Which of the following statements is most likely to be true?

   a. Fiona is better than Callie in abstract reasoning.

   b. Callie is better than Fiona in combinatorial reasoning.

   c. Fiona is more likely than Callie to focus on the tangible and real aspects of a task.

   d. Callie is better than Fiona at hypothetical reasoning.

3. By the time they reach Piaget's _____ stage, children are able to draw logical conclusions even when the conclusion contradicts what experience tells them is really true.

   a. preoperational

   b. formal-operational

   c. concrete-operational

   d. sensorimotor

4. The ability to draw appropriate conclusions from facts is referred to as

   a. deductive reasoning.

   b. divergent thinking.

   c. performing a mental operation.

   d. concrete thinking.

5. Piaget's theory has been criticized because it

   a. is vague about the processes that cause changes in cognitive development.

   b. overemphasizes the impact of sociocultural factors on cognitive development.

   c. concentrates too much on variability in children's performance.

   d. did not provide a comprehensive view of cognitive development.

6. Most thought takes place in the _____, according to information-processing theorists.

    a. sensorimotor cortex

    b. working memory

    c. long-term memory

    d. intelligence quotient

7. The _____ is a permanent storehouse of knowledge that has an unlimited capacity.

    a. sensorimotor cortex

    b. working memory

    c. long-term memory

    d. intelligence quotient

8. If seven-year-old Kevin performs like a typical young child on a memory task, he will

    a. use rehearsal to try to remember the to-be-recalled information.

    b. accurately judge the objective of a memory task.

    c. usually pick the best strategy to use to remember the to-be-recalled information.

    d. successfully monitor how much of the information he can recall.

9. Which of the following shows the correct sequence in which the events should take place for effective learning to occur?

    a. Determine task goals, select appropriate strategy, use strategy, monitor strategy

    b. Monitor strategy, determine task goals, select appropriate strategy, use strategy

    c. Select appropriate strategy, determine task goals, use strategy, monitor strategy

    d. Determine task goals, monitor strategy, select appropriate strategy, use strategy

10. Natsuki has an extensive vocabulary and excels at using language to convey ideas to others. According to Gardner's theory of multiple intelligences, Natsuki is high in the _____ component.

    a. intrapersonal intelligence

    b. logical-mathematical intelligence

    c. linguistic intelligence

    d. spatial intelligence

11. In Sternberg's theory of successful intelligence, _____ ability involves investigating problems and generating different solutions; _____ ability involves dealing adaptively with novel situations; and _____ ability involves knowing what solution or plan will actually work.

    a. analytic; creative; practical

    b. creative; analytic; practical

    c. creative; practical; analytic

    d. analytic; practical; creative

12. The difficulty of the problems that a child can solve on an intelligence test determines the child's

    a. chronological age.

    b. mental age.

    c. analytic ability.

    d. divergent reasoning.

13. Which of the following is the formula that Terman originally used to determine an intelligence quotient?

    a. IQ = MA/CA x 100

    b. IQ = CA/MA x 100

    c. IQ = MA x CA x 100

    d. IQ = CA/100 x MA

14. Who has the highest IQ?

    a. A 4-year-old with a mental age of 4

    b. A 10-year-old with a mental age of 12

    c. A 6-year-old with a mental age of 10

    d. A 5-year-old with a mental age of 3

15. If intelligence is influenced by genes, then the IQ scores of identical twins should be

    a. less similar than those of fraternal twins.

    b. less similar than those of children and their adopted siblings.

    c. less similar than those of children and their biological parents.

    d. more similar than those of other pairs of siblings.

16. If you wanted to get a culture-fair assessment of intelligence, which of the following tests would be best to use?

    a. Kaufman Assessment Battery for Children II

    b. Raven's Progressive Matrices

    c. Stanford-Binet

    d. Wechsler Intelligence Scale for Children-IV (WISC-IV)

17. Gifted children

    a. tend to have more emotional problems than their nongifted peers.

    b. often have difficulty getting along with other children.

    c. tend to be more mature than their nongifted peers.

    d. will flourish even if their talents are not nurtured by others.

18. Which of the following is NOT a prerequisite for exceptional talent?

    a. The child must love the subject and have an almost overwhelming desire to master it.

    b. The child must be instructed at an early age by an inspiring and talented teacher.

    c. The child must receive support and help from parents who are committed to promoting their child's talent.

    d. The child must demonstrate outstanding reading or math skills in an academic setting.

19. Which question requires divergent thinking?

    a. What is 3,928 + 2,432?

    b. How many different ways can you think of to use a paper clip?

    c. What is the chemical composition of water?

    d. Who was the 35th president of the United States?

20. Which of the following is NOT a defining characteristic of an intellectual disability?

    a. Substantial limitation in intellectual abilities

    b. Problems adapting to an environment

    c. Emerging before 18 years of age

    d. Exceptionally high levels of divergent thinking

21. Down syndrome is considered a(n) _____ factor that leads to intellectual disabilities.

    a. behavioral

    b. biomedical

    c. educational

    d. social

22. A child with a learning disability has

    a. difficulty in an academic subject.

    b. below average intelligence.

    c. difficulty learning due to a visual impairment.

    d. learning problems due to poor teaching.

23. Clyde is unusually energetic, has difficulty concentrating in school, and often acts without thinking. Clyde shows many of the characteristics of

    a. a learning disability.

    b. attention-deficit hyperactivity disorder.

    c. an intellectual disability.

    d. giftedness.

24. Research supports which of the following as a cause of ADHD?

    a. Food allergies

    b. Sugar

    c. Poor home life

    d. Prenatal exposure to alcohol and drugs

25. The ability to hear the distinctive sounds of letters is a skill known as

    a. phonological awareness.

    b. letter recognition.

    c. word recognition.

    d. knowledge-telling.

26. Which of the following is NOT a factor related to improved reading comprehension as children get older?

    a. Increases in working memory capacity

    b. Acquiring more knowledge of the physical, social, and psychological world

    c. Using more appropriate reading strategies

    d. Doing less monitoring of comprehension

27. Before he started to write, Billy decided what information he wanted to include and thought about how he could best organize it to get his point across. What type of strategy was Billy using?

    a. Knowledge-telling

    b. Knowledge-transforming

    c. Comprehension

    d. Phonological

28. Compared to students in other countries, U.S. students have

    a. the highest math achievement scores in the world.

    b. the lowest math achievement scores in the world.

    c. substantially lower math achievement than students in the nation with the highest level of math achievement.

    d. math achievement scores very close to those in the nation with the highest math achievement scores.

29. Which of the following comparisons between students in the U.S., Japan, and Taiwan is true?

    a. Students in Japan and Taiwan spend more time in school than students in the U.S.

    b. Students in the U.S. spend more time on homework than student in Japan and Taiwan.

    c. Parents in the U.S. have much higher standards for their children's achievement than do parents in Japan and Taiwan.

    d. Parents in the U.S. believe more strongly than parents in Japan and Taiwan that effort, not native ability, is the key factor in school success.

30. In which of the following schools would students be most likely to fail?

    a. In School A, where the school climate is safe and nurturing

    b. In School B, where parents are involved

    c. In School C, where the progress of students, teachers, and programs is monitored

    d. In School D, where many nonacademic activities are included in the school day

31. Who is likely to be the most effective teacher?

    a. Ms. Allen, who believes she is responsible for her students' learning

    b. Mr. Brown, who often lectures and then has students do worksheets

    c. Mr. Curry, who presents material at a very rapid pace

    d. Ms. Diamond, who spends a lot of time disciplining students

32. During the elementary school years,

    a. boys grow faster than girls for most years.

    b. growth occurs at a steady pace.

    c. most of the growth occurs in the trunk not the legs.

    d. growth slows down; children need to consume fewer calories than in the preschool years.

33. In regard to elementary-school-age children's motor skills,

    a. boys outperform girls on skills that require strength.

    b. boys outperform girls on skills that require balance.

    c. boys outperform girls on skills that require flexibility.

    d. there are no gender differences in performance levels.

34. Gender differences in motor skills during the elementary school years are due in part to

    a. differences in experience.

    b. girls' bodies having less fat.

    c. girls' bodies having more muscle.

    d. beliefs that physical fitness is less important for boys than for girls.

35. Participation in sports during the elementary school years

    a. is more informal today than in years past.

    b. gives children a chance to learn valuable social skills.

    c. is most beneficial when coaches emphasize competition rather than skill development.

    d. is detrimental to cognitive skill development.

ESSAY QUESTIONS

1. Your friend Sam took his children to a hands-on science museum when they were on vacation in Florida. Sam noticed that his eight-year-old son and his 12-year-old son interacted with some of the displays in very different ways. One display involved opening doors to wall safes by determining the combination. Each safe had 3, 4, or 5 buttons that had to be pressed in a particular order to open the door. Sam's eight-year-old randomly pushed the buttons and gave up before the door opened; the 12-year-old approached the task in a very systematic manner, trying all possible combinations until the doors opened. Sam wonders if his sons are typical. What can you tell Sam about the differences between concrete-operational and formal-operational thought that might explain his sons' behavior?

2. Your friends Mick and Mia are both above average in intelligence and concerned that their new son Mike will be intelligent also. They want to know how they can shape Mike's environment so that it will increase his chances of being above average in intelligence. What can you tell them about the effects of environment and heredity on intelligence?

175

3. Your friend Lola would like her five-year-old daughter, Lisa, to become a piano virtuoso at a young age. She has seen 12- and 13-year-olds winning national instrumental competitions on television, and Lola is wondering what she should be doing to increase the likelihood that Lisa will be one of those adolescents in a few short years. What can you tell Lola about the prerequisites for exceptional talent?

4. Your friend Antonio wonders if his son Claudio, who is very active, has attention-deficit hyperactivity disorder. What can you tell Antonio about the symptoms of ADHD that might help him decide if he should seek treatment for his son?

5. Your friend, Jin-pyo, is a concerned father, and he would like to do all that he can to help his four-year-old daughter, Jae-jin, learn to read. What can you tell Jin-pyo about pre-reading skills that are related to more skilled reading in first grade?

6. You are having a discussion with a friend about the differences in math achievement in children in the United States and children in Asian countries. During your discussion, your friend states, "It must be genetic. Or maybe Asian kids are just smarter than American kids." What can you tell your friend about the reasons for cultural differences in math achievement that refute his statement?

7. Your friend's first-grade son, Hasani, has been writing a story every Monday in school. Your friend is concerned about Hasani's writing because she thinks that his stories aren't very good. They often have no organization and seem very incomplete. What can you tell your friend about the changes in writing ability that might make her feel better?

8. Your friends are moving to a new community, and they are concerned about finding a good, effective school for their daughter in their new city. What can you tell your friends about the characteristics of schools where students typically succeed rather than fail?

9. At a recent parent council meeting at your child's elementary school, a group of parents raised objections to the use of computers in the classroom. They felt that teachers used computers solely to entertain the children and that computers were a waste of instructional time. What can you tell this group of parents about the benefits of using computers in the classroom?

10. Your spouse is going to coach your eight-year-old daughter's soccer team. You want this to be a positive experience for your daughter and the other girls. What can you tell your spouse about good and bad coaches that might help the experience be as positive as possible?

ANSWERS WITH PAGE REFERENCES

6.1 KNOW THE TERMS

1. mental operations (206)
2. deductive reasoning (207)
3. Working memory (208)
4. Long-term memory (208)
5. Organization (208)

6. elaboration (208)
7. Metamemory (209)
8. metacognitive knowledge (209)
9. cognitive self-regulation (209)

6.1 KNOW THE DETAILS OF COGNITIVE DEVELOPMENT

1. T, 206	5. F, 206	9. T, 208	13. T, 209
2. F, 206	6. F, 206	10. F, 208	14. T, 209
3. T, 206	7. T, 207	11. T, 208	15. T, 209
4. T, 206	8. F, 207	12. T, 208	

6.2 KNOW THE TERMS

1. psychometricians (211)
2. emotional intelligence (213)
3. Analytic ability (214)
4. Creative ability (214)
5. Practical ability (214)

6. mental age (215)
7. intelligence quotient (216)
8. culture-fair (219)
9. Stereotype threat (220)

6.2 KNOW THE DETAILS OF APTITUDES FOR SCHOOL

1. T, 211	6. T, 214	11. F, 268	16. T, 219
2. T, 212	7. T, 215	12. T, 216	17. F, 220
3. T, 213	8. F, 215	13. T, 217	
4. F, 213	9. F, 216	14. T, 218	
5. F, 214	10. T, 216	15. F, 219	

6.3 KNOW THE TERMS

1. convergent thinking (222)
2. divergent thinking (222)
3. Intellectual disability (223)
4. learning disability (224)

6.3 KNOW THE DETAILS OF SPECIAL CHILDREN, SPECIAL NEEDS

1. T, 222	5. F, 222	9. F, 224	13. F, 227
2. T, 222	6. T, 223	10. T, 224	14. F, 227
3. F, 222	7. T, 223	11. T, 226	15. F, 228
4. F, 222	8. T, 224	12. F, 226	

6.4 KNOW THE TERMS

1. word recognition (229)
2. comprehension (229)
3. phonological awareness (230)
4. knowledge-telling (232)
5. knowledge-transforming (232)

6.4 KNOW THE DETAILS OF ACADEMIC SKILLS

1. T, 229	5. T, 230	9. F, 234	13. T, 238
2. T, 229	6. F, 232	10. T, 235	14. F, 238
3. F, 230	7. T, 233	11. T, 237	15. F, 238
4. T, 230	8. T, 234	12. F, 237	

6.5 KNOW THE DETAILS OF PHYSICAL DEVELOPMENT

1. F, 239	4. T, 241	7. F, 242
2. T, 240	5. F, 241	
3. T, 240	6. T, 242	

SUMMARY

6.1 COGNITIVE DEVELOPMENT

1. egocentric (206); reverse (206); concrete (206); abstractly (206); logic (207)
2. working (208); goals (209); monitoring (209)

6.2 APTITUDES FOR SCHOOL

1. Hierarchical (212); linguistic (213); musical (213); analytic ability (214); practical ability (214)
2. intelligence quotient (216)
3. workplace (216)
4. like (217); responsive (218)
5. economically disadvantaged (219); middle-class (219)

6.3 SPECIAL CHILDREN, SPECIAL NEEDS

1. IQ (222); socially mature (222); Creativity (222); flexibly (223)
2. 70 (223); social (223); normal (224); developmental dyslexia (224)
3. inattentive (227); medication (227);

6.4 ACADEMIC SKILLS

1. sounds (230); Word recognition (230); Comprehension (231); increases (231)
2. organizing (232); revising (232)
3. counting (234); lag behind (234); attitudes (236)
4. academic excellence (237); monitors (237); parents (237); responsibility (238); mastery (238); monitor (238)

6.5 PHYSICAL DEVELOPMENT

1. legs (239); same (239); 2,400 (240); one-fourth (240)
2. fine-motor (240); strength (241); cultural expectations (241)
3. Most (242); obesity (242)
4. self-esteem (242); antisocial (242); winning (242)

TEST YOURSELF

MULTIPLE-CHOICE QUESTIONS

1. d, 206	11. a, 214	21. d, 223	31. a, 238
2. a, 206	12. b, 215	22. a, 224	32. b, 239
3. b, 207	13. a, 216	23. b, 226	33. a, 241
4. a, 207	14. c, 216	24. d, 227	34. a, 241
5. a, 208	15. d, 217	25. a, 230	35. b, 242
6. b, 208	16. b, 220	26. d, 231	
7. c, 208	17. c, 222	27. b, 232	
8. a, 208	18. d, 222	28. c, 234	
9. a, 210	19. b, 222	29. a, 235	
10. c, 213	20. d, 223	30. d, 237	

ESSAY QUESTIONS

1. The behavior of Sam's sons fits Piaget's description of formal-operational and concrete-operational thought very well. According to Piaget, children who are 12 years old would be in the period of formal operations. Formal-operational children use more sophisticated, logical, deductive reasoning to solve problems like the safe problem. However, concrete-operational children (such as the eight-year-old) use haphazard trial-and-error and often do not solve problems like the safe problem. Concrete-operational children are more likely to try to solve problems in concrete ways, such as pushing buttons, but formal-operational children can think abstractly about the possible logical combinations before attempting the button pushing. (206-208)

2. There does seem to be a hereditary component to intelligence. Studies of twins show that identical twins, who have identical genes, have more similar scores on intelligence tests than do fraternal twins or other non-twin siblings. Similarly, adopted children's IQ scores are more like their biological parents' IQ scores than their adoptive parents and become more similar to their biological parents' scores as they get older. The environment is also important in shaping one's intelligence. Children with high intelligence test scores tend to live in homes that are well-organized and have plenty of appropriate play materials. Mike will probably receive genes for above average intelligence from Mia and Mick, and they will probably provide a stimulating environment that nurtures Mike's intellectual development. (217-218)

3. First, children who develop exceptional talent in an area love the subject and have a very strong desire to master it. Second, children who develop exceptional talent begin instruction in the given area at an early age from inspiring and talented teachers. Third, these children also receive help and support from their parents, who are committed to promoting their children's talents. Lola sounds as if she is committed to supporting Lisa's piano playing and that she is willing to find inspiring and talented piano teachers for her. The critical question is whether Lisa loves to play the piano and has a strong desire to master it. (222)

4. The first symptom that Antonio should be looking for in Claudio is overactivity. Can Claudio sit still in school? Children with ADHD are energetic and unable to keep still, especially in situations like school classrooms. The second sign is inattention. Children with ADHD do not pay attention in class and find it hard to concentrate on schoolwork. The final sign is that ADHD children are impulsive; they act before they think. Not all children show these symptoms to the same degree. For example, some children suffer from more inattention and others show more hyperactivity. Because of these problems, children with ADHD often have problems with academic performance, conduct, and getting along with peers. (226-228)

5. Young children who know most of their letters and who can easily distinguish the sounds that the different letters make (phonological awareness) learn to read more readily and are more skilled readers. Jin-pyo can help Jae-jin master these skills by playing games with her that involve identifying the letters of the alphabet. Reading to Jae-jin is one of the best things that Jin-pyo can do to teach her the language-related skills that are important to prepare for reading. Also, identifying letters and their sounds while reading books to Jae-jin will increase her phonological awareness. Even in older children, phonological awareness continues to be an excellent predictor of reading ability. (229-230)

6. Students in the United States do fare poorly on tests of math skills when compared to students in many other countries, but you can tell your friend that, in fact, there are no systematic differences in general intelligence or general cognitive skills between children in the United States and those in Japan or Taiwan. Experiences at home and school seem to account for the differences in math achievement. In general, children in Japan and Taiwan spend more hours in school and spend a greater percentage of those hours engaged in academic pursuits. Children in Japan and Taiwan also spend more time per week doing homework, and they rate homework as being more valuable than do children in the United States. Parents in Japan and Taiwan have higher expectations for achievement in their children, and they believe that effort and experience are critical in determining achievement. In other words, differences in achievement stem from differences in cultural attitudes and school practices. (234-236)

7. You can tell your friend that most first-graders are not very good writers. First, their stories are often very limited because their knowledge of the world is limited. As children learn more about the world, they have more interesting information to incorporate into their stories. Second, young writers like Hasani use a knowledge-telling strategy in which they write down information on a topic as they retrieve it from memory. This often means that the writing is disorganized and disjointed. Third, as children become more proficient at the mechanical requirements of writing (e.g., spelling, punctuation, handwriting) they can devote more of their attention to the other aspects of writing that make a story more interesting. Last, as children develop, they become better editors of their own writing. Older children are more likely to find problems and revise them. So, as Hasani matures during the elementary-school years his writing should improve, and his mother shouldn't be worried about his simple-minded, unorganized stories. (232-233)

8. Schools where the students typically succeed rather than fail have a number of characteristics in common. First, both the staff and students understand that academic excellence is the primary goal of the school and of every student in the school. Second, the school environment is safe and nurturing so that students can devote their energy to learning. Third, successful schools have a high level of formal and informal parental involvement. Finally, the progress of students, teachers, and programs is monitored to determine if academic goals are being met. (237)

9. Good coaches encourage their players and emphasize skill development. When coaches act in this manner, children usually enjoy playing, often improve their skills, and show an increase in self-esteem. However, when coaches emphasize winning over skill development and criticize or punish players for mistakes, children lose interest and stop playing. (242-243)

EXPANDING SOCIAL HORIZONS

7.1 Family Relationships

7.2 Peers

7.3 Electronic Media

7.4 Understanding Others

This chapter focuses on how the child is influenced by family members, peers, electronic media, and his or her understanding of others.

7.1 FAMILY RELATIONSHIPS

TO MASTER THE LEARNING OBJECTIVES:

What is a systems approach to parenting?

- Describe the view of families as systems.

What are the primary dimensions of parenting? How do they affect children's development?

- Describe how the degree of parental warmth is related to outcomes for children.

- Explain why moderate levels of parental control are best for children.

- Describe the authoritarian, authoritative, indulgent-permissive, and indifferent-uninvolved parental styles.

- Describe how the various parental styles are related to children's developmental outcomes.

- Compare cultural and socioeconomic differences in parental warmth and control.

- Describe the parental behaviors and other factors that influence children's behavior.

- Describe how parents' marital systems influence development.

- Explain the reciprocal influence between children and their parents.

What determines how siblings get along? How do first-born, later-born, and only children differ?

- Describe how older children may react when a younger sibling is born.

- Describe how the sibling relationship changes over the first few years of life.

- Explain how gender, temperament, age, perceptions of parental treatment, and quality of the relationship between the parents are related to the quality of sibling relationships.

- Compare adopted and nonadopted children.

How do divorce and remarriage affect children?

- Describe how divorce affects children's lives.

- Describe how divorce influences development and which children are most affected by parental divorce.

- Describe how blended families with stepmothers differ from blended families with stepfathers.

What factors lead children to be maltreated?

- Define physical abuse, sexual abuse, psychological abuse, and neglect.

- Describe cultural, parental, and child factors that are related to an increased likelihood of abuse.

- Describe the effects of child abuse on the children.

- Describe some things that can be done to reduce the risk of child abuse.

184

7.1 KNOW THE TERMS

Authoritarian   Negative reinforcement trap

Authoritative   Permissive

Blended   Punishment

Counterimitation   Reinforcement

Direct instruction   Socialization

Ego resilience   Time-out

Joint custody   Uninvolved

1.   The process of teaching children the values, roles, and behaviors of their cultures is called

     _____.

2.   _____ parents show high levels of control and low levels of warmth toward their

     children.

3.   Parents who use a moderate amount of control and who are warm and responsive to their

     children are _____ parents.

4.   _____ parents are warm and caring, but they exert little control over their children.

5.   Parents who are neither warm nor controlling and who try to minimize the amount of time

     spent with their children are _____ parents.

6.   Telling a child what to do, when, and why is called _____.

7.   Observing another's behavior and learning what should not be done is known as

     _____.

8.   _____ is an action that increases the likelihood of the response that it follows.

9.   _____ is any action that discourages the reoccurrence of the response that it follows.

10. Parents may unwittingly reinforce the very behaviors that they want to discourage in a

     situation called a _____.

11. _____ involves removing children who are misbehaving from a situation to a quiet,

     unstimulating environment.

12. In _____ both parents retain legal custody of their children after divorce.

13. _____ families consist of a biological parent, a stepparent, and children.

14. Children's ability to respond adaptively and resourcefully to new situations is known as

     _____.

7.1 KNOW THE DETAILS OF FAMILY RELATIONSHIPS

1. According to the systems view, parents and children influence each other.

   TRUE or FALSE

2. Children benefit from warm and responsive parenting.

   TRUE or FALSE

3. Children do best when parents exert a high level of control.

   TRUE or FALSE

4. Authoritarian parenting combines high control with warmth and responsiveness to the children.

   TRUE or FALSE

5. Permissive parents are warm and caring but exert little control over their children.

   TRUE or FALSE

6. Children with authoritarian parents tend to be responsible, self-reliant, and friendly.

   TRUE or FALSE

7. Children with uninvolved parents more often do poorly in school and are aggressive.

   TRUE or FALSE

8. Although authoritative parenting is generally considered the most beneficial, authoritarian parenting can protect children growing up in dangerous areas.

   TRUE or FALSE

9. Direct instruction involves telling a child what to do, when, and why.

   TRUE or FALSE

10. Counterimitation involves watching the parental model and imitating what they do.

    TRUE or FALSE

11. Reinforcement is any action that increases the likelihood of the response that it follows.

    TRUE or FALSE

12. A negative reinforcement trap occurs when parents unwittingly reinforce the very behaviors they want to discourage.

    TRUE or FALSE

13. Punishment works best when it is used only occasionally after an undesired behavior.

    TRUE or FALSE

14. Time-out involves having a child who misbehaved briefly sit alone in a quiet, unstimulating location.

    TRUE or FALSE

15. Parental conflict is not harmful to children.

TRUE or FALSE

16. Children's behavior can influence the parenting style used.

TRUE or FALSE

17. The basic pattern of sibling relationship is usually established early in life and remains stable.

TRUE or FALSE

18. Sibling relations are more likely to be warm and harmonious between siblings of the opposite sex than between siblings of the same sex.

TRUE or FALSE

19. Adopted children are more prone to problems when they were adopted at an older age and when their care before adoption was poor.

TRUE or FALSE

20. Parents are usually more affectionate and more punitive with first-borns than with later-born children.

TRUE or FALSE

21. Compared to first-born children, later-born children tend to be more intelligent and more willing to conform to parents' requests.

TRUE or FALSE

22. Only children are worse off than children with siblings in terms of intelligence, leadership, autonomy, and maturity.

TRUE or FALSE

23. Children of divorce are more likely to experience conflict in their own marriages than children from intact homes.

TRUE or FALSE

24. As divorce became more common in the 1970s and 1980s, the effects on children diminished.

TRUE or FALSE

25. Children adjust to divorce more readily if their divorced parents cooperate with each other.

TRUE or FALSE

26. Children often adjust better to parental divorce when they live with the same-sex parent.

TRUE or FALSE

27. Parental divorce is more harmful for school-age children and adolescents than for preschoolers or college-age adults.

    TRUE or FALSE

28. Children whose parents are married but fight often show many of the same effects associated with parental divorce.

    TRUE or FALSE

29. Children adjust better to divorce when they keep good relationships with both parents.

    TRUE or FALSE

30. Preadolescent girls tend to adjust better than preadolescent boys to having a stepfather when their mothers remarry.

    TRUE or FALSE

31. Countries that do not approve of physical punishment tend to have lower rates of child maltreatment than the U.S.

    TRUE or FALSE

32. Older children are more likely than younger children to be the targets of abuse.

    TRUE or FALSE

33. Children who are abused tend to have poor relationships with peers.

    TRUE or FALSE

34. The effects of abuse are smallest for children with high levels of ego-resiliency.

    TRUE or FALSE

7.2 PEERS

TO MASTER THE LEARNING OBJECTIVES:

What are the benefits of friendship?

- Describe how friendship changes throughout childhood.

- Describe why intimacy and loyalty are important in friendships among adolescents.

- Explain how the source of social support changes from childhood to adolescence.

- Describe the characteristics that friends usually have in common.

- Explain the positive consequences associated with having friends.

- Describe how friendship can influence aggression and risky behavior.

What are important features of groups of children and adolescents? How do these groups influence individuals?

- Describe how the status of one's crowd is related to self-esteem.

- Explain how parents influence their adolescent children's membership in crowds.

- Describe factors that determine which children and adolescents will become leaders of their groups.

- Explain the circumstances under which peer pressure is likely to be most influential.

Why are some children more popular than others? What are the causes and consequences of being rejected?

- Describe popular, rejected, controversial, average, and neglected children.

- Describe the characteristics that are related to popularity and rejection.

What are some effects of childhood aggression? Why are some children chronic victims of aggression?

- Describe the consequences of being a rejected child.

- Explain how parental behavior and disciplinary practices are related to a child's rejection by peers.

- Define instrumental aggression and hostile aggression.

- Explain why some children are victims of aggression.

7.2 KNOW THE TERMS

Average	Friendship
Clique	Hostile aggression
Controversial	Instrumental aggression
Co-rumination	Neglected
Crowd	Popular
Dominance hierarchy	Rejected

1. _____ is a voluntary relationship between two people involving mutual liking.

2. Discussing each other's personal problems while spending time together with friends is known as _____.

3. A small group of friends who are similar in age, sex, and race is called a _____.

4. Many cliques that have similar attitudes and values may become part of a larger group known as a _____.

5. Groups often have a _____ where group members with lower status defer to the group leader.

6. Children who are _____ are liked by many classmates.

7. Children who are _____ are disliked by many classmates.

8. _____ children are both liked and disliked by many classmates.

9. Children who are _____ are liked and disliked by many classmates, but without the intensity found for popular, rejected, or controversial children.

10. Children who are _____ are ignored by classmates.

11. In _____, a child uses aggression to achieve an explicit goal.

12. _____ is unprovoked and seems to have as its sole goal to intimidate, harass, or humiliate another child.

7.2 KNOW THE DETAILS OF PEERS

1. Children begin to have friendships characterized by trust and assistance in the older elementary school years.
    TRUE or FALSE

2. Older children and adolescents emphasize a friend's role as a playmate.
    TRUE or FALSE

3. Intimacy is more common in girls' friendships than in boys' friendships.
    TRUE or FALSE

4. Adolescents depend less on friends and more on family for social support than they did earlier in childhood.
    TRUE or FALSE

5. Most friends are similar in age, sex, and race.
    TRUE or FALSE

6. Researchers generally find that friends are enjoyable but do not give children any tangible benefits.
    TRUE or FALSE

7. Boys tend to spend more time than girls engaging in co-rumination with their friends.
    TRUE or FALSE

8. Adolescents are more likely to be sexually active when their best friends are sexually active.
    TRUE or FALSE

9. Self-esteem in older children and adolescents is unrelated to the status of their crowd.
    TRUE or FALSE

10. When parents monitor their children's out-of-school behavior, their children are less likely to be in crowds that do not identify with adult standards.
    TRUE or FALSE

11. In groups of young boys, physical power is often the basis for leadership.
    TRUE or FALSE

12. Peer pressure is strongest when the standards for appropriate behavior are not clear-cut.
    TRUE or FALSE

13. Most popular children are not skilled academically.
    TRUE or FALSE

14. Many rejected children are aggressive and hostile.
    TRUE or FALSE

15. Children who are rejected by their peers are more likely to drop out of school and commit juvenile offenses.
    TRUE or FALSE

16. Inconsistent discipline is associated with antisocial, aggressive behavior in children.
    TRUE or FALSE

17. Rejected children can learn social skills that make it more likely that they will be accepted by other children.
    TRUE or FALSE

18. Instrumental aggression is unprovoked and seems to have a goal of intimidation, harassment, or humiliation of another child.
    TRUE or FALSE

19. Children's tendencies to behave aggressively are stable over time.
    TRUE or FALSE

7.3 ELECTRONIC MEDIA

TO MASTER THE LEARNING OBJECTIVES:

What is the impact of watching television on children's attitudes, behavior, and cognitive development?

- Describe how watching TV affects children.

- Describe the impact of educational TV programs on children's cognitive development.

- Describe the criticisms of TV that are supported by research.

How do children use computers at home?

- Describe how children use home computers.

- Describe the effects of playing violent video games.

7.3 KNOW THE DETAILS OF ELECTRONIC MEDIA

1. The typical high school graduate has watched 20,000 hours of TV

   TRUE or FALSE

2. Exposure to TV violence has no effect on aggression in children.

   TRUE or FALSE

3. Children who watch TV shows that emphasize prosocial behavior are more likely to behave prosocially.

   TRUE or FALSE

4. Prosocial behaviors are shown on TV programs far more frequently than aggressive behaviors.

   TRUE or FALSE

5. The time preschool children spend watching *Sesame Street* predicts their grades in high school and the amount of time spent reading as adolescents.

   TRUE or FALSE

6. TV watching reduces children's attention spans.

   TRUE or FALSE

7. Most of the impact of TV on children comes from the amount of TV watched rather than the content of TV programs watched.

   TRUE or FALSE

8.   When children frequently play computer games requiring perceptual-spatial skills, their spatial skills often improve.
     TRUE or FALSE

9.   Playing violent video games can make children more aggressive.
     TRUE or FALSE

10. Extremely high levels of video-game playing are associated with less success in school.
     TRUE or FALSE

7.4 UNDERSTANDING OTHERS

TO MASTER THE LEARNING OBJECTIVES:

As children develop, how do their descriptions of others change?

- Describe how children's descriptions of others begin with the concrete and become more conceptual with age.

How does understanding of others' thinking change as children develop?

- Explain how children's perspective-taking changes with age.
- Define recursive thinking.

When and why do children develop prejudice toward others?

- Describe how the level of prejudice typically changes during childhood.
- Describe how parents and teachers can help reduce prejudice in children.

7.4 KNOW THE DETAILS OF UNDERSTANDING OTHERS

1.   As children get older, their descriptions of other people change from being in terms of concrete features to being in terms of abstract traits.
     TRUE or FALSE

2.   Preschoolers are usually in Selman's self-reflective stage of perspective-taking.
     TRUE or FALSE

3.   Children who are in Selman's undifferentiated stage of perspective-taking know that self and others can have different thoughts and feelings, but often confuse the two.
     TRUE or FALSE

4. Adolescents are typically in Selman's social-informational stage of perspective-taking.
   TRUE or FALSE

5. Individuals who realize that a third person's perspective is influenced by broader personal, social, and cultural contexts would be in Selman's societal stage of perspective-taking.
   TRUE or FALSE

6. The third-person stage is the most advanced level of Selman's perspective-taking theory.
   TRUE or FALSE

7. Children with better perspective-taking skills tend to have more positive social interactions.
   TRUE or FALSE

8. Young children tend to be biased positively toward their own group.
   TRUE or FALSE

9. Prejudice tends to increase during early adolescence.
   TRUE or FALSE

10. Prejudice can be reduced by having children from different groups work together toward common goals.
    TRUE or FALSE

SUMMARY

7.1 FAMILY RELATIONSHIPS

1. **What is a systems approach to parenting?**
   According to the systems approach, the family consists of _____ elements; parents and children influence each other. The family itself is influenced by other social systems such as neighborhoods and religious organizations.

2. **What are the primary dimensions of parenting? How do they affect children's development?**
   One key factor in parent-child relationships is the degree of warmth that parents express. Children clearly benefit from warm, caring parents. A second factor is control, which is complicated because neither too much nor too little control is desirable. Effective parental control involves setting appropriate standards, _____ them, and trying to anticipate conflicts. Taking into account both warmth and control, four prototypic parental styles emerge: (a) authoritarian parents are _____ but uninvolved; (b) authoritative parents are fairly controlling but are also _____ to their children; (c) permissive parents are

loving but exert little control; and (d) uninvolved parents are neither warm nor controlling. _____ parenting seems best for children, in terms of both cognitive and social development. But there are important exceptions associated with culture and socioeconomic status.

Parents influence development by direct instruction and coaching. In addition, parents serve as models for their children, who sometimes imitate parents' behavior directly. Sometimes children's behavior is the opposite of what they've seen (_____). Parents also use feedback to influence children's behavior. Sometimes parents fall into the _____, inadvertently reinforcing behaviors that they want to discourage. Punishment is effective when it is prompt, _____, accompanied by an explanation, and delivered by a person with whom the child has a warm relationship. Punishment has limited value because it suppresses behaviors but does not _____ them, and it often has side effects. _____ is one useful form of punishment.

Chronic conflict is harmful to children, but children can benefit when their parents solve problems constructively. Parenting is a team sport, but not all parents play well together because they may disagree in _____ or parenting methods. Parenting is influenced by characteristics of the children themselves. A child's age and temperament will influence how a parent tries to exert control over the child.

3. **What determines how siblings get along? How do first-born, later-born, and only children differ?**

The birth of a sibling can be stressful for children, particularly when the children are still young and when parents ignore their needs. Siblings get along better when they are of the _____, believe that parents treat them _____, enter adolescence, and have parents who get along well.

As adoption became more common in the U.S., a myth grew that adopted children are more prone to problems. Research shows that adopted children are similar to children living with biological parents in many respects, but they are more prone to some problems such as _____ and conduct disorders. However, these results depend strongly on the child's _____ when adopted and the quality of care prior to adoption, which suggests that adoption *per se* is not a problem for children's development.

Parents have higher _____ for first-born children, which explains why these children are more intelligent and more likely to go to college. Later-born children are more _____ and more innovative. Contradicting the folklore, only children are almost never worse off than children with siblings, and on some dimensions (such as intelligence, achievement, autonomy), they are often better off.

4. **How do divorce and remarriage affect children?**

   Divorce can harm children in a number of areas ranging from school achievement to adjustment. The impact of divorce stems from less _____ of children following divorce, economic hardship, and _____ between parents. Children often benefit when parents have joint custody following divorce, or when they live with the _____ parent. When a mother remarries, _____ sometimes have difficulty adjusting because the new stepfather encroaches on an intimate relationship with the mother. A father's remarriage can cause problems because children fear that the stepmother will disturb intimate father-child relationships and because of tension between the stepmother and the noncustodial mother.

5. **What factors lead children to be maltreated?**

   Cultural factors contributing to child abuse include a culture's views on violence, poverty, and _____. Parents who abuse their children were often neglected or abused themselves and tend to be _____ and socially unskilled individuals. Younger or _____ children are more likely to be targets of abuse. Children who are abused often lag behind in cognitive and _____ development.

7.2 PEERS

1. **What are the benefits of friendships?**

   Friendships among younger children are based on _____ and getting along well. As children grow, loyalty, trust, and _____ become more important features in their friendships. Friends are usually similar in age, gender, _____, and race. Children with friends are _____ and better adjusted.

2. **What are the important features of groups of children and adolescents? How do these groups influence individuals?**

   Older children and adolescents often form _____—groups of like-minded individuals—that become part of a crowd. Some crowds have higher status than others, and members of higher-status crowds often have higher _____ than members of lower-status crowds. Common to most groups is a dominance hierarchy, a well-defined structure with a leader at the top. _____ often determines the dominance hierarchy, particularly among boys. However, with older children and adolescents, dominance hierarchies are more often based on _____ that are important to the group. Peer pressure is neither totally powerful nor totally evil. In fact, groups influence individuals primarily in areas where standards of behavior are unclear, such as tastes in _____ or clothing, or concerning drinking, _____, and sex.

3. **Why are some children more popular than others? What are the causes and consequences of being rejected?**

Most popular children are socially skilled. They often share, cooperate, and _____ others. A far smaller number of popular children use aggression to achieve their social goals. Some children are rejected by their peers because they are _____. Others are rejected because they are too _____ or withdrawn. Repeated peer rejection often leads to school failure and behavioral problems.

4. **What are some effects of childhood aggression? Why are some children chronic victims of aggression?**

Many highly aggressive children end up being violent and poorly adjusted adults. Children who are chronic victims of aggression either overreact or _____ themselves.

7.3 ELECTRONIC MEDIA

1. **What is the impact of watching television on children's attitudes, behavior, and cognitive development?**

TV programs can cause children to become more _____, to adopt gender stereotypes, and to act _____. TV programs designed to foster children's cognitive skills, such as *Sesame Street* are _____. Many criticisms about TV as a medium (e.g., it shortens children's attention spans) are not supported by research.

2. **How do children use computers at home?**

At home, children use computers for schoolwork, to play video games (and are influenced by the contents of the games they play) and to _____ via the Internet.

7.4 UNDERSTANDING OTHERS

1. **As children develop, how do their descriptions of others change?**

Children's descriptions of others change in much the same way that children's descriptions of themselves change. During the early elementary school years, descriptions emphasize _____ characteristics. In the late elementary school years, they emphasize _____. In adolescence, they emphasize providing an integrated picture of others.

2. **How does understanding of others' thinking change as children develop?**

According to Selman's theory, a child's understanding of how others think progresses through five stages. In the first, the undifferentiated stage, children often confuse _____ and another's view. In the last, the societal stage, adolescents can take a _____ perspective and know that this perspective is influenced by context.

197

3. **When and why do children develop prejudice toward others?**

   Prejudice emerges in the preschool years, soon after children recognize different

   _____. Prejudice often _____ in early adolescence, reflecting exposure to

   prejudiced views of others and adolescents' greater affiliation with their own group as they

   seek _____. Prejudice can be reduced with _____ between groups, role-playing,

   and greater knowledge of racism directed at minority groups.

TEST YOURSELF

MULTIPLE-CHOICE QUESTIONS

1. Children benefit most when parents exhibit _____ control over their children.

   a. no

   b. very little

   c. moderate

   d. very strong

2. Chinese parents have been found to _____ than American parents.

   a. be less controlling

   b. be more emotionally restrained

   c. be more affectionate

   d. stress individualism more

3. Jessica's parents usually explain why they set specific rules, and encourage Jessica to talk
   with them about their rules. While they do set expectations for Jessica's behavior, they are
   quite affectionate, loving, and interested in what is going on in Jessica's life. Jessica's
   parents most closely fit the _____ parenting style.

   a. authoritarian

   b. authoritative

   c. permissive

   d. uninvolved

4. Victoria's parents dote on her. They want her to have the best of everything and do what they can to cater to her sometimes frivolous whims. They are usually quite satisfied with Victoria's behavior and have rarely disciplined her. Their parenting style most closely resembles the _____ pattern.

    a. authoritarian

    b. authoritative

    c. permissive

    d. uninvolved

5. Children with _____ parents often have lower self-esteem, are unhappy, and are overaggressive.

    a. authoritarian

    b. authoritative

    c. permissive

    d. uninvolved

6. Children with _____ parents usually do poorly in school and are aggressive.

    a. authoritarian

    b. authoritative

    c. permissive

    d. uninvolved

7. Jasmine's mother told her to wash her hands before she eats, explaining that she needs to wash away the germs before she eats. Jasmine's mother was using

    a. time-out.

    b. positive reinforcement.

    c. punishment.

    d. direct instruction.

8. Josh often saw his father kick and throw things when they didn't work properly and saw his mother get upset. Josh then became less likely to kick and throw things himself. Josh's observation resulted in

    a. counterimitation.

    b. disinhibition.

    c. reinforcement.

    d. a negative reinforcement trap.

9. Punishment is most effective when

    a. it is administered with a delay after the behavior occurs.

    b. it is administered only occasionally when the misbehavior occurs.

    c. there is no explanation of why the child was punished.

    d. the child has a warm, affectionate relationship with the punisher.

10. When parents punish children by making them sit alone in a quiet, unstimulating location for a few minutes, they are using a method of discipline called

    a. time-out.

    b. disinhibition.

    c. direct instruction.

    d. inhibition.

11. Sibling relations are less likely to be harmonious when

    a. the younger sibling approaches adolescence.

    b. siblings are of the same sex.

    c. both siblings are very emotional.

    d. parents have a warm, harmonious relationship.

12. Which of the following statements concerning birth-order effects or family constellation is true?

    a. First-born children typically have higher scores on intelligence tests and are more likely than later-borns to go to college.

    b. First-born children are more innovative and popular with their peers than later-born children.

    c. Later-born children are more willing than first-borns to conform to parents' and adults' requests.

    d. Only children tend to be worse off in many ways than children with siblings.

13. The effect of divorce on children

    a. is about the same for girls and boys.

    b. is greater for preschool children than for school-age children and adolescents.

    c. became less harmful during the 1990s than it had been prior to that time.

    d. is less negative when children live with their opposite-sex parent.

14. _____ is occurring when children do not receive adequate food, clothing, or medical care.

    a. Sexual abuse

    b. Psychological abuse

    c. Physical abuse

    d. Neglect

15. Child abuse occurs more often

    a. in countries like Sweden, where physical punishment is not socially accepted, than in countries like the United States, where physical punishment is accepted.

    b. when children are older rather than younger.

    c. when parents have low expectations for their children.

    d. when families are socially isolated from other relatives or neighbors.

16. When describing her friends, six-year-old Samantha is likely to emphasize

    a. their role as a playmate.

    b. their loyalty.

    c. mutual give and take.

    d. intimacy.

17. A new aspect of friendship during adolescence is

    a. shared activities.

    b. trust.

    c. assistance.

    d. intimacy.

18. Interracial friendships

    a. are more likely to occur when classes are large.

    b. are more likely to occur when a child's school and neighborhood are ethnically diverse.

    c. made in school usually extend to out-of-school settings when neighborhoods are segregated.

    d. are as likely to occur as same-race friendships.

19. Children with friends _____ than children without friends.

    a. show less prosocial behavior

    b. adapt less readily to new schools

    c. have higher self-esteem

    d. are more likely to be victimized by their peers

20. When parents have _____ parenting styles, their children are likely to become involved with crowds that _____.

    a. uninvolved or indulgent; endorse adult standards of behavior

    b. authoritative; reject adult standards of behavior

    c. authoritarian; do not use drugs

    d. authoritative; endorse adult standards of behavior

21. Nate is the leader of a group of boys that call themselves the Arrows. The boys in the group all go along with the decisions that Nate makes about what the Arrows are going to do. The Arrows have a group structure known as

    a. power assertion.

    b. a dominance hierarchy.

    c. a blended family.

    d. authoritative.

22. Bobby, a(n) _____ child, is admired and even idolized by many of his classmates, but at the same time is detested and avoided by many of his other classmates.

    a. popular

    b. rejected

    c. controversial

    d. average

23. Popular children _____ while unpopular children _____.

    a. are more likely to share, cooperate, and help; typically do not

    b. tend to make groups adjust to them; try to fit in with groups

    c. typically have average intelligence; are quite often gifted

    d. are more likely to break rules; are less likely to do so

24. Deirdre is very aggressive with other children, often verbally attacking them for no apparent reason. Whenever someone disagrees with her, she becomes very angry and tries to get back at them in some way. Other children tend to reject her. Compared to more popular children, Deirdre is more likely to

    a. do well in school.

    b. have parents who discipline her consistently.

    c. drop out of school.

    d. have fewer behavioral problems.

25. A child who uses aggression to achieve an explicit goal is demonstrating

    a. a dominance hierarchy.

    b. hostile aggression.

    c. instrumental aggression.

    d. relational aggression.

26. An effective strategy for victimized children to use for dealing with aggression is to

    a. respond to aggression with aggression.

    b. show fear when threatened.

    c. increase their self-esteem so they are less tolerant of personal abuse.

    d. encourage them to avoid friendships with peers.

27. Michael frequently watches TV shows with high levels of violence. If Michael responds typically,

    a. his behavior is not likely to be affected by the exposure to TV violence.

    b. he is likely to become less tolerant of aggression in others.

    c. he is likely to become less aggressive.

    d. he is likely to become more aggressive.

28. Prosocial TV shows

    a. have no influence on children's prosocial behavior.

    b. have less influence on children's prosocial behavior than violent TV shows have on children's aggressive behavior.

    c. are more common than violent TV shows.

    d. can increase prosocial behavior.

29. Children who watch a lot of TV

    a. have reduced attention spans.

    b. show greater impulsivity.

    c. have reduced task persistence.

    d. do not have increased activity level.

30. Which of the following statements about the influence of computers on children is true?

    a. Playing violent video games is not related to levels of aggression in children.

    b. Extremely high levels of video-game playing is associated with greater school success.

    c. The content of video games does not affect the impact on children who play them.

    d. Communication with peers online promotes self-disclosure and can produce high-quality friendships.

31. Compared to older children's descriptions, younger children's descriptions of other people are more likely to focus on _____ traits.

    a. psychological

    b. abstract

    c. personality

    d. concrete

32. Which of Selman's stages of perspective-taking is the LEAST advanced?

    a. Social-informational

    b. Third-person

    c. Undifferentiated

    d. Societal

33. Who has the most advanced form of perspective-taking?

    a. Janda, who can step in another's shoes and view himself as others do

    b. Michael, who knows that he and others can have different thoughts and feelings but often confuses the two

    c. Brian, who can step out of the immediate situation to see how he and another person are viewed by a third person

    d. Maria, who realizes that a third person's perspective is influenced by broader personal, social, and cultural contexts

34. Prejudice

    a. decreases in early adolescence.

    b. decreases as children learn that they are part of a specific group.

    c. increases when children have more contact with children from other groups.

    d. decreases when children use role-playing to imagine what it would be like to be from a different ethnic group and experience discrimination.

ESSAY QUESTIONS

1. Your friend Shabrisha is concerned because her seven-year-old daughter and her five-year-old son seem to fight constantly. Shabrisha's daughter has always been temperamental, and Shabrisha thinks that the fighting may be her fault. Shabrisha remembers being very close to and fighting very little with her sister when they were children, and she thinks that her children must be unusual because they fight so much. What can you tell Shabrisha about the factors that are related to harmonious relationships between siblings?

2. Your friends Mark and Bianca are getting an amicable divorce and they are trying to decide what custody arrangement would be best for their 11-year-old daughter, Kelly. What can you tell them about the effects of various custody arrangements and the effects of remarriage on children, in general, and daughters, in particular?

3. Your friend Lars has noticed that his 15-year-old daughter, Ingrid, seems very concerned with how loyal her friends are to her. Lars doesn't remember being so concerned about his friends' loyalty to him when he was an adolescent. What can you tell Lars about loyalty and intimacy in the friendships of adolescent girls?

4. Your spouse is concerned that your two-year-old son grow up to be popular rather than rejected and is wondering what the two of you can do to help your son achieve this goal. What can you tell your spouse about the relation between parents' behavior and disciplinary practices and their child's popularity or rejection?

5. Your friend Chuck does not have a TV in his house because he feels that TV will only have negative effects on his children—in particular, they will become more violent, they'll ask for junky toys that they see advertised, etc. Chuck feels that nothing good can come of TV viewing. What can you tell Chuck about the research on the effects of television on children?

6. Your friend Chuck also doesn't want to have his children use a computer at home because he feels that his children will become addicted to it, become influenced by violent video games, and will have no friends since they will sit in front of the computer all of the time. What can you tell Chuck about how children use computers at home and the effects of that usage?

7. Your friend is an elementary school teacher at a multicultural school, and he is concerned that the children in his class show a lot of prejudice toward the other students who are members of other racial or ethnic groups in class. He is wondering what he can do to reduce the prejudice in his students. What can you tell him?

ANSWERS WITH PAGE REFERENCES

7.1 KNOW THE TERMS

1. socialization (248)
2. Authoritarian (250)
3. authoritative (250)
4. Permissive (250)
5. uninvolved (250)
6. direct instruction (251)
7. counterimitation (251)
8. Reinforcement (252)
9. Punishment (252)
10. negative reinforcement trap (252)
11. Time-out (253)
12. joint custody (259)
13. Blended (261)
14. ego resilience (264)

7.1 KNOW THE DETAILS OF FAMILY RELATIONSHIPS

1. T, 248
2. T, 249
3. F, 249
4. F, 250
5. T, 250
6. F, 250
7. T, 250
8. T, 251
9. T, 251
10. F, 251
11. T, 252
12. T, 252
13. F, 252
14. T, 253
15. F, 253
16. T, 255
17. T, 256
18. F, 256
19. T, 257
20. T, 257
21. F, 258
22. F, 2582
23. T, 258
24. T, 258
25. T, 259
26. T, 259
27. T, 259
28. T, 259
29. T, 260
30. F, 261
31. T, 262
32. F, 263
33. T, 263
34. T, 264

7.2 KNOW THE TERMS

1. Friendship (266)
2. co-rumination (268)
3. clique (268)
4. crowd (268)
5. dominance hierarchy (269)
6. popular (270)
7. rejected (270)
8. Controversial (270)
9. average (270)
10. neglected (270)
11. instrumental aggression (271)
12. Hostile aggression (271)

7.2 KNOW THE DETAILS OF PEERS

1. T, 266	6. F, 268	11. T, 269	16. T, 271
2. F, 266	7. F, 268	12. T, 269	17. T, 271
3. T, 266	8. T, 268	13. F, 270	18. F, 271
4. F, 267	9. F, 268	14. T, 271	19. T, 272
5. T, 267	10. T, 269	15. T, 271	

7.3 KNOW THE DETAILS OF ELECTRONIC MEDIA

1. T, 273	5. T, 274	9. T 275
2. F, 274	6. F, 274	10. T, 275
3. T, 274	7. F, 274	
4. F, 274	8. T, 275	

7.4 KNOW THE DETAILS OF UNDERSTANDING OTHERS

1. T, 277	4. F, 278	7. T, 279	10. T, 280
2. F, 278	5. T, 278	8. T, 279	
3. T, 278	6. F, 278	9. F, 280	

SUMMARY

7.1 FAMILY RELATIONSHIPS

1. interacting (248)
2. enforcing (249); controlling (250); responsive (250); Authoritative (250); counterimitation (251); negative reinforcement trap (252); consistent (252); eliminate (252); Time-out (253); child-rearing goals (253)
3. same sex (256); similarly (256); adjusting to school (257); age (257); expectations (257); popular (258)
4. supervision (259); conflict (259); same-sex (259); daughters (261)
5. social isolation (262); unhappy (262); unhealthy (263); social (263)

7.2 PEERS

1. common interests (266); intimacy (266); attitudes (267); more skilled socially (268)
2. cliques (268); self-esteem (268); Physical power (269); skills (269); music (269); drug use (269)
3. help (270); too aggressive (271) timid (271)
4. refuse to defend (272)

7.3 ELECTRONIC MEDIA

1. aggressive (274); prosocially (274); effective (274)

2. communicate with friends (275)

7.4 UNDERSTANDING OTHERS

1. concrete (276); personality traits (277)

2. their own (278); third-person's (278)

3. social groups (279); increases (280); identity (280); positive contact (280)

TEST YOURSELF

MULTIPLE-CHOICE QUESTIONS

1. c, 249	10. a, 253	19. c, 268	28. d, 274
2. b, 250	11. c, 256	20. d, 269	29. d, 274
3. b, 250	12. a, 258	21. b, 269	30. d, 275
4. c, 250	13. a, 259	22. c, 270	31. d, 276
5. a, 250	14. d, 262	23. a, 270	32. c, 278
6. d, 250	15. d, 262	24. c, 271	33. d, 278
7. d, 251	16. a, 266	25. c, 271	34. d, 280
8. a, 251	17. d, 266	26. c, 272	
9. d, 252	18. b, 267	27. d, 274	

ESSAY QUESTIONS

1. The first factor that is related to the quality of sibling relationships is gender. Same-sex sibling pairs tend to have more harmonious relationships than mixed-sex pairs. The second factor is temperament. Siblings tend to have better relationships when neither one of them is emotionally temperamental. Third, siblings' perceptions that their parents are treating them equally are more likely to lead to a compatible relationship. Fourth, relationships generally improve as the younger sibling approaches adolescence. Fifth, a better relationship between parents is related to a better relationship between siblings. Based on these factors, Shabrisha's children already have two factors working against a harmonious relationship: they are a mixed-sex pair, and one of them is emotionally temperamental. Shabrisha should also look at her treatment of the children and the quality of her relationship with her husband to see if she can change the relationships. Even if there is nothing that she can do, the sibling relationship should improve as her son approaches adolescence. (255-257)

2. Fortunately, Mark and Bianca get along and are concerned about their daughter. This one factor alone will help ease their daughter's adjustment to their divorce. Because they get along, they might want to consider joint custody where they will both maintain legal custody of Kelly. If they don't want to pursue joint custody, research has shown that children usually fare better when their same-sex parent has custody, so it might be better if Bianca has custody. However, if Bianca remarries, her preadolescent daughter may feel her new stepfather is intruding on her relationship with her mother. By adolescence, though, Kelly should adjust and benefit from the presence of a warm and caring stepfather and the involvement of two caring parents. (258-259)

3. Lars probably wasn't as concerned as his daughter is about the faithfulness of friends. Adolescent girls are more concerned than adolescent boys about loyalty because they tend to have more intimate relationships with their friends. This intimacy means that they tell private information to their friends, and they are concerned that their friends remain loyal so that this information isn't spread to other people. Lars should realize that Ingrid isn't paranoid but is reacting like many other adolescent girls. (266-267)

4. You and your spouse can help your son be popular by modeling effective social skills for him. Children who are pleasant, friendly, share, cooperate, and help are more likely to be popular while children who are rejected are more likely to use aggression and intimidation with peers. These rejected children usually have parents who have modeled aggression and intimidation as solutions to problems. Parents' disciplinary practices also are related to children's behavior with peers. Inconsistent discipline is related to antisocial, aggressive behavior that leads to rejection, and consistent discipline is related to social skills that may lead to popularity. (270-271)

5. Chuck is mostly, but not entirely, correct. A number of negative effects are associated with large amounts of television viewing: children who watch violent TV programs are more likely to behave aggressively. Children also learn gender stereotypes from TV. On the positive side, children engage in prosocial behavior if they see it modeled on TV. Watching TV can help children learn to be more generous, cooperative, and have greater self-control. Children who watch educational programs, like *Sesame Street*, are more proficient in the skills that have been taught on the programs and adjust to school more readily. The amount of time preschoolers spent watching *Sesame Street* predicts their grades in high school. Unfortunately, there are many more violent, stereotyped programs than prosocial, educational programs on television. However, if Chuck monitors what his children watch and limits their viewing, they could learn some good things from television. (273-274)

6.   Children use home computers for many different activities, including using them to look up information for homework assignments. They also use computers to communicate with friends online. This online communication seems to promote the self-disclosure that produces high-quality friendships, which in turn leads to greater well-being. Even when children use computers to play video games they may benefit by showing improved spatial skill. On the negative side, playing violent video games can make children more aggressive. But while addiction to video games is related to poor school performance, only 10% of children seem to be addicted. In general, children's use of home computers has positive effects for school work and social relationships. Even playing games on computers can have benefits that depend on the type of games played. As long as Chuck monitors their computer usage, the benefits of a home computer seem to outweigh the negatives. (275)

7.   You can tell your friend that he can take two different approaches to reducing prejudice. First, he can create group projects in which children from different groups work together toward a common goal. For example, the groups might create a mural to decorate the room or they might do a group science project. Another activity that your friend should try is role-playing. In role-playing, the children would be asked to imagine that they were insulted or not allowed to participate in a particular activity because of their race, ethnic background, or gender. For example, the children would be asked to imagine that they weren't invited to a birthday party because they are Hispanic. After the role-playing, the children are asked to reflect upon their feelings when they were the target of prejudice and discrimination. The children also are asked to think of behavior that would be fair in the situation. A third thing that your friend can do is educate the children about racism that minority groups have experienced. Children who have been taught about racism directed at African Americans had a more positive attitude toward African Americans. (280-281)

RITES OF PASSAGE

8.1 Pubertal Changes

8.2 Health

8.3 Information Processing during Adolescence

8.4 Reasoning about Moral Issues

This chapter focuses on the physical changes associated with puberty, threats to health that occur during adolescence, cognitive changes in adolescence, and changes in moral reasoning during adolescence.

8.1 PUBERTAL CHANGES

TO MASTER THE LEARNING OBJECTIVES:

What physical changes occur in adolescence that mark the transition to a mature young adult?

- Describe when the adolescent growth spurts begin and end for both boys and girls.

- Describe the physical events and their timing that occur during puberty in both boys and girls.

- Describe the development of the brain and how it is related to behavior.

- Know the difference between primary and secondary sex characteristics.

What factors cause the physical changes associated with puberty?

- Explain the causes of puberty.

- Describe how the onset of puberty is influenced by both one's genes and nutrition and health.

- Know the environmental contributions to the onset of puberty, including paternal investment theory.

How do physical changes affect adolescents' psychological development?

- Describe teenagers' body images and their reactions to spermarche and menarche.

- Explain the causes of teenage moodiness.

- Describe the costs and benefits of early maturation for both boys and girls.

8.1 KNOW THE TERMS

Menarche	Secondary sex characteristics
Primary sex characteristics	Spermarche
Puberty	

1. The physical changes that mark the transition from childhood to young adulthood are associated with _____.

2. Organs that are directly involved in reproduction are called _____.

3. Physical signs of maturity that are not linked directly to the reproductive organs are _____.

4. The onset of menstruation in girls is called _____.

5. _____ is the first spontaneous ejaculation of sperm-laden fluid.

8.1 KNOW THE DETAILS OF PUBERTAL CHANGES

1. Girls usually start the growth spurt at about 11, boys at about 13.
   TRUE or FALSE

2. Body fat increases more rapidly in adolescence for boys than for girls.
   TRUE or FALSE

3. Myelination and synaptic pruning are nearly complete in adolescence.
   TRUE or FALSE

4. Systems in the frontal cortex that are associated with deliberate control of behavior are still developing during adolescence.
   TRUE or FALSE

5. The appearance of facial hair and changes in the voice are examples of changes in primary sex characteristics.

   TRUE or FALSE

6. Menarche typically occurs at about age 13.

   TRUE or FALSE

7. Spermarche refers to the first spontaneous ejaculation of sperm-laden fluid.

   TRUE or FALSE

8. The pituitary gland has a key role in regulating pubertal changes.

   TRUE or FALSE

9. The timing of puberty is determined by genetic factors, with the environment having very little influence on it.

   TRUE or FALSE

10. Puberty has been reached at about the same age for many generations.

    TRUE or FALSE

11. Menarche occurs later in girls who experience chronic stress.

    TRUE or FALSE

12. The paternal investment theory proposes that when fathers are invested in child-rearing, their daughters reach maturation earlier.

    TRUE or FALSE

13. Adolescents are more concerned with their appearance than children or adults.

    TRUE or FALSE

14. Adolescent boys and girls are equally likely to be dissatisfied with their appearance.

    TRUE or FALSE

15. The primary reason that adolescents are moodier than adults is fluctuating hormone levels.

    TRUE or FALSE

16. Early maturation has more harmful effects for girls than it does for boys.

    TRUE or FALSE

8.2 HEALTH

TO MASTER THE LEARNING OBJECTIVES:

What are the elements of a healthy diet for adolescents? Why do some adolescents suffer from eating disorders?

- Describe a healthy diet for teenagers and the typical teenager's diet.
- Describe the causes, effects, and treatments of being overweight.
- Describe the causes of anorexia and bulimia.

Do adolescents get enough exercise? What are the pros and cons of participating in sports in high school?

- Describe the amount of exercise that the typical American teen gets.
- Describe the benefits and problems associated with sports participation.

What are common obstacles to healthy growth in adolescence?

- Describe how the causes of death in teens differ by gender and ethnicity.
- Explain why teens engage in risky behavior.

8.2 KNOW THE TERMS

Anorexia nervosa	Basal metabolic rate
Body mass index (BMI)	Bulimia nervosa

1. The _____ is an adjusted ratio of weight to height.

2. The _____ is the speed at which the body consumes calories.

3. The eating disorder that is marked by a persistent refusal to eat and an irrational fear of being overweight is called _____.

4. Individuals with _____ alternate between periods of binge eating and purging through self-induced vomiting or the use of laxatives.

8.2 KNOW THE DETAILS OF HEALTH

1. A typical teenage girl should eat about 2,200 calories a day whereas a typical boy should have about 2,700 calories.
   TRUE or FALSE

2. Children and adolescents who are in the upper 5% of body mass index are defined as being overweight.

   TRUE or FALSE

3. Overweight children and adolescents are frequently less popular and have lower self-esteem than children of normal weight.

   TRUE or FALSE

4. Heredity has a strong influence on juvenile obesity.

   TRUE or FALSE

5. Adolescents with a lower basal metabolic rate burn off calories more quickly.

   TRUE or FALSE

6. Relying on internal rather than external cues to stop eating encourages obesity.

   TRUE or FALSE

7. Anorexic teenagers usually have an accurate body image, understanding that they are extremely underweight.

   TRUE or FALSE

8. Males and females are equally likely to suffer from anorexia or bulimia.

   TRUE or FALSE

9. Eating disorders are more likely when parents give daughters a great deal of freedom.

   TRUE or FALSE

10. Most adolescents do not get enough regular exercise.

    TRUE or FALSE

11. Anabolic steroids increase muscle size and strength but can cause both physical and mental health problems.

    TRUE or FALSE

12. Among male and female adolescents, most deaths are due to natural causes.

    TRUE or FALSE

13. Adolescents tend to take more risks than adults.

    TRUE or FALSE

8.3 INFORMATION PROCESSING DURING ADOLESCENCE

TO MASTER THE LEARNING OBJECTIVES:

How do working memory and processing speed change in adolescence?

- Describe the changes in working memory and processing speed.

How do increases in content knowledge, strategies, and metacognitive skill influence adolescent cognition?

- Explain the changes in content knowledge, strategies, and metacognitive skill and how those changes influence cognition.

What change in problem-solving and reasoning take place in adolescence?

- Explain the difference between heuristic and analytic solutions.
- Describe adolescents' ability to detect flawed arguments.

8.3 KNOW THE DETAILS OF INFORMATION PROCESSING DURING ADOLESCENCE

1. Information-processing theorists believe that major qualitative changes in cognition occur during adolescence.
    TRUE or FALSE

2. Adolescents' working memory has about the same capacity as adults' working memory.
    TRUE or FALSE

3. Adolescents usually process information more slowly than adults.
    TRUE or FALSE

4. Adolescents become better at selecting appropriate strategies and monitoring their progress when trying to complete a task.
    TRUE or FALSE

5. Adolescents are more likely than children to rely on heuristics to solve problems.
    TRUE or FALSE

6. The ability to detect flawed arguments improves significantly during adolescence.
    TRUE or FALSE

7. Adolescents' beliefs can interfere with their reasoning.
    TRUE or FALSE

8.4 REASONING ABOUT MORAL ISSUES

TO MASTER THE LEARNING OBJECTIVES:

How do adolescents reason about moral issues?

- Define moral reasoning.

- Describe how moral reasoning differs at Kohlberg's three levels.

- Describe the research on Kohlberg's theory regarding progression through the stages.

- Describe the research that supports a link between moral reasoning and moral behavior.

- Describe how consistent moral reasoning is.

Is moral reasoning similar in all cultures?

- Describe research on cultural differences in moral reasoning.

How do concern for justice and caring for other people contribute to moral reasoning?

- Explain the difference between Gilligan's view and Kohlberg's view of moral reasoning.

What factors help promote more sophisticated reasoning about moral issues?

- Describe the effects of exposure to more advanced moral reasoning and exposure to just communities on moral reasoning.

8.4 KNOW THE TERMS

Conventional	Preconventional
Interpersonal norms	Social contract
Instrumental	Social system
Obedience	Universal ethical
Postconventional	

1. At Kohlberg's _____ level, moral reasoning is based on external forces.

2. People using Kohlberg's Stage 1 of moral reasoning have an _____ orientation where they believe that authority figures know what is right and what is wrong.

3. People in Kohlberg's Stage 2 of moral reasoning have an _____ orientation where they look out for their own needs.

4. Adolescents and adults in Kohlberg's _____ level of moral reasoning look to society's norms for moral guidance.

217

5. Individuals in Kohlberg's Stage 3 base their moral reasoning on _____ and winning the approval of others.

6. Kohlberg's Stage 4 morality is based on maintenance of order in society, or _____ morality.

7. Moral reasoning at Kohlberg's _____ level is based on a personal moral code.

8. Kohlberg's Stage 5 morality is based on a _____, or the belief that laws and expectations are for the good of all members of society.

9. Kohlberg's Stage 6 moral reasoning is based on _____ principles.

8.4 KNOW THE DETAILS OF REASONING ABOUT MORAL ISSUES

1. In the earliest stages of Kohlberg's theory, moral reasoning is based on external forces such as reward and punishment.
   TRUE or FALSE

2. When people look out for their own needs when reasoning about a moral dilemma, they are at the preconventional level.
   TRUE or FALSE

3. At the conventional level of Kohlberg's theory, moral reasoning is based on a personal moral code.
   TRUE or FALSE

4. The postconventional level focuses on society's norms for moral guidance.
   TRUE or FALSE

5. At the highest stage of Kohlberg's theory, moral reasoning is determined by universal ethical principles.
   TRUE or FALSE

6. Kohlberg stated that individuals often skip stages of moral reasoning and move back and forth between stages.
   TRUE or FALSE

7. Moral reasoning is not related to moral behavior.
   TRUE or FALSE

8. Moral reasoning is influenced by cultural standards.
   TRUE or FALSE

9. Gilligan criticized Kohlberg's theory for emphasizing justice over caring and responsibility.
   TRUE or FALSE

10. Adolescents who are more involved with religion show more concern for others.
    TRUE or FALSE

11. Moral reasoning can be advanced by exposure to others who have more advanced moral reasoning.
    TRUE or FALSE

SUMMARY

8.1 PUBERTAL CHANGES

1. **What physical changes occur in adolescence that mark the transition to a mature young adult?**

   Puberty includes bodily changes in _____ and weight as well as sexual maturation. Girls typically begin the growth spurt earlier than boys, who acquire more muscle, _____, and greater heart and lung capacity. The brain communicates more effectively and the frontal cortex continues to mature. Sexual maturation, which includes primary and secondary sex characteristics, occurs in _____ sequences for boys and girls.

2. **What factors cause the physical changes associated with puberty?**

   Pubertal changes take place when the pituitary gland signals the adrenal gland, ovaries, and _____ to secrete hormones that initiate physical changes. The timing of puberty is influenced strongly by health and _____. In addition, the timing of puberty is influenced by the social environment, coming earlier when girls experience family conflict or _____.

3. **How do physical changes affect adolescents' psychological development?**

   Pubertal changes affect adolescents' psychological functioning. Teens, particularly girls, become concerned about their _____. When forewarned, adolescents respond positively to menarche and spermarche. Adolescents are _____ than children or adults, primarily because their mood shifts in response to frequent changes in activities and social setting. Early maturation tends to be harmful to _____.

8.2 HEALTH

1. **What are the elements of a healthy diet for adolescents? Why do some adolescents suffer from eating disorder?**

   For proper growth, teenagers need to consume adequate calories, calcium, and iron. Unfortunately, many teenagers do not eat properly and do not receive adequate nutrition. Anorexia nervosa and bulimia, eating disorders that typically affect adolescent girls, are characterized by an irrational fear of being _____. Several factors contribute to these disorders, including heredity, a childhood history of _____, and (during adolescence) _____ and a preoccupation with one's body and weight. Treatment and prevention programs emphasize changing adolescents' views toward thinness and their eating-related behaviors.

2. **Do adolescents get enough exercise? What are the pros and cons of participating in sports in high school?**

   Individuals who work out at least three times weekly often have improved physical and _____ health. Unfortunately, many high school students do not get enough exercise. Millions of American boys and girls participate in sports. Football and _____ are the most popular sports for boys and girls, respectively. The benefits of participating in sports include improved physical fitness, enhanced _____, and understanding teamwork. The potential costs include _____ or abuse of performance-enhancing drugs.

3. **What are common obstacles to healthy growth in adolescence?**

   Accidents involving automobiles or _____ are the most common cause of death in American teenagers. Many of these deaths could be prevented if, for example, adolescents did not drive recklessly (e.g., too fast and without wearing seat belts). Adolescents often _____ the harm of risky behavior in general, but they don't believe they're at risk _____ and they often place greater value on the _____ associated with risky behavior.

8.3 INFORMATION PROCESSING DURING ADOLESCENCE

1. **How do working memory and processing speed change in adolescence?**

   Working memory _____ and processing speed becomes _____. Both achieve adult-like levels during adolescence.

2. **How do increases in content knowledge, strategies, and metacognitive skill influence adolescent cognition?**

   Content knowledge increases to _____ levels in some domains; strategies and metacognitive skills become more sophisticated.

3. **What changes in problem-solving and reasoning take place in adolescence?**

   Adolescents often solve problems _____, using mathematics or logic. They also acquire skill in detecting weaknesses in scientific evidence and in _____ arguments.

8.4 REASONING ABOUT MORAL ISSUES

1. **How do adolescents reason about moral issues?**

   Kohlberg proposed that moral reasoning includes preconventional, conventional, and postconventional levels. In the early stages, moral reasoning is based on _____; in the latter stages, on _____ moral codes. As predicted by the theory, people progress through the stages in sequence, _____ regress, and morally advanced reasoning is associated with more frequent moral behavior. However, few people attain the most advanced levels of reasoning, and _____ differ in the bases for moral reasoning.

2. **Is moral reasoning similar in all cultures?**

   Not all cultures emphasize justice in moral reasoning. The Hindu religion emphasizes duty and _____ to others, and consistent with these beliefs, Hindu children and Indians emphasize _____ other people in their moral reasoning.

3. **How do concern for justice and caring for other people contribute to moral reasoning?**

   Gilligan proposed that females' moral reasoning is often based on caring and _____, not justice. Research does not support consistent sex differences in moral reasoning but has found that males and females both consider caring as well as _____ in their moral judgments, depending upon the situation.

4. **What factors help promote more sophisticated reasoning about moral issues?**

   Many factors can promote more sophisticated moral reasoning, including (a) noticing that one's current thinking is _____ (is contradictory or does not lead to clear actions), (b) observing that others reason at more _____ levels, and (c) _____ moral issues with peers, teachers, and parents, and (d) involvement in a religious community that connects adolescents to a network of caring peers and adults.

TEST YOURSELF

MULTIPLE-CHOICE QUESTIONS

1. The collection of physical changes that occur during early adolescence is called

    a. puberty.

    b. menarche.

    c. spermarche.

    d. physical growth.

2. Changes in primary sex characteristics include changes in

    a. breasts.

    b. ovaries.

    c. the voice.

    d. body hair.

3. The beginning of puberty is marked by _____ in girls and by _____ in boys.

    a. the onset of menstruation; the growth of the testes and scrotum

    b. the appearance of pubic hair; the first spontaneous ejaculation

    c. the onset of menstruation; the first spontaneous ejaculation

    d. the growth of the breasts; the growth of the testes and scrotum

4. Puberty occurs

    a. earlier in adolescents who are well-nourished and healthy.

    b. earlier in girls who are lighter and shorter.

    c. later in girls who experience much family conflict.

    d. later in Western European and North American countries than in African countries.

5. What are the psychological consequences of early maturation?

    a. Both boys and girls who mature early are likely to be more self-confident.

    b. Girls who mature early are likely to be more popular with peers.

    c. Girls who mature early are likely to smoke and drink.

    d. Early studies suggested that early maturation is harmful to boys.

6. If Myra's basal metabolic rate is significantly higher than Lilly's, you would expect to find that

   a. Myra gains weight more easily than Lilly.

   b. Lilly gains weight more easily than Myra.

   c. Lilly exercises more than Myra.

   d. Lilly consumes more calories than Myra.

7. According to what we know from research about obesity,

   a. obesity is almost entirely due to environmental factors.

   b. obesity is a result of both genetic and environmental factors.

   c. when obese children lose weight, they are usually able to reach and maintain a healthy weight.

   d. obese youth will not be able to lose weight.

8. You watch an infomercial about a weight loss program for adolescents. Which of these components would you NOT expect the program to have if it is indeed an effective program?

   a. Having adolescents monitor their own eating, exercise, and sedentary behavior

   b. Training parents to help children set realistic goals

   c. Having parents monitor their own lifestyles to be sure they aren't encouraging the child's obesity

   d. Emphasizing external eating signals rather than internal ones

9. Heather sometimes eats uncontrollably and then vomits or takes laxatives. Heather appears to have

   a. bulimia nervosa.

   b. anorexia nervosa.

   c. a basal metabolic rate.

   d. obesity.

10. Anorexia is most likely to occur in

   a. early childhood.

   b. males.

   c. adolescents with a history of eating problems as children.

   d. adolescents with positive self-esteem.

11. Which of the following statements about causes of death during adolescence in the U.S. is true?

    a. Most adolescent deaths are due to disease.

    b. Causes of death do not differ by ethnicity during adolescence.

    c. Among boys, most deaths are due to natural causes or firearms.

    d. Among girls, most deaths are due to natural causes or accidents involving motor vehicles.

12. During adolescence,

    a. working memory capacity is less than it will be during adulthood.

    b. information-processing speed is faster than it was during childhood.

    c. increased knowledge interferes with information-processing ability.

    d. there is unlikely to be any monitoring of the effectiveness of strategies used for a task.

13. When adolescents were asked to rate the quality of scientific studies, some of which were favorable to their religious affiliation and some of which were unfavorable,

    a. they tended to rate the quality of the study objectively, not being influenced by its consistency with their beliefs.

    b. they were more critical of studies that were unfavorable to their beliefs than those that were favorable.

    c. they were more critical of studies that were favorable to their beliefs than those that were unfavorable.

    d. they became more biased in their ratings the older they were.

14. In Kohlberg's theory, moral reasoning is based on external forces at the _____ level.

    a. care-based

    b. preconventional

    c. conventional

    d. postconventional

15. An adolescent who makes a decision about a moral dilemma based on what is best for her own needs is in Kohlberg's _____ stage of moral reasoning.

    a. obedience orientation

    b. interpersonal norms

    c. instrumental orientation

    d. social system morality

16. Someone in Kohlberg's _____ stage of moral reasoning might respond to the Heinz dilemma by saying the man should steal the drug for his wife because that is what a "good" husband would do.

    a. obedience orientation

    b. interpersonal norms

    c. universal ethical principles

    d. social contract

17. A person who is in Kohlberg's conventional level of moral reasoning might decide to help someone because

    a. they would be punished if they didn't.

    b. helping is part of their personal moral code.

    c. the other person might help them in return.

    d. helping is part of society's norms for morality.

18. The highest level of moral reasoning in Kohlberg's theory is the stage of

    a. obedience orientation.

    b. social system morality.

    c. universal ethical principles.

    d. instrumental orientation.

19. The Real People feature concerning the movie *Schindler's List* described how Oskar Schindler's moral reasoning underwent a shift from the _____ level to the _____ level over the course of the movie.

    a. preconventional; postconventional

    b. conventional; postconventional

    c. postconventional; preconventional

    d. preconventional; conventional

20. When asked to respond to a moral dilemma, people living in the U.S. were more likely to choose a _____ solution whereas people living in India more often chose a _____ solution.

    a. reward-based; punishment-based

    b. punishment-based; reward-based

    c. justice-based; care-based

    d. care-based; justice-based

21. Carol Gilligan criticized Kohlberg's theory for

    a. claiming that moral development proceeds through stages.

    b. emphasizing the association between cognitive development and moral reasoning.

    c. ignoring the importance of justice in moral reasoning.

    d. downplaying the importance of care and responsibility in interpersonal relationships to moral reasoning.

22. Research suggests that people develop more advanced forms of moral reasoning

    a. through biological maturation.

    b. as a result of rewards and punishments.

    c. through discussion about moral issues with people who are at a higher level of moral reasoning.

    d. when they are exposed to people with lower levels of moral reasoning than their own.

ESSAY QUESTIONS

1. You have an 11-year-old daughter and your best friend has an 11-year-old son. Your friend thinks that your daughter has entered puberty and is wondering when his son will begin puberty and what physical events will occur during it. What can you tell your friend about puberty in general and the differences in its onset for boys and girls?

2. Your friend Wanda is upset because her adopted 13-year-old daughter is overweight. No one else in the family has a problem with obesity. What can you tell Wanda about the influence of heredity and environment on one's weight? What advice can you give Wanda about weight loss in children?

3. Your friend, Felicia, is the mother of a 13-year-old daughter, Yvonne. Felicia is concerned that Yvonne is anorexic because she "eats like a bird." What can you tell Felicia about the causes and symptoms of anorexia that will help her identify if Yvonne is anorexic?

4. Recently, you and a friend were at a ski resort. You both noticed a group of teenagers who were engaged in very reckless behavior on the slopes. Your friend said to you, "Teenagers are so stupid and they make so many irrational decisions. Obviously, they don't know or seriously underestimate how harmful their risky behavior is." What can you tell your friend about the factors that influence teenagers' risky behavior?

5. You and three of your friends were talking about Kohlberg's Heinz Dilemma. One of your friends said that Heinz should not steal the drug for his wife because it is illegal and laws are in place to protect people and property. Your other friend, who is a Hindu, said that Heinz should steal the drug because it is a husband's responsibility to care for his wife. After these two friends left, your third friend commented on the differences between the two answers. What can you tell your friend about cultural differences in moral reasoning?

ANSWERS WITH PAGE REFERENCES

8.1 KNOW THE TERMS

1. puberty (286)
2. primary sex characteristics (288)
3. secondary sex characteristics (288)
4. menarche (288)
5. Spermarche (289)

8.1 KNOW THE DETAILS OF PUBERTAL CHANGES

1. T, 287	5. F, 288	9. F, 289	13. T, 290
2. F, 287	6. T, 288	10. F, 289	14. F, 290
3. T, 287	7. T, 289	11. F, 289	15. F, 291
4. T, 288	8. T, 289	12. F, 290	16. T, 292

8.2 KNOW THE TERMS

1. body mass index (295)
2. basal metabolic rate (295)
3. anorexia nervosa (296)
4. bulimia nervosa (296)

8.2 KNOW THE DETAILS OF HEALTH

1. T, 295	5. F, 295	9. F, 297	13. T, 300
2. T, 295	6. F, 295	10. T, 297	
3. T, 295	7. F, 296	11. T, 298	
4. T, 295	8. F, 297	12. F, 299	

8.3 KNOW THE DETAILS OF INFORMATION PROCESSING DURING ADOLESCENCE

1. F, 301	3. F, 302	5. F, 302	7. T, 304
2. T, 301	4. T, 302	6. T, 303	

8.4 KNOW THE TERMS

1. preconventional (306)
2. obedience (306)
3. instrumental (306)
4. conventional (307)
5. interpersonal norms (307)

6. social system (307)
7. postconventional (307)
8. social contract (307)
9. universal ethical (307)

8.4 KNOW THE DETAILS OF REASONING ABOUT MORAL ISSUES

1. T, 306	4. F, 307	7. F, 308	10. T, 310
2. T, 306	5. T, 307	8. T, 309	11. T, 310
3. F, 307	6. F, 308	9. T, 310	

SUMMARY

8.1 PUBERTAL CHANGES

1. height (286); less fat (297); predictable (288)
2. testes (289); nutrition (289); depression (289)
3. appearance (290); moodier (291); girls (292).

8.2 HEALTH

1. overweight (295); eating problems (296); negative self-esteem (297)
2. mental (297); track (298); self-esteem (298); injury (298)
3. firearms (299); overestimate (300); personally (300); rewards (300)

8.3 INFORMATION PROCESSING DURING ADOLESCENCE

1. increases in capacity (301); faster (301)
2. adultlike (302)
3. analytically (302); logical (302)

8.4 REASONING ABOUT MORAL ISSUES

1. rewards and punishments (306); personal (307); do not (308); cultures (309)
2. responsibility (309); caring for (309)
3. responsibility for others (310); justice (310)
4. inadequate (310); advanced (311); discussing (311)

TEST YOURSELF

MULTIPLE-CHOICE QUESTIONS

1. a, 286	7. b, 295	13. b, 304	19. a, 308
2. b, 288	8. d, 296	14. b, 306	20. c, 309
3. d, 288	9. a, 296	15. c, 306	21. d, 310
4. a, 289	10. c, 296	16. b, 307	22. c, 311
5. c, 292	11. d, 299	17. d, 307	
6. b, 295	12. b, 301	18. c, 307	

ESSAY QUESTIONS

1. Puberty is characterized by many physical changes, which usually begin at age 11 in girls and at about age 13 in boys. The adolescent growth spurt is a period of very rapid growth when adolescents put on both height and weight. This growth spurt usually lasts about four years. In girls, puberty begins with the growth of the breasts, the start of the adolescent growth spurt, the emergence of pubic hair, and finally the onset of menstruation, or menarche, which usually occurs around age 13. For boys, puberty usually begins with the growth of the testes and scrotum, followed by the appearance of pubic hair, the start of the growth spurt, and growth of the penis. At about age 13, boys experience spermarche, the first spontaneous ejaculation of sperm-laden fluid. Because girls tend to begin puberty at earlier ages than do boys, it is quite likely that your daughter has entered puberty and that your friend's son has not. Tell your friend not to worry because his son has not yet reached the average age at which boys enter puberty. (286-289)

229

2.   Tell Wanda that heredity plays an important role in juvenile obesity. Adopted children's weight is related to the weight of their biological parents and not to the weight of their adoptive parents. Genetic influence may contribute to obesity by determining a person's activity level and one's basal metabolic rate (the speed with which the body consumes calories). A less active person with a slower basal metabolic rate will be more likely to be overweight than someone who is active and has a faster basal metabolic rate. Wanda may also be providing an environment that encourages her daughter to eat even when she is not hungry. For example, many parents encourage their children to clean their plates at the dinner table even though the child may be full. Wanda's daughter can lose weight, but she should remember that weight loss in obese children and adolescents is most successful if the whole family is involved in decreasing the number of calories consumed and increasing the amount of exercise. The most effective weight-loss programs involve monitoring eating, exercise, and sedentary behavior. Parents should help children set realistic goals and use behavioral principles to help children meet these goals. Parents should also evaluate their own lifestyles to be sure they are not inadvertently fostering their child's obesity. (295-296)

3.   Tell Felicia that the typical anorexic is an adolescent female like Yvonne. Anorexics often have a childhood history of eating problems such as being a picky eater or eating non-food objects. During adolescence, anorexics often have negative self-esteem, or a mood or anxiety disorder. The most important risk factor is being overly concerned about body size and weight. Anorexics' homes often have overprotective parents. Even if Yvonne and her family match this description, however, she may not be anorexic. An anorexic will limit food intake to such a great extent that she will become painfully thin but will perceive herself as being overweight. If Yvonne shows any of these signs, she should seek medical treatment right away. If left untreated, anorexia can lead to death. (296-297)

4.   Adolescents' risky behavior may appear stupid and adolescents may seem to be ignorant of the consequences of risky behavior, but, in fact, they do know the consequences of risky behavior. They even overestimate the actual likelihood of harm associated with risky behavior. However, they believe that they personally are not likely to experience those harmful consequences. In other words, they believe that "*other* reckless drivers have car accidents, but I don't." Adolescents also find the rewards associated with risky behavior to be much more appealing than adults do. This may be related to the maturation of the adolescent brain. The limbic system, which is associated with experiencing pleasure and emotion, matures earlier than the frontal cortex which is associated with deliberate control of behavior. Even though adolescents may know the risks associated with risky behavior, the potential rewards and pleasure of the risky behavior may be stronger than the ability to control their behavior. (300)

5. Cross-cultural research has shown that children and adolescents in North America reason at Stages 2 and 3, which is similar to findings in other cultures. However, adults in many non-Western cultures do not emphasize justice in moral reasoning. The emphasis on justice is apparent in cultures where the rights of the individual are emphasized. In cultures where the primary religion emphasizes different values, principles other than justice are used in moral reasoning. For example, the Hindu religion emphasizes duties and responsibilities toward others. In fact, research has shown that those reared with traditional Hindu beliefs do emphasize care and responsibility to others in moral reasoning. So, what you and your friend observed was a cultural difference in moral reasoning. (309)

MOVING INTO THE ADULT SOCIAL WORLD

9.1   Identity and Self-Esteem

9.2   Romantic Relationships and Sexuality

9.3   The World of Work

9.4   The Dark Side

This chapter focuses on the challenging issues that face adolescents: the search for identity, romantic and sexual relationships, work, and problems of adolescence.

9.1 IDENTITY AND SELF-ESTEEM

TO MASTER THE LEARNING OBJECTIVES:

How do adolescents achieve an identity?

- Describe the developmental crisis during adolescence of identity versus role confusion.

- Describe Marcia's four identity statuses—achievement, moratorium, foreclosure, and diffusion—and describe the likelihood of occurrence throughout adolescence.

233

- Define adolescent egocentrism, imaginary audience, the personal fable, and the illusion of invulnerability.
- Describe how adolescents' identity formation is related to their parents' styles of parenting.

What are the stages and results of acquiring an ethnic identity?

- Describe the three phases of achieving ethnic identity.
- Describe the development of ethnic identity in immigrant adolescents.
- Describe the benefits of having a strong ethnic identity.
- Describe ethnic identity in biracial adolescents.

How does self-esteem change in adolescence?

- Describe changes in self-esteem in different domains.
- Describe the things that influence self-esteem in adolescence.
- Explain how most adolescents feel about their parents.

9.1 KNOW THE TERMS

Adolescent egocentrism	Imaginary audience
Ethnic identity	Personal fable
Illusion of invulnerability	

1. The self-absorption that is characteristic of teenagers as they search for identity is called _____.

2. Many adolescents feel that their behavior is constantly being watched by their peers. This phenomenon is called the _____.

3. The _____ is the feeling that many adolescents have that their feelings and experiences are unique and have never been experienced by anyone else before.

4. The belief that misfortune only happens to others is called an _____.

5. Feeling a part of ones ethnic group and learning the special customs and traditions of their group's culture and heritage is known as _____.

9.1 KNOW THE DETAILS OF IDENTITY AND SELF-ESTEEM

1. According to Erik Erikson, persons who are confused about their identity will never experience intimate human relationships.
    TRUE or FALSE

2. While in the moratorium identity status, individuals have an identity that is based on advice from adults rather than from personal exploration of alternatives.
    TRUE or FALSE

3. Achievement and moratorium identity statuses become more common during later adolescence and young adulthood.
    TRUE or FALSE

4. Individuals in the achievement identity status have no identity and are doing nothing to achieve one.
    TRUE or FALSE

5. The feeling adolescents have that their peers are watching their behavior is called adolescent egocentrism.
    TRUE or FALSE

6. The tendency of adolescents to believe that their experiences and feelings are unique and that no one else has ever felt or thought as they do is called the personal fable.
    TRUE or FALSE

7. Parents who encourage discussion and adolescent autonomy have adolescents more likely to reach achievement identity status.
    TRUE or FALSE

8. When parents set rules with little explanation, adolescents are more likely to stay in the foreclosure identity status.
    TRUE or FALSE

9. Adolescents in the first phase of achieving ethnic identity have spent a lot of time exploring their ethnic roots.
    TRUE or FALSE

10. Adolescents in the second phase of achieving ethnic identity have begun to explore the personal impact of their ethnic heritage.
    TRUE or FALSE

11. Adolescents who have attained an ethnic identity tend to have lower levels of self-esteem than those who have not.

    TRUE or FALSE

12. Adolescents with a strong ethnic identity tend to do better in school than adolescents whose ethnic identities are weaker.

    TRUE or FALSE

13. Self-esteem becomes more differentiated as children enter adolescence.

    TRUE or FALSE

14. Self-esteem remains stable with age and across settings.

    TRUE or FALSE

15. Parents who don't set rules tend to have adolescents with higher self-esteem.

    TRUE or FALSE

16. Most teenagers adopt many of their parents' values.

    TRUE or FALSE

17. Over the course of adolescence, parent-teen relationships become more egalitarian.

    TRUE or FALSE

9.2 ROMANTIC RELATIONSHIPS AND SEXUALITY

TO MASTER THE LEARNING OBJECTIVES:

Why do teenagers date?

- Describe the changing functions of dating as adolescents grow older.

- Explain the ethnic differences in dating patterns.

- Describe the effects of dating.

Why are some adolescents sexually active? Why do so few use contraceptives?

- Describe how peers' and parents' attitudes influence sexual activity in teens.

- Describe the different attitudes of boys and girls to sexual activity.

- Explain why adolescents are susceptible to contracting sexually transmitted diseases such as AIDS.

- Describe the frequency with which most teens use contraception and the common reasons for not using contraception.

- Describe the sex education programs that seem to be the most effective in getting teens to either abstain from sex or to use contraception when they are sexually active.

What determines an adolescent's sexual orientation?

- Describe how attraction to the same sex might develop differently for males and females.

- Describe the challenges that gay and lesbian adolescents face.

What circumstances can make dating violence especially likely?

- Explain the factors that are related to sexual violence.

- Describe the characteristics of boys who are more likely to commit sexual violence.

9.2 KNOW THE DETAILS OF ROMANTIC RELATIONSHIPS AND SEXUALITY

1. Hispanic-American and Asian-American adolescents often begin dating at an earlier age than European-American adolescents.
    TRUE or FALSE

2. Adolescents are more likely to have sex when they believe that their friends are also sexually active.
    TRUE or FALSE

3. Girls are more likely to describe their first sexual partner as a "casual date" whereas boys tend to describe their first sexual partner as "someone they love."
    TRUE or FALSE

4. Most sexually transmitted diseases can be cured with antibiotics.
    TRUE or FALSE

5. Adolescents are especially susceptible to AIDS because they are more likely than adults to engage in unprotected sex and to use intravenous drugs.
    TRUE or FALSE

6. Most adolescents in the U.S. use contraceptives when they first have intercourse.
    TRUE or FALSE

7. Common reasons why adolescents do not use birth control include ignorance about facts of conception, an illusion of invulnerability, and a desire to become pregnant.
   TRUE or FALSE

8. Most adolescents who are emotionally or sexually attracted to a person of their own sex eventually identify themselves as gay.
   TRUE or FALSE

9. Boys raised by a domineering mother are likely to become gay.
   TRUE or FALSE

10. Genes and hormones seem to play a role in males becoming gay.
    TRUE or FALSE

11. Gay and lesbian youth often experience mental health problems.
    TRUE or FALSE

12. Drinking alcohol heavily increases the risk of date rape.
    TRUE or FALSE

9.3 THE WORLD OF WORK

TO MASTER THE LEARNING OBJECTIVES:

How do adolescents select an occupation?

- List and describe Super's three phases of vocational choice.
- List and describe Holland's six personality prototypes and how they are related to vocational choice.

What is the impact of part-time employment on adolescents?

- Describe the extent of part-time employment in teens.
- Describe the three problems associated with part-time employment of teens during the school year.
- Describe the factors that can make part-time employment a good experience.

9.3 KNOW THE TERMS

Crystallization	**Personality-type theory**
Implementation	**Specification**

1. A 13-year-old in Super's _____ phase has decided that he likes to play the piano and that he might like to be a concert pianist.

2. When the budding concert pianist is 18 years old, he learns that being a concert pianist requires many hours of practicing each day and that very few jobs in this area exist, so he decides that being a music teacher might be a better job for him. He is in Super's _____ phase.

3. A 23-year-old who has just graduated from college with a degree in music education and has begun a job as a high school music teacher would be in Super's _____ phase.

4. According to Holland's _____, people find their work fulfilling when the important features of a job or profession fit the workers' personalities.

9.3 KNOW THE DETAILS OF THE WORLD OF WORK

1. According to Super, identity is a key factor in determining an adolescent's career choice.
   TRUE or FALSE

2. During Super's crystallization phase, adolescents enter the workforce and learn firsthand about jobs.
   TRUE or FALSE

3. During Super's specification phase, adolescents limit their career possibilities by learning more about specific types of work and starting to obtain the training that is required for a job.
   TRUE or FALSE

4. According to Holland, personality type is related to how fulfilling people find a profession to be.
   TRUE or FALSE

5. A person with an investigative personality type is skilled verbally and interpersonally and enjoys solving problems using these skills.
   TRUE or FALSE

6. An individual with a conventional personality type is well-suited for professions such as poet, musician, and actor.

   TRUE or FALSE

7. Less than half of all high school seniors have a part-time job.

   TRUE or FALSE

8. Part-time work does not affect high school performance.

   TRUE or FALSE

9. Adolescents who work more than 15 or 20 hours a week are more likely to experience anxiety and depression.

   TRUE or FALSE

10. Extensive part-time work is associated with increased substance abuse.

    TRUE or FALSE

11. Working part-time helps adolescents develop more realistic expectations about how income can be allocated.

    TRUE or FALSE

9.4 THE DARK SIDE

TO MASTER THE LEARNING OBJECTIVES:

Why do teenagers drink and use drugs?

- Describe how the attitudes and behavior of family and peers concerning drinking are related to teenage drinking.

- Describe changes in the incidence of teenage smoking and the factors that are related to teenage smoking.

- Describe the programs that are most effective in reducing teenage smoking.

What leads some adolescents to become depressed? How can depression be treated?

- Describe the possible causes and treatments of depression.

- Describe the warning signs of suicide.

What are the causes of juvenile delinquency?

- Explain the differences between life-course persistent antisocial behavior and adolescent-limited antisocial behavior.

- Describe how poverty, family processes, cognitive processes, and biology are related to juvenile delinquency.

- Describe the factors related to successful treatment and prevention of juvenile delinquency.

9.4 KNOW THE TERMS

Adolescent-limited	**Juvenile delinquency**
Depression	**Life-course persistent**

1. _____ is a disorder characterized by pervasive feelings of sadness, irritability, and low self-esteem.

2. Adolescents who commit illegal acts as well as acts that are destructive to themselves and others are engaged in _____.

3. _____ antisocial behavior refers to youth who engage in relatively minor criminal acts yet aren't consistently antisocial.

4. Antisocial behavior that emerges at an early age and continues throughout life is known as _____ antisocial behavior.

9.4 KNOW THE DETAILS OF THE DARK SIDE

1. Many teenagers drink because their peers pressure them to.
   TRUE or FALSE

2. When drinking is an important part of their parents' social lives, adolescents are more likely to drink.
   TRUE or FALSE

3. In the U.S., teenage smoking typically begins between sixth and ninth grades.
   TRUE or FALSE

4. Teens are less likely to smoke when their parents have an authoritative parenting style.
   TRUE or FALSE

5. Adolescent boys are depressed more often than girls.
   TRUE or FALSE

Chapter 9

6. Depressed adolescents are unhappy, angry, and irritable.

   TRUE or FALSE

7. Adolescents who are less able to regulate their emotions are more prone to depression.

   TRUE or FALSE

8. Depression-prone adolescents are more likely to blame others than themselves for failure.

   TRUE or FALSE

9. Heredity appears to play a part in depression.

   TRUE or FALSE

10. Both antidepressant drugs and psychotherapy are often used to treat depression.

   TRUE or FALSE

11. Teen suicide is more common among boys than girls.

   TRUE or FALSE

12. In most cases of teen suicide, there are warning signals before it occurs.

   TRUE or FALSE

13. When a teenager shows common signs of suicide, the threats should be treated lightly or ignored.

   TRUE or FALSE

14. Adolescent-limited antisocial behavior refers to antisocial behavior that emerges at an early age and continues throughout life.

   TRUE or FALSE

15. Some children inherit factors that place them at risk for violent or aggressive behavior.

   TRUE or FALSE

16. Antisocial youth tend to be impulsive and have difficulty delaying gratification.

   TRUE or FALSE

17. Adolescents whose parents use harsh discipline or don't monitor effectively are more likely to engage in delinquent acts.

   TRUE or FALSE

SUMMARY

9.1 IDENTITY AND SELF-ESTEEM

1. **How do adolescents achieve an identity?**

   The task for adolescents is to find an identity. This search for identity typically involves four statuses. Diffusion and _____ are more common in early adolescence; _____ and achievement are more common in late adolescence and young adulthood. As they seek identity, adolescents often believe that others are always watching them and that no one else has felt as they do. Adolescents are more likely to achieve identity when parents encourage _____ and recognize their autonomy; they are least likely to achieve identity when parents set rules and enforce them without explanation.

2. **What is an ethnic identity? What are the stages in acquiring an ethnic identity?**

   Adolescents from ethnic groups often progress through three phases in acquiring an ethnic identity: initial disinterest, _____, and identity _____. Achieving an ethnic identity usually results in higher _____ but is not consistently related to the strength of one's identification with mainstream culture.

3. **How does self-esteem change in adolescence?**

   Social comparisons begin anew when children move from elementary school to junior high school, and, consequently, self-esteem usually _____ somewhat during this transition. However, self-esteem begins to rise in middle and late adolescence as teenagers see themselves acquiring more adult-like skills and _____. Self-esteem is linked to adolescents' actual competence in domains that matter _____ and is also linked to how parents and peers view them.

   The parent-child relationship becomes more egalitarian during the adolescent years, reflecting adolescents' growing independence. Contrary to myth, adolescence is not usually a period of storm and stress. Most adolescents love their parents, rely upon them for _____, and adopt their _____.

9.2 ROMANTIC RELATIONSHIPS AND SEXUALITY

1. **Why do teenagers date?**

   Romantic relationships emerge in mid-adolescence. For younger adolescents, dating is for both companionship and sexual exploration; for older adolescents, it is a source of trust and _____. Adolescents in romantic relationships are more _____ but also report more emotional upheaval.

2. **Why are some adolescents sexually active? Why do so few use contraceptives?**

    By the end of adolescence, most American boys and girls have had sexual intercourse, which boys view as _____ but girls see as romantic. Adolescents are more likely to be sexually active if they believe that their parents and peers approve of sex. Adolescents do not use birth control consistently because they do not understand conception, don't know where to _____ contraceptives, and sometimes find pregnancy appealing. Because they do not use contraception frequently, they are at risk for sexually transmitted diseases and becoming _____.

3. **What determines an adolescent's sexual orientation?**

    A small percentage of adolescents are attracted to members of their own sex. Attraction to same-sex individuals follows a _____ path in boys and girls. For boys, the first step involves feeling _____ and becoming interested in gender-typical activities. In contrast, for girls, the first step often involves strong feelings toward _____ female. Gay and lesbian youth face many special challenges and consequently often suffer from _____ problems.

4. **What circumstances make dating violence likely?**

    Many adolescents experience dating violence, with teenage girls sometimes forced into sex against their will. Girls are more likely to be victims of sexual violence when they've been _____ and they hold traditional views of gender. Boys are more likely to perpetrate violence when they've experienced violence at _____, when they drink, and when their _____ perpetrate sexual violence. Date-rape workshops work to improve communication between males and females.

9.3 THE WORLD OF WORK

1. **How do adolescents select an occupation?**

    In his theory of vocational choice, Super proposes three phases of vocational development during adolescence and young adulthood: _____, in which basic interests are identified; specification, in which jobs associated with interests are identified; and _____, which marks entry into the workforce. Holland proposed six different work-related _____: realistic, investigative, social, conventional, enterprising, and artistic. Each is uniquely suited to certain jobs. People are _____ when their personality fits their job and less happy when it does not.

2. **What is the impact of part-time employment on adolescents?**

    Most adolescents in the United States have part-time jobs. Adolescents who are employed more than _____ hours per week during the school year typically do poorly in school, often have lowered _____ and increased anxiety, and have problems interacting with others. Employed adolescents save relatively _____ of their income and, instead, spend most of it on clothing, food, and entertainment for themselves, which can give misleading expectations about how to allocate income. Part-time employment can be beneficial if adolescents work relatively few hours, if the work allows them to use existing _____ or to acquire new ones, and if teens _____ some of their earnings. Summer employment, because it does not conflict with the demands of school, can also be beneficial.

9.4 THE DARK SIDE

1. **Why do teenagers drunk and use drugs?**

    Today, many adolescents drink alcohol regularly. The primary factors that influence whether adolescents drink is when they get _____ from others (parents and peers) and stress. Similarly, teenage smoking is influenced by parents and peers.

2. **What leads some adolescents to become depressed? How can depression be treated?**

    Depressed adolescents have little enthusiasm for life, believe that others are _____, and wish to be left alone. Depression can be triggered by a negative event: those who are most likely to be affected are those who can't control their _____ and who see themselves in a negative light. Treating depression relies upon medications that correct the levels of _____ and therapy designed to improve social skills and restructure adolescents' _____ of life events.

3. **What are the causes of juvenile delinquency?**

    Many young people engage in antisocial behavior briefly during adolescence. In contrast, the small percentage of adolescents who engage in life-course persistent antisocial behavior are involved in one-fourth to one-half of the serious crimes committed in the United States. Life-course persistent antisocial behavior has been linked to poverty, _____, cognitive processes, and _____. Efforts to reduce adolescent criminal activity must address all of these variables.

TEST YOURSELF

MULTIPLE-CHOICE QUESTIONS

1. According to Erikson, the developmental task of adolescence is to

    a. establish intimacy with another person.

    b. establish a sense of trust.

    c. achieve an identity.

    d. achieve generativity.

2. Teens in the _____ and _____ identity statuses have not explored alternative identities.

    a. achievement; moratorium

    b. diffusion; foreclosure

    c. diffusion; achievement

    d. moratorium; foreclosure

3. Individuals who are examining different alternatives, but have yet to find a satisfactory identity, are in the _____ identity status.

    a. diffusion

    b. foreclosure

    c. moratorium

    d. achievement

4. Which of the following is true of attaining identity?

    a. Once the achievement status is attained, an individual's identity remains constant throughout the life-span.

    b. An individual may not reach achievement status for all aspects of identity at the same time.

    c. Most people attain an identity during early adolescence.

    d. Parents do not influence teens' identity status.

5. Tori is a 15-year-old who feels that everyone at school is watching her and will notice her new haircut. Tori is experiencing

    a. the imaginary audience.

    b. the personal fable.

    c. identity foreclosure.

    d. identity achievement.

6. Natalie thought that there was no way anyone else could understand how upset she was when her boyfriend broke up with her. This kind of thinking is most strongly associated with which feature of adolescent thinking?

   a. Imaginary audience

   b. Personal fable

   c. Illusion of invulnerability

   d. Adolescent egocentrism

7. Achievement status is associated with parents who

   a. encourage discussion and recognize children's autonomy.

   b. set rules with little justification or explanation.

   c. provide children with explicit direction for their identities.

   d. discourage their children from experimenting with different identities.

8. Maria is interested in learning more about her culture. She has not yet achieved a distinct ethnic self-concept, but she has begun reading books, attending festivals, and talking to her grandmother about her Mexican-American heritage. Maria is in the _____ phase of achieving ethnic identity.

   a. first

   b. second

   c. third

   d. fourth

9. Compared to adolescents who do not have a strong ethnic identity, those adolescents with a strong ethnic identity tend to

   a. have higher self-esteem.

   b. find their interactions with family and friends less satisfying.

   c. do worse in school.

   d. have a more negative view of their own ethnic group.

10. Children are more likely to have higher self-esteem when

   a. parents do not set rules.

   b. they do well in something important to them and are valued by those important to them.

   c. they do not participate in extracurricular activities.

   d. teachers do not seem to care about them or listen to them.

11. Most adolescents

    a. have happy and satisfying relationships with their parents.

    b. do not rely on their parents for advice.

    c. do not accept many of their parents' values.

    d. feel unloved by their parents.

12. Teens

    a. spend less time with their parents than they did when they were younger.

    b. are more affectionate with their parents than they were when they were younger.

    c. have a less egalitarian relationship with their parents as they get older.

    d. argue less often with their parents than they did when they were younger.

13. Darrell is less likely to be sexually active as an adolescent if

    a. his parents don't monitor his activities closely.

    b. he believes that his friends are sexually active.

    c. his peers do not approve of having sex.

    d. his parents have permissive attitudes toward sex.

14. Which of the following is most likely to keep Shannon, a teenage girl, from becoming a teenage mother?

    a. Having an illusion of invulnerability

    b. Lack of access to contraceptives

    c. Participating in a comprehensive sex education program

    d. Not knowing the facts of conception

15. Which of the following statements about determinants of sexual orientation is true?

    a. Sons become gay when raised by a domineering mother and a weak father.

    b. Girls are more likely to become lesbians when their father is their primary role model.

    c. For females who later identify as lesbians, attraction to other females usually emerges in early adolescence.

    d. Attraction to same-sex individuals comes about differently in males and females.

16. Date rape is least likely to occur when

    a. the woman has a clear and consistent sexual policy.

    b. the woman involved has a traditional gender-role orientation.

    c. the male has a friend who has perpetrated dating violence.

    d. the woman reasons with the man but does not struggle or scream.

17. In Super's theory of vocational choice, individuals go through the phases of choosing a career in which of the following sequences?

    a. Specification, implementation, crystallization

    b. Specification, crystallization, implementation

    c. Crystallization, specification, implementation

    d. Crystallization, implementation, specification

18. Jane enjoys taking care of her little sister's scraped knees and is fascinated by her high school biology class. She doesn't know much about the kind of training involved, but thinks she might want to go into a healthcare profession. Jane is in Super's _____ phase of vocational choice.

    a. specification

    b. crystallization

    c. establishment

    d. implementation

19. Steve has always enjoyed sports, is going to college on a basketball scholarship, and now thinks he might want to have a career in coaching. He has talked with his high school and college coaches about the opportunities available at different levels. Steve liked working with high school students at summer basketball camps, and he decided to major in education in order to be prepared to teach and coach at the high school level. Steve is in Super's _____ phase of career development.

    a. specification

    b. crystallization

    c. establishment

    d. implementation

20. Individuals enter the workforce and learn first-hand about jobs during Super's _____ phase of career development.

    a. specification

    b. crystallization

    c. establishment

    d. implementation

21. According to Holland, people find work most fulfilling when

    a. they are highly compensated financially.

    b. the job requirements fit the worker's personality.

    c. they are in the specification phase of career development.

    d. they have a realistic personality type.

22. Nick has an enterprising personality type. Which career is he likely to find most fulfilling?

    a. Scientist

    b. Counselor

    c. Real estate agent

    d. Bank teller

23. Sarah is task-oriented and enjoys thinking about abstract relations. She would best be described as having a(n) _____ personality type.

    a. realistic

    b. enterprising

    c. conventional

    d. investigative

24. Compared to adolescents who do not have a part-time job, adolescents who work long hours

    a. are likely to have higher self-esteem.

    b. are less likely to be anxious and depressed.

    c. have a more realistic understanding of how to manage money.

    d. tend to argue with their parents more.

25. Chad, a high school junior, is eager to work. His parents are not so sure he should, though. Which of the following contingencies should Chad's parents set on his employment situation to make it less likely that working would be harmful for Chad?

    a. Have him work at a simple, repetitive job rather than a more demanding, skill-oriented job

    b. Make sure he takes the summer off and works only during the school year

    c. Allow him to work no more than 5 to 10 hours a week

    d. Working is harmful for high school students under all circumstances, so Chad should not work at all

26. Which of the following substances is most likely to be used by adolescents?

    a. Marijuana

    b. Cocaine

    c. Amphetamines

    d. Alcohol

27. Which of the following statements concerning the decisions made by adolescents about whether to drink or not is true?

    a. Peers are influential in the decision to drink, but parents are not.

    b. Parents are influential in the decision to drink, but peers are not.

    c. Both parents and peers play a part in a teenager's decision to drink or not.

    d. Most teenagers make the decision about whether to drink or not solely on the basis of how alcohol makes them feel.

28. Pervasive feelings of sadness, irritability, and low self-esteem characterize an individual

    a. with depression.

    b. who has a drinking problem.

    c. with an addiction to drugs.

    d. who engages in delinquent acts.

29. Depression

    a. is associated with increased levels of neurotransmitters.

    b. is more common in males than in females.

    c. can be triggered by feelings of helplessness.

    d. cannot be treated successfully.

30. Suicide

    a. is more common among boys than girls.

    b. is the most frequent cause of death among U.S. adolescents.

    c. is common before 15 years of age.

    d. rates are higher in Asian-American than in Native-American teenage boys.

31. Recently, Maxie has lost interest in shopping, which used to be one of her favorite activities, has changed from being a very happy-go-lucky girl to being very quiet and serious, and has given her favorite possessions to her best friend. Maxie

    a. appears to be making a typical transition from adolescence to adulthood.

    b. is showing signs that she may be considering suicide.

    c. appears to have fallen in love.

    d. probably has a drug addiction.

32. Which of the teenagers described below is most at risk for engaging in delinquent acts?

    a. Jared, who is not very emotional and doesn't get irritated easily

    b. Lyle, whose mother is always home after school because she doesn't trust Lyle to stay home alone

    c. Wayne, who is very good at interpreting other people's intentions

    d. Jake, who is living in poverty

ESSAY QUESTIONS

1. Your friend thinks that there is something wrong with her 16-year-old son. One week he says that he wants to be a famous rock-and-roll drummer and the next he says that he wants to be a pediatrician. Your friend doesn't believe that a normal adolescent can change identities so rapidly. Based on what you know about achieving an identity in adolescence, what can you tell your friend to make her feel better?

2. Another friend is having trouble with her teenage daughter. She thinks that her daughter must feel unloved and has rejected all of her parents' values because they argue all the time about her daughter's choice of music and clothes. What can you tell your friend about adolescents to make her feel better?

3. At a recent parent council meeting at your son's high school, another parent suggested that condoms should be sold at school at a low price to slow down the increasing number of teenage pregnancies at school. This parent stated that many teens don't use contraceptives because they don't know how to obtain them or can't afford them. This other parent also said that teens will have sex no matter what so they might as well have contraceptives readily available to them. What can you tell the parent council about programs that seem to be effective in delaying sexual intercourse and increasing the use of contraceptives by teens?

4. Your friend Enrique has a coworker that he thinks is gay. Enrique said that he thought that his coworker was gay because the coworker's mother must have been domineering, and his coworker could become heterosexual if he really wanted. What can you tell Enrique about the myths surrounding the causes of homosexuality and the role of biology in determining sexual orientation?

5. Your artistic, unconventional teenage daughter has told you that she would like to be a research scientist and discover the cure for heart disease when she grows up. You are not so sure that this is a good idea. What can you tell her about Holland's personality-type theory of occupational choice that might change her mind?

6. Your 16-year-old son wants to get a part-time job at the local fast food restaurant. This job would involve working about 20 hours per week during the school year. Your spouse thinks that this is a great idea and that a part-time job will make your son more responsible and will teach him the value of money. You, however, have read this textbook and don't think that the part-time job during the school year is a good idea. What can you tell your spouse about part-time employment during the school year for teens and the negative effects associated with it?

7. Your friend Jevan is concerned that his teenage daughter, Antigone, might be drinking. What can you tell Jevan about the factors associated with teenage alcohol abuse that might help him and his daughter?

8. Your brother is worried that his daughter Yolanda might be depressed and suicidal. What can you tell your brother about the signs of suicide and the course of action if these signs are present that could help him and your niece?

ANSWERS WITH PAGE REFERENCES

9.1 KNOW THE TERMS

1. adolescent egocentrism (317)
2. imaginary audience (318)
3. personal fable (318)
4. illusion of invulnerability (318)
5. ethnic identity (318)

9.1 KNOW THE DETAILS OF IDENTITY AND SELF-ESTEEM

1. T, 316	6. T, 318	11. F, 319	16. T, 322
2. F, 316	7. T, 318	12. T, 319	17. T, 322
3. T, 316	8. T, 318	13. T, 320	
4. F, 317	9. F, 318	14. F, 320	
5. F, 318	10. T, 318	15. F, 321	

9.2 KNOW THE DETAILS OF ROMANTIC RELATIONSHIPS AND SEXUALITY

1. F, 324	4. T, 326	7. T, 326	10. T, 327
2. T, 325	5. T, 326	8. F, 326	11. T, 327
3. F, 325	6. F, 326	9. F, 327	12. T, 327

9.3 KNOW THE TERMS

1. crystallization (329)
2. specification (330)
3. implementation (330)
4. personality-type theory (331)

9.3 KNOW THE DETAILS OF THE WORLD OF WORK

1. T, 329	4. T, 331	7. F, 332	10. T, 332
2. F, 329	5. F, 331	8. F, 332	11. F, 332
3. T, 330	6. F, 331	9. T, 332	

9.4 KNOW THE TERMS

1. Depression (335)
2. Juvenile delinquency (337)
3. Adolescent-limited (337)
4. life-course persistent (337)

9.4 KNOW THE DETAILS OF THE DARK SIDE

1. T, 334	6. T, 335	11. T, 336	16. T, 338
2. T, 334	7. T, 336	12. T, 337	17. T, 338
3. T, 335	8. F, 336	13. F, 337	
4. T, 335	9. T, 336	14. F, 337	
5. F, 335	10. T, 336	15. T, 338	

SUMMARY

9.1 IDENTITY AND SELF-ESTEEM

1. foreclosure (317); moratorium (317); encourage discussion (318)

2. exploration (318); achievement (319); self-esteem (319)

3. declines (320); responsibilities (321); to them (321); advice (322); values (322)

9.2 ROMANTIC RELATIONSHIPS AND SEXUALITY

1. support (324); self-confident (324)

2. recreational (325); buy (326): pregnant (326)

3. different (327); different (327); one particular (327); mental-health (327)

4. drinking (328); home (327); friends (328)

9.3 THE WORLD OF WORK

1. crystallization (329); implementation (330); personality (331); happier (331)

2. 15 (332); self-esteem (332); little (332); skills (333); save (333)

9.4 THE DARK SIDE

1. encouragement (334)

2. unfriendly (335); emotions (336); neurotransmitters (336); interpretation (336)

3. family processes (338); biology (337).

TEST YOURSELF

MULTIPLE-CHOICE QUESTIONS

1. c, 316	10. b, 321	19. a, 330	28. a, 335
2. b, 316	11. a, 322	20. d, 330	29. c, 335
3. c, 317	12. a, 322	21. b, 331	30. a, 336
4. b, 317	13. c, 325	22. c, 331	31. b, 337
5. a, 318	14. c, 326	23. d, 331	32. d, 338
6. b, 318	15. d, 327	24. d, 333	
7. a, 318	16. a, 328	25. c, 333	
8. b, 318	17. c, 329	26. d, 334	
9. a, 319	18. b, 329	27. c, 334	

ESSAY QUESTIONS

1. During early adolescence, most teens either have no identity (diffusion status) or have chosen an identity that is based on advice from adults (foreclosure status). As teens progress through adolescence they begin to "try on" different identities to see how each one fits (moratorium status). These different identities may be as diverse as a rock-and-roll drummer or a pediatrician. Eventually, during late adolescence or early adulthood, after trying many different identities, one finds an identity that "fits" and one in which the person feels secure (achievement status). In other words, your friend's son is acting like other teens, and he probably won't settle on an identity for a few years yet. (316-318)

2. Research findings do not support the view that adolescence is a time of storm and stress. In fact, most adolescents love their parents, turn to their parents for advice, accept many of their parents' values, and feel loved by their parents. However, as teens become more independent, they may seem as if they do not love their parents as much, because they spend less time with them, are less affectionate with them, and argue about topics such as music, clothes, and freedom. While your friend's daughter may be typical of other teens, your friend probably finds these arguments more distressing than her daughter does, but only 25% of conflicts between adolescents and their parents are associated with behavior problems. (322-323)

3. You can tell the parent council that while it is true that some teens do not use contraceptives because they are not readily available and are too expensive, there are many other factors that are related to teenage sexual activity and contraceptive use. Teens don't use contraceptives consistently because they are often ignorant of the true facts about conception and the transmission of sexually transmitted diseases. Also, because of the illusion of invulnerability, teens think pregnancy only happens to others. For some teens, becoming pregnant is appealing. Programs that seem to be most effective in preventing teenage pregnancy and sexually transmitted diseases are ones that teach the biological facts and also focus on responsible sexual behavior or abstaining from premarital sex altogether. These also include discussing the pressure to become sexually active and role-playing strategies for responding to these pressures. Students who participate in these programs are less likely to have intercourse; when they do have intercourse, they are more likely to use contraceptives. (326)

4. Enrique should know that research has shown that a number of the myths that people have about sexual orientation are wrong. The myths include the belief that sons become gay when they are reared by a domineering mother and that girls become lesbians because their fathers are their primary role models. In fact, many scientists now believe that genes and hormones influence sexual orientation, particularly in males. These genes and hormones may lead some boys to feel "different" during early adolescence, and these feelings lead to an interest in gender-atypical activities and a later attraction to other males. In other words, Enrique's coworker probably won't be able to change his sexual orientation by simply "wanting to" any more than he could change the color of his eyes. (326-327)

5. According to Holland's personality-type theory of vocational choice, one's personality should be a major factor in choosing a vocation. Holland suggested that people will feel more satisfied with their jobs and be more productive if they choose jobs that fit their personality characteristics. Holland suggested six personality types. The first type is the realistic person who likes physical labor and likes to solve concrete problems. The second type is the investigative person who is task-oriented and enjoys thinking abstractly. The artistic person likes to express himself through unstructured tasks. The enterprising person likes to use verbal skill in positions of power or leadership. The conventional person likes to apply verbal and quantitative skill to well-defined tasks that are assigned by others. Finally, the social person is skilled verbally and socially and likes to use those skills to solve problems. Your daughter fits the artistic personality, but the job of scientist fits the investigative personality. According to Holland, if your daughter would become a scientist, she may not enjoy the job. (331-332)

6. Tell your spouse that part-time employment of over 15 hours during the school year for teens is associated with a number of negative outcomes. First, school performance drops because teens who are employed part-time don't seem to use their free time efficiently to do their homework. Second, teens who work over 15 hours per week during the school year are more likely to be depressed and suffer from anxiety. Even though many part-time jobs are boring and repetitive, they may still be very stressful during busy times, which may lead to anxiety. This anxiety may also be related to increased substance abuse and problem behavior that is seen in teens who work many hours per week. Third, these part-time jobs rarely teach teens the value of money. Teens rarely save their money for college or help their parents pay for necessary items. Instead teens tend to spend most of their money on entertainment and personal items such as cosmetics or music. Because such a large percentage of their paychecks go toward "fun" items, teens develop very unrealistic expectations about finances and budgeting. However, there is one long-term benefit. People who have stressful part-time jobs as adolescents are better able to cope with stressful jobs as adults. (332-333)

7. You can tell Jevan that adolescents often drink because their peers do and they pressure them to join them. However, the family atmosphere and the example that parents set for drinking behavior are also important. If drinking is an important part of their parents' social lives, teens are more likely to drink. Teens are also more likely to drink if their parents set arbitrary or unreasonable standards for them or are uninvolved parents. Many teens drink to reduce stress such as problems with parents, friends, or school. In particular, teens are more likely to drink to reduce stress if family problems are frequent. Jevan can help his daughter by helping her reduce stress in her life and by setting a good example of responsible drinking behavior. (334)

8. If Yolanda has been depressed or if she has engaged in substance abuse, your brother should be worried because these are two common precursors of suicide. Some other warning signs include the person threatening to commit suicide, being preoccupied with death, changing her eating or sleeping habits, losing interest in activities that used to be important, exhibiting marked changes in personality, expressing persistent feelings of gloom and helplessness, and giving away valued possessions. If Yolanda shows any of these signs, your brother should NOT ignore them but should ask Yolanda if she is planning to hurt herself. Your brother should remain calm and supportive. If Yolanda appears to have made preparations to commit suicide, she shouldn't be left alone. Your brother should also insist that Yolanda seek professional help to treat her feelings of depression and hopelessness that may be leading to the suicidal thoughts. (336-337)

BECOMING AN ADULT

10.1 Emerging Adulthood

10.2 Physical Development and Health

10.3 Cognitive Development

10.4 Who Do You Want to Be? Personality in Young Adulthood

This chapter focuses on the transition to adulthood and the physical, cognitive, and personality changes that occur during young adulthood.

10.1 EMERGING ADULTHOOD

TO MASTER THE LEARNING OBJECTIVES:

What role transitions mark entry into adulthood?

- Define emerging adulthood.

- Define role transitions and how they are related to age.

- Describe rites of passage and indicators of adulthood that can be found in non-Western and Western cultures.

How does going to college reflect the transition to adulthood?

- Compare returning adult students to traditional-aged college students.

What behavioral criteria mark the transition to adulthood?

- Explain how adolescents and adults differ in terms of engaging in reckless behavior.

- Describe Erikson's psychosocial conflict of intimacy versus isolation, and explain how this conflict relates to achieving identity.

- Describe the pattern of behavior for forming an identity and establishing intimacy in both men and women.

How does achieving financial independence reflect the transition to adulthood?

- **Describe the trend in the age of financial independence.**

When do people become adults?

- Describe the characteristics of the *quarterlife crisis*.

10.1 KNOW THE TERMS

Edgework	Returning adult
Emerging adulthood	Rites of passage
Intimacy versus isolation	Role transitions

1. _____ is a period between late teens and mid- to late-20s when individuals are not adolescents but are not yet fully adults.

2. _____ involve assuming new responsibilities and duties and are often used to determine whether a person has attained adulthood.

3. Rituals that mark the initiation into adulthood are called _____.

4. College students over the age of 25 years are often referred to as _____ students.

5. The desire to live life on the edge through physically and emotionally threatening situations is called _____.

6. According to Erikson, the psychosocial conflict of young adulthood is one of _____.

10.1 KNOW THE DETAILS OF EMERGING ADULTHOOD

1. The markers for entrance into adulthood tend to be clearer in the culture of developing countries than in the culture of Western societies.

   TRUE or FALSE

2. Rites of passage are rituals that mark initiation into adulthood.
    TRUE or FALSE

3. In Western cultures, role transitions are the most widely used criteria for deciding whether a person has reached adulthood.
    TRUE or FALSE

4. The average age for completing education has increased since the early 1900s.
    TRUE or FALSE

5. Returning adult students tend to be less pragmatic and self-directed than traditional-aged college students.
    TRUE or FALSE

6. The frequency of reckless behavior decreases significantly between adolescence and middle age.
    TRUE or FALSE

7. According to Erikson, the major task for young adults is dealing with the psychosocial conflict of trust versus mistrust.
    TRUE or FALSE

8. Most men resolve intimacy issues before identity issues.
    TRUE or FALSE

9. Living with one's parents slows the process of becoming an independent adult.
    TRUE or FALSE

10.2 PHYSICAL DEVELOPMENT AND HEALTH

TO MASTER THE LEARNING OBJECTIVES:

In what respects are young adults at their physical peak?

-   Describe physical functioning in young adults.

-   Describe sensory acuity during young adulthood.

How healthy are young adults in general?

-   Explain the general, overall health found in young adults in the United States.

-   Describe the frequency of death from disease and death from accidents during young adulthood.

-   Explain the gender and ethnic differences in causes of death in young adults.

261

How do smoking, drinking alcohol, and nutrition affect young adults' health?

- Describe the negative health effects of smoking and second-hand smoke and the health benefits of quitting smoking.

- Describe the factors related to, negative effects of, and prevention of binge drinking.

- Describe the consequences associated with alcohol addiction.

- Describe the nutritional requirements and eating habits of young adults.

- Explain how dietary fat intake and cholesterol levels are related to cardiovascular disease.

- Define BMI, and describe how it is related to health.

How does the health of young adults differ as a function of socioeconomic status, gender, and ethnicity?

- Describe how income and level of education are linked to health in the United States.

- Describe how men and women differ in health.

10.2 KNOW THE TERMS

Addiction	**High-density**
Binge drinking	**Low-density**
Body mass index (BMI)	**Metabolism**

1. Consuming four or more drinks in a row within a two-week period is _____.

2. People who have an _____ are physically dependent on a particular substance, such as alcohol, and suffer from withdrawal symptoms when they do not use the substance.

3. How much energy one's body needs is known as _____.

4. _____ lipoproteins cause fatty acids to accumulate in arteries, which impedes the flow of blood.

5. _____ lipoproteins help clear arteries and break down LDLs.

6. The ratio of body weight and height, which is related to total body fat, is known as _____.

10.2 KNOW THE DETAILS OF PHYSICAL DEVELOPMENT AND HEALTH

1. Physical functioning peaks during middle adulthood.

    TRUE or FALSE

2. Sensory acuity is at its peak in the early 20s.

    TRUE or FALSE

3. Accidents are the leading cause of death between the ages of 25 and 44.

    TRUE or FALSE

4. Young adult men are nearly 2.5 times as likely to die as women of the same age.

    TRUE or FALSE

5. Alcohol is the single biggest contributor to health problems.

    TRUE or FALSE

6. Exposure to second-hand smoke increases the risk of smoking-related diseases.

    TRUE or FALSE

7. Total consumption of alcohol in industrialized countries has increased for the past few decades.

    TRUE or FALSE

8. Binge drinking increases the likelihood of engaging in unwanted sexual behavior.

    TRUE or FALSE

9. More men than women are alcohol dependent.

    TRUE or FALSE

10. Nutrition directly affects one's mental, emotional, and physical functioning.

    TRUE or FALSE

11. Body metabolism speeds up with age.

    TRUE or FALSE

12. Body mass index is related to the risk of serious medical conditions and mortality.

    TRUE or FALSE

13. Socioeconomic status and education are the two most important social influences on health.

    TRUE or FALSE

14. On average, women live longer than men.

    TRUE or FALSE

10.3 COGNITIVE DEVELOPMENT

TO MASTER THE LEARNING OBJECTIVES:

What is intelligence in adulthood?

- Explain what is meant by multidimensional and multidirectional intelligence.

- Explain what is meant by interindividual variability and plasticity in intelligence.

What are primary and secondary mental abilities? How do they change?

- Define primary and secondary mental abilities.

- Describe age differences and cohort differences in primary mental abilities.

- List and describe the variables that are related to reduced cognitive decline in old age.

What are fluid and crystallized intelligence? How do they change?

- Explain the difference between fluid intelligence and crystallized intelligence, and explain how each changes with age.

How has neuroscience research furthered our understanding of intelligence in adulthood?

- Describe the P-FIT theory.

What is postformal thought? How does it differ from formal operations?

- Explain how adults' thinking differs from the formal-operational thought that is seen in adolescence.

- Describe how thought changes during the college years.

- Define postformal thought and reflective judgment.

- Describe the progression from prereflective reasoning to reflective reasoning.

- Describe the importance of emotion and logic throughout adolescence and adulthood.

How do emotion and logic become integrated in adulthood?

- Describe how problem analysis and decision-making shift from young adulthood to middle age.

- Describe how social beliefs change with age.

10.3 KNOW THE TERMS

Crystallized	Plasticity
Fluid	Postformal
Interindividual variability	Primary mental
Multidimensional	Reflective judgment
Multidirectionality	Secondary mental
Parieto-Frontal Integration Theory (P-FIT)	

1. Most theories of intelligence are _____ because they identify many different areas of intellectual abilities.

2. Intellectual abilities show _____ because some aspects of intelligence improve and other aspects decline across adulthood.

3. _____ means that the patterns of change in intelligence are different for different people.

4. _____ in intellectual ability also occurs when certain conditions modify one's ability at any point during adulthood.

5. Groups of related intellectual skills (e.g., spatial skill, mathematical skill, etc.) are called _____ abilities.

6. Broader categories of intellectual skills that subsume and organize the primary abilities are called _____ abilities.

7. _____ intelligence includes abilities such as thinking in a flexible, adaptive manner, drawing inferences, and understanding relations between concepts.

8. _____ intelligence reflects knowledge that has been acquired through experience and education in a particular culture.

9. _____ proposes that intelligence comes from a distributed and integrated network of neurons in the parietal and frontal lobes of the brain.

10. Thought that is characterized by the realization that the correct answer may vary from situation to situation, that problem solutions must be realistic, that most situations are ambiguous, and that emotion and other subjective factors are an important part of thought is called _____ thought.

11. _____ is a way in which adults reason about dilemmas involving current affairs, religion, science, and personal relationships.

10.3 KNOW THE DETAILS OF COGNITIVE DEVELOPMENT

1. Interindividual variability refers to some aspects of intelligence improving and others declining during adulthood.
    TRUE or FALSE

2. Plasticity refers to the modifiability of people's abilities.
    TRUE or FALSE

3. Schaie's Seattle Longitudinal Study found that older cohorts outperformed younger cohorts on all primary mental abilities.
    TRUE or FALSE

4. Adults who remain cognitively active through reading and lifelong learning have a lower risk of cognitive decline in old age.
    TRUE or FALSE

5. Patterns of intellectual change over the course of adulthood vary a great deal from person to person.
    TRUE or FALSE

6. Fluid and crystallized intelligence are called primary mental abilities.
    TRUE or FALSE

7. Factual knowledge is a form of fluid intelligence.
    TRUE or FALSE

8. Fluid intelligence increases throughout adulthood.
    TRUE or FALSE

9. Crystallized intelligence increases throughout adulthood.
    TRUE or FALSE

10. Research suggests that certain areas in the brain are associated with intellectual abilities, and that developmental changes in these areas should be related to changes in performance.
    TRUE or FALSE

11. Adults are more likely than adolescents to consider situational constraints and circumstances when solving problems.
    TRUE or FALSE

266

12. As they go through the college years, students increasingly rely on the expertise of authority figures to determine which ways of thinking are right and which are wrong.
TRUE or FALSE

13. Postformal thought is characterized by logical, deductive reasoning that is not influenced by emotion or subjective factors.
TRUE or FALSE

14. Individuals in the stages of prereflective thought do not acknowledge that knowledge is uncertain.
TRUE or FALSE

15. Mature adult thinking is marked by the tendency to separate emotion and logic.
TRUE or FALSE

16. Strongly held social beliefs vary across cohorts as a result of how particular generations were socialized.
TRUE or FALSE

10.4 WHO DO YOU WANT TO BE? PERSONALITY IN YOUNG ADULTHOOD

TO MASTER THE LEARNING OBJECTIVES:

What is the life-span construct? How do adults create scenarios and life stories?

- Define life-span construct, and list the factors that lead to the development of one.
- Define scenario, and explain how it is related to a social clock.
- Define life story, and explain why distortions may occur in one's memory for autobiographical events.

What are possible selves? Do they show differences during adulthood?

- Describe possible selves, and explain how they motivate behavior.
- Explain how concerns about and the number of possible selves change with age.

Chapter 10

What are personal control beliefs?

- Define personal control beliefs, and explain how they may vary across different domains of one's life.

- Know the difference between primary and secondary control and how they change with age.

10.4 KNOW THE TERMS

Life-span construct   Possible selves

Life story   Scenario

Personal control   Secondary control

Primary control   Social clock

1. A _____ is a unified sense of the past, present, and future that is based on one's own experiences and input from others.

2. The first manifestation of the life-span construct that consists of expectations about the future is called a _____.

3. Associating future events with a time or age by which one expects to complete them creates a _____.

4. The second manifestation of the life-span construct, the _____, is a personal narrative that organizes past events into a coherent sequence.

5. _____ represents what one could become, what one would like to become, and what one is afraid of becoming.

6. _____ beliefs are beliefs about the degree to which one's performance in a situation is within one's control.

7. _____ is behavior that is aimed at affecting the individual's external world such as working a second job to increase one's income.

8. _____ is behavior or cognition aimed at affecting an individual's internal world such as believing that one can succeed in spite of challenges.

10.4 KNOW THE DETAILS OF PERSONALITY IN YOUNG ADULTHOOD

1. A life-span construct is created from personal experience and input from other people and represents a unified sense of the past, present, and future.

   TRUE or FALSE

2. Tagging future events with a particular time or age by which they are to be completed creates a life story.

   TRUE or FALSE

3. Possible selves represent what we could become, what we would like to become, and what we are afraid of becoming.

   TRUE or FALSE

4. Health tends to become a less important aspect of feared self as people get older.

   TRUE or FALSE

5. Personal control beliefs are generally similar across different domains.

   TRUE or FALSE

SUMMARY

10.1 WHEN DOES ADULTHOOD BEGIN?

1. **What role transitions mark entry into adulthood?**

   The most widely used criteria for deciding whether a person has reached adulthood are role transitions, which involve assuming new _____ and duties. Some societies use rituals, called _____, to mark this transition clearly. However, such rituals are largely absent in Western culture.

2. **How does going to college reflect the transition to adulthood?**

   Over half of all college students are _____. These returning adult students tend to be more _____ and have many other positive characteristics. College also serves as a catalyst for cognitive development.

3. **What behavioral criteria mark the transition to adulthood?**

   A major difference between adolescents and adults is a drop in the rate of participation in _____. Young adults grapple with issues relating to _____, although whether this occurs only after the issue of _____ is resolved differs across gender.

4. **How does achieving financial independence reflect the transition to adulthood?**

   Launching oneself as financially _____ is a major marker of achieving adulthood in Western society. This can be achieved in many ways, such as a series of part-time jobs, joining the _____, or going to college and then entering the workforce.

5. **So when do people become adults?**

   There are many challenges faced by adults in their 20s termed the _____. Adjustment to adulthood is more difficult when the process of transition is _____ clear.

10.2 PHYSICAL DEVELOPMENT AND HEALTH

1. **In what respects are young adults at their physical peak?**

   Young adulthood is the time when height and several physical abilities peak: strength, _____, coordination, dexterity, and _____. Most of these abilities begin to decline in middle age.

2. **How healthy are young adults in general?**

   Young adults are also at the peak of health. Death from disease is relatively _____, especially during the 20s. Accidents are the leading cause of death. However, homicide and _____ are major factors in some groups. Poor ethnic minorities have less access to good healthcare, and _____ is also a major barrier to good health.

3. **How do smoking, drinking alcohol, and nutrition affect young adults' health?**

   Smoking is the single biggest contributor to health problems. It is related to half of all cancers and is a primary cause of respiratory and _____ disease. Although it is difficult, quitting smoking has many health benefits. For most people, drinking alcohol poses few health risks. Several treatment approaches have been used for alcoholics. Nutritional needs change somewhat across adulthood, mostly due to changes in _____. Some nutrient needs, such as carbohydrates, change. The ratio of LDLs to HDLs in serum cholesterol, which can be controlled through diet or _____ in most people, is an important risk factor in _____ disease

4. **How does young adults' health differ as a function of socioeconomic status, gender, and ethnicity?**

   The two most important social factors in health are socioeconomic status and _____. The poorest health conditions exist for _____ living in poor, inner-city neighborhoods. Other ethnic groups who have limited access to healthcare also suffer. Whether women or men are healthier is a difficult question to answer because women have been _____ from much health research. Higher education is associated with better health due to better access to healthcare and more _____ about proper diet and life style.

10.3 COGNITIVE DEVELOPMENT

1. **What is intelligence in adulthood?**

   Most modern theories of intelligence are _____. For instance, Baltes' research shows that development varies among individuals and across different categories of abilities.

2. **What are primary and secondary mental abilities? How do they change?**

Intellectual abilities can be studied as groups of related skills called primary mental abilities. Clusters of related primary abilities are called _____ mental abilities, and they are not measured directly. These abilities develop differently and change in succeeding _____. More recent cohorts perform better on some skills, such as _____ reasoning, but older cohorts perform better on number skills.

3. **What are fluid and crystallized intelligence? How do they change?**

Fluid intelligence consists of abilities that make people flexible and adaptive thinkers. Fluid abilities generally _____ during adulthood. Crystallized intelligence reflects knowledge that people acquire through life _____ and education in a particular culture. Crystallized abilities _____ until late life.

4. **How has neuroscience research furthered our understanding of intelligence in adulthood?**

Neuroscience research has begun mapping specific areas in the brain associated with _____. One prominent theory based on this work is the Parieto-Frontal Integration Theory (P-FIT). Neuroscience research may provide insight into controversies surrounding when cognitive abilities begin to show decline, which some researchers claim begins in the _____.

5. **What is postformal thought? How does it differ from formal operations?**

Postformal thought is characterized by a recognition that _____ may vary from one situation to another, that solutions must be realistic, that ambiguity and _____ are the rule, and that _____ and subjectivity play a role in thinking. One example of postformal thought is reflective judgment.

6. **How do emotion and logic become integrated in adulthood?**

Cognition and emotion become integrated during _____ and middle age. This means that the way people approach and solve _____ problems in life differs from adolescence through middle age.

10.4 WHO DO YOU WANT TO BE? PERSONALITY IN YOUNG ADULTHOOD

1. **What is the life-span construct? How do adults create scenarios and life stories?**

Young adults create a _____ that represents a unified sense of the past, present, and future. This is manifested in two ways: through a scenario that maps out the _____ based on a social clock and in the life story, which creates an autobiography.

2. **What are possible selves? Do they show differences during adulthood?**

People create possible selves by projecting themselves into the future and thinking about what they would like to become, what they could become, and what they are _____ of becoming. Age differences in these projections depend on the dimension examined. In hoped-for selves, 18- to 24-year-olds and 40- to 59-year-olds report _____ issues as most important, whereas 25- to 39-year-olds and older adults report personal issues to be most important. All groups include _____ aspects as their most feared selves.

3. **What are personal control beliefs?**

Personal control is an important concept with broad applicability. However, the developmental trends are complex, because personal control beliefs _____ considerably from one domain to another.

TEST YOURSELF

MULTIPLE-CHOICE QUESTIONS

1. _____ involve assuming new responsibilities, which indicate that an individual has moved into the next stage of development.
   a. **Role transitions**
   b. **Possible selves**
   c. **Rites of passage**
   d. **Personal control beliefs**

2. _____ is the most important rite of passage to adulthood in most cultures.
   a. **Beginning a full-time job**
   b. **Completing one's education**
   c. **Getting married**
   d. **Becoming a parent**

3. Ron is a returning adult student. He is likely to
   a. **be less pragmatic than younger students.**
   b. **have life experiences that relate to course work.**
   c. **need a high level of direction from others.**
   d. **have difficulty with problem-solving.**

4. The desire to live life through physically and emotionally threatening situations on the boundary between life and death is known ass
   a. rites of passage.
   b. role transitions.
   c. edgework.
   d. personal control beliefs.

5. According to Erikson, the major issue during young adulthood involves
   a. trust versus mistrust.
   b. identity versus role confusion.
   c. intimacy versus isolation.
   d. integrity versus despair.

6. Research on Erikson's theory suggests that
   a. most men and career-oriented women resolve identity issues before intimacy issues.
   b. most men resolve intimacy issues before identity issues.
   c. most women, including those who are and who are not career-oriented, tend to resolve intimacy issues before identity issues.
   d. only career-oriented women tend to resolve intimacy issues before identity issues.

7. Who is most likely to be at the peak of physical strength for his lifetime?
   a. 18-year-old Cassius
   b. 28-year-old Joe
   c. 38-year-old Rocky
   d. 48-year-old George

8. _____ often starts to decline in the late 20s.
   a. Vision
   b. Taste
   c. Smell
   d. Hearing

9. The leading cause of death for young adults is
   a. AIDS.
   b. accidents.
   c. cancer.
   d. cardiovascular disease.

273

10. Which of the following lifestyle factors is the greatest contributor to health problems in our society today?

    a. Lack of exercise

    b. Drinking

    c. Smoking

    d. Poor nutrition

11. Binge drinking is more common

    a. among 17- to 23-year-olds than among older students.

    b. in students who are not in a fraternity.

    c. in females than in males.

    d. in non-European Americans than in European Americans.

12. Body metabolism _____ with age.

    a. decreases

    b. increases

    c. decreases in females and increases in males

    d. does not change

13. High levels of _____ is a protective health factor.

    a. high density lipoproteins

    b. low density lipoproteins

    c. sodium

    d. fat

14. Which of the following statements about factors related to health is true?

    a. The best health conditions are found in poor, inner-city urban settings.

    b. Women are more likely than men to die from homicide.

    c. Higher socioeconomic status is positively related to health.

    d. Education level is negatively related to health.

15. Theories of intelligence that identify different domains of intellectual abilities are

    a. addressing interindividual variability.

    b. multidirectional.

    c. multidimensional.

    d. addressing plasticity.

16. Number, word fluency, verbal meaning, inductive reasoning, and spatial orientation are
    a. primary mental abilities.
    b. secondary mental abilities.
    c. forms of fluid intelligence.
    d. forms of crystallized intelligence.

17. Schaie's longitudinal study of adult intelligence found that older cohorts outperformed younger cohorts on tasks that involved
    a. inductive reasoning.
    b. number skills.
    c. verbal meaning.
    d. word fluency.

18. Adults' scores on tests of primary mental abilities tend to improve until the
    a. late 20s or early 30s.
    b. late 30s or early 40s.
    c. late 50s or early 60s.
    d. late 60s or early 70s.

19. Who of the following 60-year-olds has the lowest risk of cognitive decline in old age?
    a. Ruth, who is not yet satisfied with her life achievements
    b. Mary, who recently went back to school
    c. Louise, who has a rigid personality style
    d. Betty, who suffers from cardiovascular disease

20. Which of the following tasks requires the use of fluid intelligence?
    a. Defining the word "intelligence"
    b. Naming the first president of the United States
    c. Describing the main features of the three periods of prenatal development
    d. Finding the shortest way from Point A to Point B in a maze

21. Fluid intelligence _____ throughout adulthood while crystallized intelligence _____.
    a. declines; improves
    b. improves; declines
    c. declines; also declines
    d. improves; also improves

22. _____ is associated with the idea that intelligence comes from a distributed and integrated network of neurons in the parietal and frontal lobes of the brain.

    a. Parieto-Frontal Integration Theory

    b. Postformal thought

    c. Primary mental abilities

    d. Plasticity

23. _____ thought is marked by an understanding that truth may vary from situation to situation, that solutions must be realistic, and that emotion and subjective factors usually play a role in thinking.

    a. Formal-operational

    b. Absolutist

    c. Postformal

    d. Concrete-operational

24. A _____ represents a unified sense of the past, present, and future.

    a. life-span construct

    b. social clock

    c. scenario

    d. life story

25. Jasmine plans to get her engineering degree when she is 22, get married by the time she is 25, have two children by the time she is 30, and retire at age 55. Jennifer's personal timetable for important events in her future is called a

    a. life-span construct.

    b. social clock.

    c. scenario.

    d. life story.

26. At age 22, Jerry envisions himself as an entrepreneur who will use his talents to start and successfully run his own business in the future. Jerry's future view of himself is called a

    a. social clock.

    b. life story.

    c. scenario.

    d. life-span construct.

27. **At age 42, Jerry is successfully running his own business and has two failed marriages behind him. Although he was very upset about his marital breakups at the time they occurred, he now looks at them as inevitable due to the hours he was spending at work and has decided they were good learning experiences. Jerry's organization of his past life events is called a**

    a. life-span construct.

    b. scenario.

    c. possible self.

    d. life story.

28. **Young adults, 18- to 24-year-olds, most commonly mention _____ issues when asked about their hoped-for selves.**

    a. family

    b. career

    c. personal

    d. physical

29. **Enrique believes that the degree of success he has in college will be highly related to how much he goes to class and how hard he studies. Enrique has a strong sense of**

    a. self-concept.

    b. perceived competence.

    c. possible self.

    d. personal control.

ESSAY QUESTIONS

1. Your two younger sisters seem to be very different. Ashlee is 25 and has started a career in an area that she loves; she is engaged to be married. The other sister, Jessica, is 27, has changed jobs frequently since college, and doesn't seem to really have an established identity. Everyone in the family is worried that until Jessica establishes an identity, she will never get married. What can you tell your family about the research on identity and intimacy in women that might relieve some of their anxieties?

2. Your friend Frank, a smoker, is upset about the decreasing number of places where he is allowed to smoke. He thinks smokers are singled out and picked on unfairly. Frank feels that if someone wants to smoke, they should be able to when and where they want. What can you tell Frank about the effects of second-hand smoke?

3.   Your friend, Julian, is thin and never watches what he eats. He thinks that all of the recommendations about dietary fat are to help people lose weight and because he doesn't need to lose weight, he doesn't need to worry about dietary fat. What can you tell Julian about problems other than obesity that are related to dietary fat intake?

4.   The other day a friend of yours said, "We had better enjoy being smart now because when we get older, intelligence really goes downhill." After reading this section of the text on intelligence, what can you tell your friend that contradicts this statement?

5.   You and your two brothers are talking about your sister and her husband who are having marital problems. Your 17-year-old brother says, "She should leave him because he is a jerk." Your 35-year-old brother says, "Well, he may be a jerk, but how will she support herself and the two kids? And she does love him even if he is a jerk." Your 17-year-old brother then told your 35-year-old brother to stop being so wishy-washy. What can you tell your 17-year-old brother about postformal thought?

6.   You and two friends are talking one day about your lives. Your friend Erik said that he was glad that he had spent a lot of time with his kids when he was in graduate school, even if it meant that it took him 10 years to get his degree. When Erik left, your friend Sandy said that she remembers that when Erik started graduate school he was very enthusiastic and planned to get his degree in four years and make a name for himself in his field within 10 years. What can you tell Sandy about distortions in autobiographical events as one constructs a life story?

ANSWERS WITH PAGE REFERENCES

10.1 KNOW THE TERMS

1. Emerging adulthood (346)
2. Role transitions (347)
3. rites of passage (347)
4. returning adult (348)
5. edgework (350)
6. intimacy versus isolation (351)

10.1 KNOW THE DETAILS OF BECOMING AN ADULT

1. T, 347	4. T, 348	7. T, 351
2. T, 347	5. F, 348	8. F, 351
3. T, 347	6. T, 350	9. T, 352

10.2 KNOW THE TERMS

1. binge drinking (356)
2. addiction (358)
3. metabolism (359)
4. Low-density (360)
5. High-density (360)
6. body mass index (360)

10.2 KNOW THE DETAILS OF PHYSICAL DEVELOPMENT AND HEALTH

1. F, 354	5. F, 355	9. T, 358	13. T, 361
2. T, 354	6. T, 355	10. T, 359	14. T, 361
3. T, 355	7. F, 356	11. F, 359	
4. T, 355	8. T, 357	12. T, 360	

10.3 KNOW THE TERMS

1. multidimensional (363)
2. multidirectionality (363)
3. Interindividual variability (363)
4. Plasticity (363)
5. primary mental (363)
6. secondary mental (363)
7. Fluid (366)
8. Crystallized (366)
9. Parieto-Frontal Integration Theory (368)
10. postformal (369)
11. Reflective judgment (369)

10.3 KNOW THE DETAILS OF COGNITIVE DEVELOPMENT

1. F, 363	5. T, 365	9. T, 366	13. F, 369
2. T, 363	6. F, 366	10. T, 368	14. T, 369
3. F, 364	7. F, 366	11. T, 369	15. F, 371
4. T, 365	8. F, 366	12. F, 369	16. T, 372

279

10.4 KNOW THE TERMS

1. life-span construct (374)
2. scenario (374)
3. social clock (374)
4. life story (375)

5. Possible selves (376)
6. Personal control (377)
7. Primary control (378)
8. Secondary control (378)

10.4 KNOW THE DETAILS OF PERSONALITY IN YOUNG ADULTHOOD

1. T, 374
2. F, 374

3. T, 376
4. F, 376

5. F, 378

SUMMARY

10.1 WHEN DOES ADULTHOOD BEGIN?

1. responsibilities (347); rites of passage (347)
2. over age 25 (348); motivated (348)
3. reckless behavior (350); intimacy (351); identity (351)
4. independent (351); military (352)
5. quarterlife crisis (352); less (352)

10.2 PHYSICAL DEVELOPMENT AND HEALTH

1. muscle development (354); sensory acuity (354).
2. rare (354); violence (355); poverty (355)
3. cardiovascular (355); metabolism (359); medication (360); cardiovascular (360)
4. education (361).; African Americans (361); excluded (361); knowledge (361)

10.3 COGNITIVE DEVELOPMENT

1. multidimensional (363)
2. secondary (363); cohorts (364); inductive reasoning (364)
3. decline (366); experiences (366); improve (366)
4. intelligence (367); 20s (368)
5. truth (369); contradiction (369); emotion (369)
6. young adulthood (371); practical (372)

10.4 WHO DO YOU WANT TO BE? PERSONALITY IN YOUNG ADULTHOOD

1. life-span construct (374); future (374)
2. afraid (376); family (377); personal (377)
3. vary (378)

TEST YOURSELF

MULTIPLE-CHOICE QUESTIONS

1. a, 347	9. b, 355	17. b, 364	25. b, 374
2. c, 347	10. c, 355	18. b, 364	26. c, 374
3. b, 347	11. a, 357	19. b, 365	27. d, 375
4. c, 350	12. a, 359	20. d, 366	28. a, 376
5. c, 351	13. a, 360	21. a, 366	29. d, 377
6. a, 351	14. c, 361	22. a, 368	
7. b, 354	15. c, 363	23. c, 369	
8. d, 354	16. a, 363	24. a, 374	

ESSAY QUESTIONS

1. Erik Erikson said that young adults must establish an identity before they can create a shared identity with another person, which is an essential ingredient for true intimacy. Some research has supported Erikson's theory. Young adults who have achieved an identity status are more likely to be in committed relationships. However, this seems to be true for men and career-oriented women but not for all women. Some women attain intimacy before attaining identity while other women resolve intimacy and identity issues simultaneously, and they do not conform to the pattern suggested by Erikson. As far as your sisters, Ashlee seems to conform to the pattern suggested by Erikson, but Jessica does not. This does not mean, though, that Jessica will not develop an intimate relationship until she establishes an identity. Jessica may be one of the women who will establish intimacy before, or simultaneously with, establishing her identity. (351)

2. Research points to the fact that the negative health effects associated with smoking are NOT limited to smokers, but people who breathe second-hand smoke are at risk, too. Nonsmokers who are exposed to second-hand smoke have a greater risk for developing lung cancer and cardiovascular disease. Children who are exposed to second-hand smoke may develop lung problems. Treating the effects of second-hand smoke costs about $10 billion in healthcare. So, smoking in public places such as a workplace does have negative effects on the health of those who breathe smokers' second-hand smoke, and the increasing number of bans on smoking is not just an unfair attack on smokers. (355-356)

3. Dietary fat, particularly saturated fat, is related not only to being overweight but also to incidence of cardiovascular disease. By replacing foods high in saturated fat with low-fat foods, one can reduce the level of cholesterol in the blood. There are two types of cholesterol: low-density lipoproteins (LDLs) and high-density lipoproteins (HDLs). LDLs cause fatty deposits to accumulate in arteries and impede blood flow, but HDLs keep arteries clear and break down LDLs. High levels of HDLs are considered a protective factor in cardiovascular disease. HDL levels can be raised through exercise and high-fiber diet. So, while Julian may not be concerned about his weight, he could be increasing his risk for cardiovascular disease by eating large amounts of fat in his diet. (360)

4. The first fact to tell your friend is that intelligence is multidimensional. In other words, there are many different aspects of intelligence. Second, intellectual development is also multidirectional, which means that these different aspects of intelligence are not affected in the same way by aging. In fact, fluid intelligence seems to decline with age, but crystallized intelligence, which includes knowledge acquired from education and experience, seems to increase until late old age. Third, intellectual aging also shows interindividual variability. In other words, some people show the general age-related trends in intellectual functioning and others don't. Fourth, people's abilities show plasticity, which means that their abilities are not fixed and can be modified at any point. Therefore, your friend's statement isn't accurate on many dimensions. (363-367)

5. You can tell your 17-year-old brother that your other brother is not being wishy-washy but is displaying postformal thought, which is typical of middle-aged adults. Your 17-year-old brother is using formal operational thought, and he thinks that he is right because he used logical thinking to formulate his solution: if one is married to a jerk, then one should dump him. Your 35-year-old brother is using postformal thought. He is considering the pragmatic and emotional aspects of the situation. He realizes that all of these things are important and do not lead to an easy, logical answer, and he is not being wishy-washy. (368-370)

6. People use life-span constructs to link their identities with a view of themselves. Initially, a person may develop a scenario of what they would like to become. The completion of the goal in this scenario is usually linked to an age or time that creates a social clock. When Erik began graduate school, he created a scenario about graduate school and a career including a social clock for completion of graduate school and "making it" in his field. However, it took Erik much longer than he had planned to finish graduate school and now his memories of life events have been distorted so he can see himself in a more favorable light, or so he can soothe his ego for not attaining his goals. In any case, he has taken the past events of his life and has constructed a life story that fits the events. (374-375)

CHAPTER 11

BEING WITH OTHERS

This chapter focuses on adults' relationships, lifestyle choices, the family life cycle, and divorce and remarriage.

11.1 RELATIONSHIPS

TO MASTER THE LEARNING OBJECTIVES:

What types of friendships do adults have? How do adult friendships develop?

- Describe the ABCDE stages of adult friendships.

- Describe how friendships change from adolescence to young adulthood.

- Describe the three themes that underlie adult friendships.

- Know the characteristics and development of online friendships.

- Describe the differences in men's and women's friendships.

- Describe the benefits and problems associated with cross-sex friendships.

What is love? How does it begin? How does it develop through adulthood?

- Describe Sternberg's three components of love: passion, intimacy, and commitment.

- Describe how different forms of love become dominant at different points during the course of a relationship.

- Describe the aspects of love relationships that remain constant across different ages.

- Describe the factors that are important in choosing a mate.

- Describe speed dating and online dating.

- Explain the cross-cultural research on the effects of culture and gender on mate selection.

- Describe how developmental forces influence relationships.

What is the nature of abuse in some relationships?

- Describe the continuum of aggressive behaviors that occur in abusive relationships.

- Explain how the causes of aggressive behavior change as the level of aggression changes.

- Explain how gender and culture influence aggressive behavior.

11.1 KNOW THE TERMS

Abusive	**Battered woman syndrome**
Assortative mating	

1. The theory stating that people find partners based on their similarity to each other is

   _____.

2. An _____ relationship is one in which one partner becomes aggressive toward the other partner.

3. The _____ occurs when a woman believes that she cannot leave an abusive situation.

11.1 KNOW THE DETAILS OF RELATIONSHIPS

1. Acquaintanceship, buildup, continuation, deterioration, and ending are the stages of adult friendship.
   TRUE or FALSE

2. People tend to have more friends during the period of late adulthood than at any other time in life.
   TRUE or FALSE

3. Life satisfaction is strongly related to the quantity and quality of contacts with friends.

   TRUE or FALSE

4. Online environments are less conducive to developing friendships for people who are lonely.

   TRUE or FALSE

5. Intimacy and emotional sharing are a bigger part of men's friendships than women's friendships.

   TRUE or FALSE

6. Shared activities are often a part of men's friendships.

   TRUE or FALSE

7. Men tend to overperceive and women tend to underperceive their cross-sex friends' sexual interest in them.

   TRUE or FALSE

8. Passion, intimacy, and commitment are the three basic components of love.

   TRUE or FALSE

9. Early in a relationship, intimacy tends to be high, but passion and commitment tend to be low.

   TRUE or FALSE

10. The theory of assortative mating states that people find partners based on their similarity to each other.

    TRUE or FALSE

11. Nearly 1 in 5 couples in the United States meet online.

    TRUE or FALSE

12. Around the world, men value chastity in women, and women look for physically attractive men.

    TRUE or FALSE

13. Characteristics that are valued in a mate in one culture may not be valued in another culture.

    TRUE or FALSE

14. Battered woman syndrome occurs when a woman believes that she cannot leave the abusive situation; she may even go so far as to kill her abuser.

    TRUE or FALSE

15. The most pertinent causes of verbal aggression are the need to control, misuse of power, and jealousy.

TRUE or FALSE

16. The incidence of abuse is higher in cultures that emphasize honor and where female passivity, nurturing support of men's activities, and sacrifice for families are valued.

TRUE or FALSE

11.2 LIFESTYLES

TO MASTER THE LEARNING OBJECTIVES:

Why do some people decide not to marry, and what are these people like?

- Describe the gender differences in singlehood.

- Describe ethnic differences in singlehood.

- Describe the transition to permanent singlehood.

What are the characteristics of cohabiting people?

- Describe differences in cohabitation as a function of education and ethnicity.

- List the three main reasons for cohabiting.

- Describe cultural differences in cohabiting.

- Describe the effects that cohabiting may have on a later marriage.

What are gay and lesbian relationships like?

- Compare heterosexual couples and gay and lesbian couples.

- Describe gender differences in homosexual relationships.

- Describe some of the problems with family and society that gay and lesbian couples must face.

What is marriage like through the course of adulthood?

- Describe how age at the time of first marriage is related to marital success.

- Define marital success, marital quality, marital adjustment, and marital satisfaction.

- Define homogamy and exchange theory, and explain how they are related to marital success.

- Describe the course of marital satisfaction.

- Describe the *vulnerability-stress-adaptation model* of marriage.

- Explain how children affect marital satisfaction.
- Explain how military deployment is related to marital satisfaction.
- Describe the characteristics of happy marriages.

11.2 KNOW THE TERMS

Cohabitation	Marital quality
Exchange	Marital satisfaction
Homogamy	Marital success
Marital adjustment	Vulnerability-stress-adaption

1. Living with someone with whom one has a committed, intimate, sexual relationship is called _____.

2. The umbrella term for any marital outcome such as staying married or getting divorced is _____.

3. The subjective evaluation of a couple's relationship on a number of different dimensions is called _____.

4. The degree to which a husband and wife accommodate each other is _____.

5. The global assessment of one's marriage is _____.

6. Similarity of values and interests is called _____.

7. According to _____ theory, marriage is based on each partner contributing something to the relationship that the other would be hard-pressed to provide.

8. The _____ model views marital quality as a dynamic process that is the result of the couple's handling stressful situations.

11.2 KNOW THE DETAILS OF LIFESTYLES

1. In early adulthood, increasing numbers of adults are choosing to stay single.
   TRUE or FALSE

2. Fewer women than men remain unmarried throughout adulthood.
   TRUE or FALSE

3. Single people receive less compensation at work than married people.
   TRUE or FALSE

4. More African Americans than European Americans are single during young adulthood.
   TRUE or FALSE

289

5. Most never-married women over 40 are content with their lives.

TRUE or FALSE

6. In the U.S., cohabitation has become less common in recent years.

TRUE or FALSE

7. In the U.S., cohabitation before marriage results in happier marriages.

TRUE or FALSE

8. Lesbians are likely to have fewer, longer-lasting relationships than gay men.

TRUE or FALSE

9. Gay and lesbian couples tend to get less support from family members than do married couples.

TRUE or FALSE

10. The median age at first marriage in the U.S. has been rising for several decades.

TRUE or FALSE

11. The similarity of partners' values and interests is an important predictor of a successful marriage.

TRUE or FALSE

12. Marriages are more successful when one partner contributes more to the relationship than the other.

TRUE or FALSE

13. Marital satisfaction tends to be lowest early in a marriage.

TRUE or FALSE

14. Marital satisfaction usually increases in later life.

TRUE or FALSE

15. For most couples, marital satisfaction increases after the birth of the first child.

TRUE or FALSE

16. Divorce rates are higher for male service members who are deployed than they are for women service members who are deployed.

TRUE or FALSE

17. Successful couples find a way to keep romance alive in the relationship.

TRUE or FALSE

11.3 THE FAMILY LIFE CYCLE

TO MASTER THE LEARNING OBJECTIVES:

What are the common forms of families?

- **Define nuclear family and extended family.**

Why do people have children?

- Describe the factors that are related to the decision to have children.

- **Describe the costs of having children.**

- **Describe the trends in child-free couples.**

What is it like to be a parent? What differences are there in different types of parenting?

- Describe the advantages of being an older parent.

- Describe how ethnic background influences parenting.

- Explain the feelings that are typical of most divorced single parents and describe the problems that single parents face.

- Describe the obstacles that may interfere with foster, adoptive, or stepchildren forming bonds with his or her new parents.

- Describe the problems associated with forming attachments in foster parent-child relationships.

- Describe the effects associated with being raised by gay or lesbian parents.

11.3 KNOW THE TERMS

Extended	Nuclear
Familism	

1. The most common family form in Western societies is the _____ family, which consists of parents and children.

2. The most common family form around the world is the _____ family, which consists of parents, children, grandparents, and other relatives living together.

3. The idea that the well-being of the family takes precedence over the concerns of individual family members is called _____.

11.3 KNOWTHE DETAILS OF THE FAMILY LIFE CYCLE

1. Although the most common form of family in Western societies is the extended family, the most common form around the world is the nuclear family.

    TRUE or FALSE

2. In an extended family, grandparents and other relatives live with parents and children.

    TRUE or FALSE

3. Child-free couples tend to have happier marriages than couples with children.

    TRUE or FALSE

4. Compared to older mothers, younger mothers are more at ease with being parents, spend more time with their babies, and are more affectionate and sensitive to them.

    TRUE or FALSE

5. Men who become fathers in their 30s are more invested in their paternal role than men who become fathers in their 20s.

    TRUE or FALSE

6. Fathers are usually as involved in child-rearing tasks as mothers.

    TRUE or FALSE

7. African-American husbands are more likely than European-American men to help with household chores and help with childcare.

    TRUE or FALSE

8. Two key values among Latino-American families are familism and the extended family.

    TRUE or FALSE

9. The proportion of births to unwed mothers is at an all-time high in the U.S.

    TRUE or FALSE

10. Single parents are usually as well off financially as married parents.

    TRUE or FALSE

11. Many stepparents and stepchildren develop good relationships with each other.

    TRUE or FALSE

12. Children raised by gay or lesbian parents are more likely to develop sexual identity problems.

    TRUE or FALSE

11.4 DIVORCE AND REMARRIAGE

TO MASTER THE LEARNING OBJECTIVES:

Who gets divorced? How does divorce affect parental relationships with children?

- Compare the divorce rate in the United States to those found in other industrialized countries.

- Explain how the divorce rate differs for various ethnic groups in the United States.

- List the common reasons that men and women give for getting a divorce.

- Know the predictors of early and later divorce.

- Describe the psychological effects of divorce on the divorced couple.

- Describe the different effects of divorce for men and women.

- Describe the effects of divorce for middle-aged and elderly adults.

- Describe the effects of divorce when the couple has children.

What are remarriages like? How are they similar to and different from first marriages?

- Describe how the likelihood of remarriage varies by gender, ethnicity, education, and cohort.

11.4 KNOW THE DETAILS OF DIVORCE AND REMARRIAGE

1. Today, about 50% of marriages in the U.S. end in divorce.
   TRUE or FALSE

2. Ethnically mixed marriages are at greater risk of divorce than ethnically homogenous ones.
   TRUE or FALSE

3. Infidelity is the most commonly reported cause of divorce.
   TRUE or FALSE

4. Negative emotions displayed during conflict between a couple predicts early divorce but not later divorce.
   TRUE or FALSE

5. The absence of positive emotions during discussion of daily events has been found to be related to later divorce more than early divorce.
   TRUE or FALSE

6. Under a covenant marriage, divorces are easier to obtain.
   TRUE or FALSE

7. Divorced people are generally unhappy, at least for a while.
   TRUE or FALSE

8. Low preoccupation with thoughts of a former partner is a key to healthy post-divorce relationships.
   TRUE or FALSE

9. Women who initiated divorce in middle age report self-focused growth and optimism.
   TRUE or FALSE

10. Fathers are given custody of their children about 50% of the time.
    TRUE or FALSE

11. After a divorce, most fathers remain active and involved in their children's lives.
    TRUE or FALSE

12. Adults whose parents divorce are unlikely to be emotionally affected by the divorce.
    TRUE or FALSE

13. The divorce rate for remarriages is higher than the divorce rate for first marriages.
    TRUE or FALSE

SUMMARY

11.1 RELATIONSHIPS

1. **What type of friendships do adults have? How do adult friendships develop?**

   People tend to have more friendships during _____ than during any other period.

   Friendships are especially important for maintaining life satisfaction throughout adulthood.

   Men tend to have fewer close friends and base them on _____, such as sports.

   Women tend to have more close friendships and base them on _____ and emotional

   sharing. Gender differences in same-gender friendship patterns may explain the difficulties

   men and women have forming cross-gender friendships.

2. **What is love? How does it begin? How does it develop through adulthood?**

_____, intimacy, and commitment are the key components of love. Although styles of love change with age, the priorities within relationships do not. As the length of the relationship increases, intimacy and passion _____, but commitment increases. Selecting a mate works best when there are _____ values, goals, and interests. The importance of these individual aspects differs across cultures.

3. **What is the nature of abuse in some relationships?**

Levels of aggressive behavior range from _____ aggression, to physical aggression, to _____ one's partner. The causes of aggressive behaviors become more _____ as the level of aggression increases. People remain in abusive relationships for many reasons, including _____ and the belief that they cannot leave.

11.2 LIFESTYLES

1. **Why do some people decide not to marry, and what are these people like?**

Most adults decide by age 30 whether they plan on getting married. Never-married adults often develop a strong network of _____. Dealing with other people's expectations that they should _____ is often difficult for single people.

2. **What are the characteristics of cohabiting people?**

Young adults usually cohabit as a _____ toward marriage, and adults of all ages may also cohabit for financial reasons. In the United States, cohabitation is only rarely seen as an _____ to marriage. Overall, more similarities than differences exist between cohabiting and married couples.

3. **What are gay and lesbian relationships like?**

Gay and lesbian relationships are _____ to marriages in terms of relationship issues. Some countries and some states in the United States now permit same-sex marriages. _____ couples tend to be more egalitarian, and are _____ likely to remain together than gay couples.

4. **What is marriage like through the course of adulthood?**

The most important factors in creating stable marriages are creating a stable sense of identity as a foundation for _____, _____ of values and interests, effective communication, and the contribution of unique skills by each partner. For couples with children, marital satisfaction tends to _____ until the children leave home, although individual differences are apparent, especially in long-term marriages. Most long-term marriages are happy.

11.3 THE FAMILY LIFE CYCLE

1. **What are the common forms of families?**

   Although the _____ family is the most common form of family in Western societies, the most common form around the world is the _____ family.

2. **Why do people have children?**

   Although having children is stressful and very _____, most people do it anyway. However, the number of child-free couples is increasing.

3. **What is it like to be a parent? What differences are there in different types of parenting?**

   The timing of parenthood is important in how involved parents are in their families as opposed to their _____. Single parents are faced with many problems, especially if they are women and are divorced. The main problem is significantly reduced _____ resources. A major issue for adoptive, foster, and stepparents is how strongly the child will _____ with them. Each of these relationships has some special characteristics. Gay and lesbian parents also face numerous obstacles, but usually prove to be good parents.

11.4 DIVORCE AND REMARRIAGE

1. **Who gets divorced? How does divorce affect parental relationships with children?**

   Currently, odds are about _____ that a new marriage will end in divorce. _____ styles can predict who will divorce. Recovery from divorce is different for men and women. Men tend to have a tougher time in the short run, but women clearly have a harder time in the long run, often because of _____ reasons. Difficulties between divorced partners usually involve _____ and child support. Disruptions also occur in divorced parents' relationships with their children, whether the children are young or are adults themselves.

2. **What are remarriages like? How are they similar to and different from first marriages?**

   Most divorced couples remarry. Second marriages are especially vulnerable to stress if spouses must adjust to having _____. Remarriage in middle age and beyond tends to be happy.

TEST YOURSELF

MULTIPLE-CHOICE QUESTIONS

1. Three broad themes that underlie adult friendships are

    a. passion, intimacy, and commitment.

    b. affective basis, shared or communal aspects, and sociability and compatibility.

    c. stimulus, values, and role.

    d. traditional versus Western-industrial values, importance of education and intelligence, and chastity.

2. Women tend to base friendships on _____ while men are more likely to base friendships on _____.

    a. shared activities; competition

    b. intimacy and emotional sharing; shared activities

    c. shared interests; emotional sharing

    d. competition; discussing personal matters

3. Which of the following is NOT one of Sternberg's components of love?

    a. Passion

    b. Intimacy

    c. Commitment

    d. Sociability

4. Early in a relationship

    a. passion and intimacy are high, but commitment is usually low.

    b. passion and commitment are high, but intimacy is usually low.

    c. intimacy is high, but passion and commitment tend to be low.

    d. passion is high, but intimacy and commitment tend to be low.

5. According to the theory of assortative mating, who is most likely to become partners?

    a. Ted, who is Jewish, and Sarah, who is Catholic

    b. Josh, who is 42, and Kelly, who is 22

    c. Eric, who is intelligent, and Jackie, who is also intelligent

    d. Andrew, who is a Democrat, and Elizabeth, who is a Republican

6. Cross-cultural research has found that in cultures around the world men look for _____ in a mate and women look for _____.

    a. physical attractiveness; men who will be good providers

    b. physical attractiveness; physical attractiveness, too

    c. chastity; love

    d. intelligence; a pleasing disposition

7. Lana's husband, Luther, severely abused her both verbally and physically and told her that he would never let her leave him. One day, as Luther approached her with his belt in his hand, Lana shot him, killing him instantly. Lana's behavior was most likely caused by

    a. a need to control.

    b. jealousy.

    c. misuse of power.

    d. battered woman syndrome.

8. Singlehood

    a. is decreasing among Latinos.

    b. has become less common among young adults in recent years.

    c. is more common among African Americans than among European Americans during young adulthood.

    d. is more common among men than among women throughout adulthood.

9. Cohabitation

    a. is most commonly used by young adults as a substitute to marriage.

    b. has been increasing in the U.S. over the past three decades.

    c. is associated with better and happier marriages.

    d. is a more common alternative to marriage in the U.S. than in the Netherlands, Norway, and Sweden.

10. Lesbian couples

    a. report more support from family than do married heterosexual couples.

    b. tend to make a commitment and cohabit faster than heterosexual couples.

    c. have less egalitarian relationships than heterosexual couples.

    d. are less likely to be in dual-worker relationships than are heterosexual couples.

11. Marital _____ is an umbrella term that refers to any marital outcome.

    a. adjustment

    b. quality

    c. satisfaction

    d. success

12. Which of the following is associated with greater marital satisfaction?

    a. Being over 20 rather than under 20 at the time of marriage

    b. Having dissimilar values and interests

    c. Having one partner contribute more to the relationship

    d. Cohabiting prior to marriage

13. Similarity of values and interests is referred to as

    a. exchange theory.

    b. homogamy.

    c. assortative mating.

    d. nuclear family.

14. Mike and Yolanda are preparing for the birth of their first child. If they are like most couples, what will happen to their marital satisfaction after the birth of their child?

    a. Their marital satisfaction will increase.

    b. They will experience no change in marital satisfaction.

    c. Their marital satisfaction will decrease.

    d. Yolanda's marital satisfaction will increase while Mike's will decrease.

15. The most common form of family in Western societies is the

    a. nuclear family.

    b. extended family.

    c. life-cycle family.

    d. empty-nest family.

16. Childless couples

    a. have less happy marriages.

    b. have less freedom.

    c. have lower standards of living.

    d. are increasing in numbers.

17. Today, couples in the United States have
    a. their first child later than in the past.
    b. their first child earlier than in the past.
    c. their first child at about the same time as in the past.
    d. more children than in the past.

18. Frank first became a father at age 36. His brother, Ben, had his first child at age 22. Which of the following statements about Frank and Ben is most likely to be true?
    a. Ben is likely to be more invested in his paternal role than Frank is.
    b. Frank is likely to spend more time than Ben caring for his child.
    c. Frank is less likely to have his involvement with his child supported by societal attitudes.
    d. Frank and Ben probably do not differ in their paternal roles.

19. The idea that the well-being of the family takes precedence over the concerns of individual family members is known as
    a. the nuclear family.
    b. the extended family.
    c. familism.
    d. homogamy.

20. _____ must be willing to tolerate considerable ambiguity in their relationships with their children and have few expectations about the future.
    a. Stepparents
    b. Adoptive parents
    c. Foster parents
    d. Gay male and lesbian parents

21. Compared to children reared by heterosexual couples, children reared by lesbian couples
    a. are more likely to develop problems of sexual identity.
    b. show deficits in cognitive development.
    c. have more problems in school.
    d. no greater likelihood of adverse consequences.

22. Which of the following statements about divorce is FALSE?

    a. Divorce is more common in the U.S. than in many countries around the world.

    b. African-American and Asian-American couples tend to be married shorter at the time of divorce than European-American couples.

    c. Infidelity is the most commonly reported reason for divorce.

    d. Men are more likely than women to have initiated the divorce.

23. Doug and Marsha are divorcing after 20 years of marriage. Which of the following statements is true?

    a. Doug and Marsha are equally likely to get remarried.

    b. Doug is more likely to get custody of the children.

    c. A support group is most likely to help Marsha adjust if it provides emotional support.

    d. A support group is most likely to help Marsha adjust if it's a large group.

24. Which of the following statements about remarriage is true?

    a. Men and women typically wait about eight years before they remarry.

    b. Compared to older generations, younger generations tend to remarry at a higher rate.

    c. The effects of remarriage on children are generally positive.

    d. For most ethnic groups, the divorce rate for remarriages is lower than for first marriages.

ESSAY QUESTIONS

1. Your brother and sister were talking, and your brother told your sister that he thought that she and her friends were boring because the only thing that she does with her friends is sit around and talk. What can you tell your brother about gender differences in friendships?

2. Recently, you and your friends Ishan and Lola were talking. Ishan mentioned that he had just broken up with his girlfriend, Hedda. Lola said, "But, Ishan, just three months ago, you told us that Hedda was the one and only one for you, that this was true love, and that she was definitely Ms. Right." Ishan replied that he had broken up with Hedda because things weren't as good as they had been before. Lola was amazed that anyone could change his mind so drastically about a relationship in such a short time. How would you explain Ishan's behavior in terms of Sternberg's three elements of passion, intimacy, and commitment?

3. Your friend Fritz has decided to marry Marie. Fritz has told you that he likes Marie because "she is so different." For example, Fritz and Marie come from different ethnic backgrounds, Fritz is very open to new experiences, and Marie doesn't like to try new things; Fritz is very liberal, and Marie is very conservative. What can you tell Fritz about the importance of assortative mating and homogamy to marital success?

4. Your friends Nick and Nora are trying to decide if they want to become parents. They have a very companionable marriage, both are invested in their careers, and they like to travel. What can you tell them about the factors they should consider and some of the benefits of remaining child-free?

5. Your friend Lisa recently got a divorce, and she is feeling depressed. She was the one who wanted to end the marriage, and she thinks that it is abnormal that she is feeling depressed. What can you tell Lisa about the psychological effects of divorce on the divorced couple?

ANSWERS WITH PAGE REFERENCES

11.1 KNOW THE TERMS

1. assortative mating (387)

2. abusive (391)

3. battered woman syndrome (392)

11.1 KNOW THE DETAILS OF RELATIONSHIPS

1. T, 384	5. F, 386	9. F, 387	13. T, 389
2. F, 385	6. T, 386	10. T, 387	14. T, 392
3. T, 385	7. T, 386	11. T, 388	15. T, 392
4. F, 385	8. T, 386	12. F, 389	16. T, 393

11.2 KNOW THE TERMS

1. cohabitation (395)

2. marital success (398)

3. marital quality (398)

4. marital adjustment (398)

5. marital satisfaction (398)

6. homogamy (399)

7. exchange (399)

8. vulnerability-stress-adaptation (400)

11.2 KNOW THE DETAILS OF LIFESTYLES

1. T, 394	6. T, 395	11. T, 399	16. F, 402
2. F, 394	7. F, 396	12. F, 399	17. T, 402
3. T, 394	8. F, 397	13. F, 400	
4. T, 395	9. T, 397	14. T, 400	
5. T, 395	10. T, 398	15. F, 400	

11.3 KNOW THE TERMS

1. nuclear (403)	2. extended (403)	3. familism (405)

11.3 KNOW THE DETAILS OF THE FAMILY LIFE CYCLE

1. F, 403	4. F, 404	7. T, 405	10. F, 407
2. T, 403	5. T, 404	8. T, 405	11. T, 407
3. T, 404	6. F, 405	9. T, 406	12. F, 408

11.4 KNOW THE DETAILS OF DIVORCE AND REMARRIAGE

1. T, 409	5. T, 411	9. T, 413	13. T, 414
2. T, 410	6. F, 412	10. F, 413	
3. T, 410	7. T, 412	11. F, 413	
4. T, 410	8. T, 413	12. F, 414	

SUMMARY

11.1 RELATIONSHIPS

1. young adulthood (384); shared activities (386); intimacy (386)
2. Passion (386); decrease (387); shared (387)
3. verbal (392); murdering (392); complex (392); low self-esteem (393)

11.2 LIFESTYLES

1. close friends (394); marry (394)
2. step (396); alternative (396)
3. similar (397); Lesbian (397); more (397)
4. intimacy (399); similarity (399); decline (400)

11.3 THE FAMILY LIFE CYCLE

1. nuclear (403); extended (403)
2. expensive (404),
3. careers (404); financial (404); bond (407)

11.4 DIVORCE AND REMARRIAGE

1. 50-50 (409); conflict (410); financial (413); visitation (413)
2. stepchildren (414).

TEST YOURSELF

MULTIPLE-CHOICE QUESTIONS

1. b, 385	8. c, 395	15. a, 403	22. c, 410
2. b, 386	9. b, 396	16. d, 404	23. c, 413
3. d, 386	10. b, 397	17. a, 404	24. c, 415
4. d, 386	11. d, 398	18. b, 404	
5. c, 387	12. a, 399	19. c, 405	
6. a, 389	13. b, 399	20. c, 408	
7. d, 392	14. c, 400	21. d, 408	

ESSAY QUESTIONS

1.   In young adulthood, women tend to base friendships on intimacy and emotional sharing. When women get together with friends, they confide in each other and discuss personal matters. So, it is not unusual for women to spend time together "just sitting around and talking." Men, however, tend to base friendships on shared activities and interests, and when they get together, they participate in those shared activities, which are often competitive. In general, men's friendships do not involve intimacy. So, both your brother and sister seem to have friendships that are gender-typical. (386)

2.   According to Sternberg, love has three components: 1) passion, an intense physical desire for someone; 2) intimacy, the feeling that one can share all of one's thoughts and actions with another; and 3) commitment, the willingness to stay with a person through good times and bad times. At the beginning of a relationship, passion is usually very high, but intimacy and commitment are low. This combination of passion, intimacy, and commitment is known as infatuation. Infatuation usually doesn't last long, and as passion fades, the relationship needs to acquire emotional intimacy or it will probably end. So, Ishan showed lots of passion in his relationship with Hedda, but as the passion faded and intimacy did not occur, the relationship ended. (386-387)

3.   An important factor related to marital success is assortative mating, which means that people find partners who share similar goals, values, attitudes, and ethnic backgrounds. The fact that Fritz and Marie are so different may be a problem later in their marriage. The lack of similarity to each other in the relationship may be a source of marital problems. For example, couples have higher marital satisfaction when they are similar in terms of openness to new experiences. Perhaps they should rethink, or postpone, the decision to marry. (387-388)

4.   Some of the benefits of having children are personal satisfaction, fulfilling personal needs, continuing the family line, and companionship. Having children also has negative effects such as creating a financial drain, drastically changing the couple's lifestyle, decreasing marital satisfaction, and competing with one's career. Couples who decide to remain child-free tend to have happier marriages, more freedom, and higher standards of living. Given that Nick and Nora are both highly invested in their careers, that they enjoy the freedom to travel, and that they have a very close marriage, they may be better candidates for a child-free lifestyle. (403-404)

5.   Negative psychological effects are common after divorce. In fact, feeling unhappy is a common feeling of divorced people. Other common feelings are deep disappointment, feeling misunderstood, feeling like a failure, and feeling rejected. "Divorce hangover" reflects the inability to let go, develop new friendships, or reorient as a single parent. Some people are preoccupied with the former spouse and may have financial difficulties. People who are able to let go, develop new friendships, or reorient themselves as single parents tend to adjust better to divorce. So, Lisa's feelings are not abnormal, nor atypical, even though she wanted the divorce. Lisa might benefit from a support group that provides emotional support as she adjusts to her divorce. (412-413)

WORK AND LEISURE

12.1 Occupational Selection and Development

12.2 Gender, Ethnicity, and Discrimination Issues

12.3 Occupational Transitions

12.4 Work and Family

12.5 Time to Relax: Leisure Activities

This chapter focuses on occupational selection and development, discrimination in the workplace, occupational transitions, managing the demands of work and family, and relaxing away from the workplace.

12.1 OCCUPATIONAL SELECTION AND DEVELOPMENT

TO MASTER THE LEARNING OBJECTIVES:

How do people view work? How do occupational priorities vary with age?

- Explain the meanings associated with work.
- Define meaning-mission fit.

How do people choose their occupations?

- **Define social cognitive career theory (SCCT).**

- Describe how well Holland's theory and SCCT explain actual career choices.

What factors influence occupational development?

- Describe Super's developmental tasks of implementation, stabilization, and consolidation.

- Describe how occupational expectations are related to occupational goals.

- Describe cohort differences in occupational expectations.

- Describe the four phases of mentorship.

- Describe how mentors are related to occupational success and the relation between generativity and mentoring.

- Describe the problems that women have in establishing good mentor relationships.

What is the relation between job satisfaction and age?

- Describe the factors that are related to increasing job satisfaction with age.

- Describe the factors that are related to feelings of alienation on the job.

- Describe the things that employers can do to avoid feelings of alienation in their workers.

- Define burnout, and describe the factors that are related to it.

- Describe how passion may be related to burnout.

12.1 KNOW THE TERMS

Alienation	Passion
Burnout	Reality shock
Job satisfaction	Social cognitive career theory (SCCT)
Meaning-mission fit	Vocational maturity
Mentor	

1. _____ occurs when corporate executives have a good match between their personal intentions and their firm's mission but care more about employees' happiness, job satisfaction, and emotional well-being.

2. The _____ emphasizes that career choice is influenced by people's ideas about what they think they can do and how well they can do it.

3. The match between vocational behaviors and what is expected of a worker at different ages is a measure of _____.

4. _____ occurs when someone realizes that what they learned in college doesn't transfer directly to a job, and it does not represent all that someone needs to know for the job.

5. A person who facilitates on-the-job learning, helps a new hire do her job, and who prepares the person for the future is called a _____.

6. _____ is the positive feeling that results from an appraisal of one's work.

7. A feeling of _____ results when one feels that what one does on the job is meaningless, not valued, or unrelated to the final product.

8. Depletion of energy and motivation, loss of occupational idealism, and feeling one is being exploited on the job is called _____.

9. A _____ is a strong inclination toward an activity that individuals like, value, and in which they invest time and energy.

12.1 KNOW THE DETAILS OF OCCUPATIONAL SELECTION AND DEVELOPMENT

1. Four common meanings of work are developing and becoming self, union with others, expressing self, and serving others.
   TRUE or FALSE

2. Occupation is often an important part of identity.
   TRUE or FALSE

3. Holland's theory states that people choose occupations to optimize the fit between their individual traits and their occupational interests.
   TRUE or FALSE

4. Social cognitive career theories emphasize that how people choose careers is influenced by what they think they can do and how well they can do it, as well as how motivated they are.
   TRUE or FALSE

5. Men and women are equally distributed among Holland's personality types.
   TRUE or FALSE

6. In Super's theory of occupational development, people go through stages related to changing self-concepts and adaptation to an occupational role throughout adulthood.
   TRUE or FALSE

7. Super's consolidation task involves taking a series of temporary jobs to learn firsthand about work roles and try out some possible career choices.

TRUE or FALSE

8. People change career goals as a result of experience.

TRUE or FALSE

9. Millennials are less likely to change jobs as often as earlier generations.

TRUE or FALSE

10. Occupational success often depends on the quality of the mentor-protégé relationship.

TRUE or FALSE

11. Women and minorities have an especially important need for mentors.

TRUE or FALSE

12. Job satisfaction tends to decrease with age.

TRUE or FALSE

13. Burnout is least common among people in the helping professions, such as healthcare and teaching.

TRUE or FALSE

14. Burnout can be minimized by practicing stress-reduction techniques, cognitively restructuring the work situation, and finding alternative ways to enhance personal growth and identity.

TRUE or FALSE

12.2 GENDER, ETHNICITY, AND DISCRIMINATION ISSUES

TO MASTER THE LEARNING OBJECTIVES:

How do women's and men's occupational expectations differ? How are people viewed when they enter occupations that are not traditional for their gender?

- Describe the factors that are related to women choosing nontraditional occupations.

- Describe how women in male-dominated occupations are viewed.

What factors are related to women's occupational development?

- Describe the important family and work issues of women who are working full-time.

What factors affect ethnic minority workers' occupational experiences and occupational development?

- Explain how African-American women prepare for nontraditional occupations.
- Describe how occupational aspirations are related to ethnicity.

What types of bias and discrimination hinder occupational development of women and ethnic minority workers?

- Describe how gender discrimination, glass ceiling, and glass cliff influence women's occupational advancement.
- Describe the pay gap between women and men.
- Explain the effects of sexual harassment.
- Explain cultural differences in perceptions of sexual harassment.
- Define the reasonable person standard.
- Define age discrimination, and describe many ways in which it occurs in the workplace.

12.2 KNOW THE TERMS

Age discrimination	Glass ceiling
Gender discrimination	Glass cliff

1. Denying a job to someone solely on the basis of whether the person is a man or woman is known as _____.

2. The highest level to which women rise and then stop in an organization is known as the _____.

3. Women in leadership positions often confront a _____ in which their leadership position is precarious.

4. Denying a job or promotion to someone solely on the basis of age is known as _____.

12.2 KNOW THE DETAILS OF GENDER, ETHNICITY, AND DISCRIMINATION ISSUES

1. Women who choose nontraditional occupations are more likely to be viewed negatively.
   TRUE or FALSE

311

2. Women in previous generations had fewer occupational choices than women today.
    TRUE or FALSE

3. Even when millennial generation college women explore nontraditional occupational options, they generally commit to more traditional ones.
    TRUE or FALSE

4. The most important workplace issues for women who work full-time are unsupportive work environments, organizational politics, and lack of occupational development opportunities.
    TRUE or FALSE

5. European-American women are more likely than African-American women to enter nontraditional occupations.
    TRUE or FALSE

6. The responsiveness of an organization to the needs of ethnic minorities makes little difference to employees.
    TRUE or FALSE

7. Same-ethnicity mentors provide more psychosocial support than cross-ethnicity mentors.
    TRUE or FALSE

8. Gender discrimination in the workplace is no longer common.
    TRUE or FALSE

9. Women are paid about 80% of what men are paid on an average annual basis.
    TRUE or FALSE

10. Being sexually harassed is associated with negative job-related, psychological, and physical health outcomes.
    TRUE or FALSE

11. In the U.S., women are more likely than men to view specific interactions as harassment.
    TRUE or FALSE

12. In the U.S., it is legal for employers to refuse to hire or discharge a worker solely on the basis of age.
    TRUE or FALSE

12.3 OCCUPATIONAL TRANSITIONS

TO MASTER THE LEARNING OBJECTIVES:

Why do people change occupations?

- Describe the factors related to occupational changes.

- Describe the situations that make retraining necessary.

- Define career plateauing.

Is worrying about potential job loss a major source of stress?

- Describe the effects of worrying about one's job.

How does job loss affect the amount of stress experienced?

- Describe the effects of losing one's job, particularly for middle-aged men.

- Describe how the effects of job loss differ depending on when during the adult life cycle the loss occurs.

12.3 KNOW THE DETAILS OF OCCUPATIONAL TRANSITIONS

1. Changing jobs several times during adulthood is more common today than it was in the past.
   TRUE or FALSE

2. Retraining is often a successful way of dealing with career plateauing or job loss.
   TRUE or FALSE

3. Feelings of job insecurity can negatively impact physical and psychological well-being.
   TRUE or FALSE

4. Unemployment is related to declines in life satisfaction and physical health.
   TRUE or FALSE

5. Middle-aged men are less vulnerable to negative effects of job loss than are older or younger men.
   TRUE or FALSE

6. Women report fewer long-term negative effects of job loss than do men.
   TRUE or FALSE

7. Unemployment rates for many ethnic minority groups are substantially higher than they are for European Americans.

TRUE or FALSE

12.4 WORK AND FAMILY

TO MASTER THE LEARNING OBJECTIVES:

What are the issues faced by employed people who care for dependents?

- Describe how financial need and attachment to one's job influences why women return to work after having children.

- Describe the negative effects on work and workers of providing dependent care.

- Describe the things that employers can do to reduce work-family conflicts.

- Define backup care.

How do partners view the division of household chores? What is work-family conflict, and how does it affect couples' lives?

- Explain how dual-earner couples divide household and childcare responsibilities.

- Describe the division of household tasks that men find fair and that women find fair.

- Describe ethnic and cross-cultural differences in the division of household tasks in dual-worker couples.

- Describe how occupational and family roles are related to each other.

- Describe the factors that are related to the successful combination of family and occupational responsibilities in dual-worker couples.

- Explain the cross-cultural and gender differences in burnout from work and parenting.

12.4 KNOW THE TERMS

Backup care   Work-family conflict

1. Emergency care for dependent children or adults so an employee doesn't lose a day of work is called _____.

2. The feeling of being pulled in multiple directions by incompatible demands from job and family is called _____.

12.4 KNOW THE DETAILS OF WORK AND FAMILY

1. The number of families in which both parents are employed has decreased over the past few decades.
    TRUE or FALSE

2. The degree to which women are attached to their work influences whether they decide to return to work after having children.
    TRUE or FALSE

3. Women and men who are responsible for dependent care do not report negative effects on their work or higher levels of stress.
    TRUE or FALSE

4. When supervisors are sympathetic and supportive regarding family issues and daycare, parents have higher absenteeism.
    TRUE or FALSE

5. In dual-earner couples today, most men and women share household and childcare tasks equally.
    TRUE or FALSE

6. Women have decreased the amount of time they spend on housework since the 1970s.
    TRUE or FALSE

7. Women are most satisfied with the division of labor regarding household tasks when men are willing to perform women's traditional chores.
    TRUE or FALSE

8. European-American men tend to spend more time doing household tasks than do African-American and Hispanic-American men.
    TRUE or FALSE

9. Work-family conflict is greatest when there are preschoolers at home.
    TRUE or FALSE

10. Burnout from work and parenting is equally likely to affect men and women.
    TRUE or FALSE

315

12.5 TIME TO RELAX: LEISURE ACTIVITIES

TO MASTER THE LEARNING OBJECTIVES:

What activities are leisure activities? How do people choose among them?

- Describe how frequency of leisure activities is related to depression and dementia.

- Describe the factors that influence which activities are in leisure repertoires.

What changes in leisure activities occur with age?

- Explain what cross-sectional and longitudinal studies tell us about age differences in leisure activities.

What do people derive from leisure activities?

- Describe the benefits of leisure activities.

12.5 KNOW THE DETAILS OF TIME TO RELAX: LEISURE ACTIVITIES

1. Work is defined as discretionary activity, which includes simple relaxation, activities for enjoyment, and creative pursuits.
   TRUE or FALSE

2. People tend to select leisure activities based on perceived competence and psychological comfort with the activity.
   TRUE or FALSE

3. Middle-aged adults participate in a greater range of leisure activities than do young adults.
   TRUE or FALSE

4. Young adults tend to prefer more physically intense leisure activities than do middle-aged adults.
   TRUE or FALSE

5. Preferences for certain types of leisure activities are established early in life.
   TRUE or FALSE

6. Involvement in leisure activities is related to well-being.
   TRUE or FALSE

SUMMARY

12.1 OCCUPATIONAL SELECTION AND DEVELOPMENT

1. **How do people view work?**

    Although most people work for _____, other reasons are highly variable.

2. **How do people choose their occupations?**

    Holland's theory is based on the idea that people choose occupations to optimize the fit between their individual traits and their occupational _____. Six personality types that represent different combinations of these have been identified. Support for these types has been found in several studies. Social cognitive career theory emphasizes that how people choose careers is also influenced by what they _____ they can do and _____ they can do it, as well as how motivated they are to pursue a career.

3. **What factors influence occupational development?**

    Super's developmental view of occupations is based on _____ and adaptation to an occupational role. Super describes five stages: implementation, _____, maintenance, deceleration, and _____. _____ is the realization that one's expectations about an occupation are different from the reality one _____ experiences, and is common among young workers. Few differences exist across generations in terms of their _____. A mentor is a coworker who teaches a new employee the _____ rules and fosters occupational development. Mentor-protégé relationships, like other relationships, develop through stages over time.

4. **What is the relationship between job satisfaction and age?**

    Older workers report _____ job satisfaction than younger workers, but this may be partly due to _____; unhappy workers may quit. Other reasons for this difference include intrinsic satisfaction, good fit, _____ importance of work, finding nonwork diversions, and life-cycle factors. _____ and burnout are important considerations in understanding job satisfaction. Both involve significant stress for workers. Vallerand's Passion Model proposes that people develop a passion toward enjoyable activities that are incorporated into identity. _____ passion happens when people experience an uncontrollable urge to engage in the activity; _____ passion results when individuals have freely accepted the activity as important for them without any contingencies attached to it.

317

12.2 GENDER, ETHNICITY, AND DISCRIMINATION ISSUES

1. **How do women's and men's occupational expectations differ? How are people viewed when they enter occupations that are not traditional for their gender?**

    Boys and girls are socialized differently for work, and their occupational choices are affected as a result. Women choose nontraditional occupations for many reasons, including expectations and personal feelings. Women in such occupations are still viewed more _____ than men in the same occupations.

2. **What factors are related to women's occupational development?**

    Women leave well-paid occupations for many reasons, including _____ obligations and the workplace environment. Women who continue to work full-time have _____ and look for ways to further their occupational development. The _____, which limits women's occupational attainment, and the glass cliff, which puts women leaders in a precarious position, affect how often women achieve top executive positions and how _____ women leaders are.

3. **What factors affect ethnic minority workers' occupational experiences and occupational development?**

    Vocational identity and vocational goals vary in different ethnic groups. Whether an organization is sensitive to ethnicity issues is a strong predictor of _____ among ethnic minorities.

4. **What types of bias and discrimination hinder the occupational development of women and ethnic minority workers?**

    Gender bias remains the chief barrier to women's occupational development. In many cases, this operates as a glass ceiling, which _____ women's occupational advancement. _____ inequity is also a problem. Sexual harassment is a problem in the workplace. Current criteria for judging harassment are based on the _____ standard. Denying employment to anyone over the age of 40 because of age is age discrimination.

12.3 OCCUPATIONAL TRANSITIONS

1. **Why do people change occupations?**

    Important reasons people change occupations include personality, _____, and economic trends. To adapt to the effects of a _____ economy and an _____ workforce, many corporations are providing retraining opportunities for workers. Retraining is especially important in cases of outdated skills and _____.

2. **Is worrying about potential job loss a major source of stress?**

   Occupational insecurity is a growing problem. Fear that one may lose one's job is a better predictor of _____ than actual likelihood of job loss.

3. **How does job loss affect the amount of stress experienced?**

   Job loss is a traumatic event that can affect _____ aspect of a person's life. Degree of _____ distress and the extent of _____ to the job are the best predictors of distress.

12.4 WORK AND FAMILY

1. **What are the issues faced by employed people who care for dependents?**

   Caring for children or aging parents creates dilemmas for workers. Whether a woman returns to work after having a child depends largely on how _____ she is to her work. Simply providing childcare on-site does not always result in higher job satisfaction. A more important factor is the degree to which supervisors are _____ regarding childcare issues.

2. **How do partners view the division of household chores? What is work-family conflict? How does it affect couples' lives?**

   Although women have _____ the amount of time they spend on household tasks over the past two decades, they still do most of the work. European-American men are _____ likely than either African-American or Latino-American men to help with traditionally _____ household tasks. Recent evidence shows that work stress has a much _____ impact on family life than family stress has on work performance. Some women pay a high personal price for having careers.

12.5 TIME TO RELAX: LEISURE ACTIVITIES

1. **What activities are leisure activities? How do people choose among them?**

   _____ can be simple relaxation, activities for enjoyment, or creative pursuits. Views of leisure activities vary by gender, _____, and age.

2. **What changes in leisure activities occur with age?**

   As people grow older, they tend to engage in leisure activities that are less _____ and more _____ oriented. Leisure preferences in adulthood are a reflection of those established _____ in life.

3. **What do people derive from leisure activities?**

   Leisure activities _____ and can benefit all aspects of people's lives.

319

TEST YOURSELF

MULTIPLE-CHOICE QUESTIONS

1. Holland's theory of occupational choice

    a. focuses on the context in which occupational decisions are made.

    b. proposes stages of occupational interests that occur throughout adulthood.

    c. considers the fit between individuals' traits and their occupational interests.

    d. accounts for ethnic differences in occupational interests.

2. Women are more likely than men to be in Holland's _____ personality types.

    a. social, artistic, and conventional

    b. investigative, social, and enterprising

    c. realistic, conventional, and investigative

    d. artistic, enterprising, and investigative

3. Twenty-two-year-old Darrell is considering a career in physical therapy and has taken a summer job as an aide in a physical therapy clinic. Darrell is engaged in Super's _____ task.

    a. stabilization

    b. consolidation

    c. crystallization

    d. implementation

4. Thirty-four-year-old Peter is advancing up the career ladder in an accounting firm. He is involved in Super's _____ task.

    a. stabilization

    b. consolidation

    c. crystallization

    d. implementation

5. Twenty-eight-year-old Sonya decided to become a social worker and has been working in that role for three years now. She is engaged in Super's _____ task.

    a. stabilization

    b. consolidation

    c. crystallization

    d. implementation

6. During Kramer's _____ phase of mentor relationships, the mentor-protégé relationship either ends or is transformed into a different type of relationship.

   a. initiation

   b. cultivation

   c. separation

   d. redefinition

   e. mentors

7. Job satisfaction

   a. tends to increase with age.

   b. tends to decrease with age.

   c. tends to increase with age for women and decrease with age for men.

   d. tends to increase with age for men and decrease with age for women.

8. Ike works in a box factory, assembling boxes. He feels that his job is very unimportant, that no one appreciates the work he does, and feels frustrated because he never sees the boxes used for anything. Ike is likely to

   a. have high job satisfaction.

   b. develop a sense of alienation.

   c. develop burnout.

   d. have a low absenteeism rate.

9. Women in nontraditional occupations for females tend to be viewed

   a. positively.

   b. as having negative interpersonal characteristics.

   c. as more respectable than men in the same occupations.

   d. as giving, honest, and collaborative.

10. Which of the following statements concerning women and occupational development is true?

   a. The characteristics and aspirations of women who entered the workforce in the 1950s and those from Generation X are very similar.

   b. Working mothers are usually viewed as being a team player in the work environment.

   c. Women tend to value working interdependently with others more than men do.

   d. Women feel very connected to the workplace.

11. Which of the following statements concerning ethnicity and occupational development is true?

    a. More African-American than European-American women choose nontraditional occupations.

    b. African-American workers have significantly lower leadership aspirations than European-American workers do.

    c. Latino Americans and European Americans have different occupational development and work values.

    d. African-American women who choose nontraditional occupations tend to plan for less formal education than necessary to achieve their goals.

12. The level to which women may rise in a company but beyond which they may not go is referred to as

    a. vocational maturity.

    b. a career plateau.

    c. a glass cliff.

    d. a glass ceiling.

13. The standard by which sexual harassment is judged is

    a. pay equity.

    b. the reasonable person standard.

    c. gender discrimination.

    d. the glass ceiling.

14. The U.S. Age Discrimination in Employment Act of 1986 protects workers over the age of

    a. 40.

    b. 50.

    c. 60.

    d. 70.

15. Career _____ occurs when there is either a lack of promotional opportunity in the organization or when a person decides not to seek advancement.

    a. burnout

    b. alienation

    c. plateauing

    d. retraining

16. Forty-six-year-old Allan, a European-American mid-level manager, lost his job in a recent downsizing in the corporation where he had worked for 20 years. He is likely to experience
    a. decreased physical health, life satisfaction, and physical health.
    b. less distress than a female in a similar position.
    c. less distress than a young adult in a similar position.
    d. more distress than an African-American male in a similar position.

17. Who is most likely to experience negative effects as a result of losing a job?
    a. Young men
    b. Middle-aged men
    c. Older men
    d. Young, middle-aged, and older men are equally vulnerable to negative effects

18. In dual-career households,
    a. most couples share household and childcare tasks equally.
    b. men assume the greatest responsibility for household and childcare tasks.
    c. women perform the majority of housework.
    d. European-American men spend more time doing household tasks than Hispanic or African-American men.

19. Men are most satisfied when the division of labor for household tasks is based on _____, whereas women are most satisfied when _____.
    a. traditional gender-typing of chores; it's divided by hours spent performing tasks
    b. women performing men's traditional chores; men perform men's traditional chores
    c. the number of hours spent; men perform women's traditional chores
    d. the amount of income each spouse brings in; it's divided by the number of hours spent

20. Sherry has a meeting with her regional boss scheduled for the same time that her daughter is competing in the high school state swimming finals. These competing demands cause
    a. work-family conflict.
    b. burnout.
    c. plateauing.
    d. alienation.

21. Jack's favorite leisure activities include volunteering at a homeless shelter and luncheon meetings for community organizations. Jack's leisure activities tend to be in the _____ classification.

    a. developmental
    b. social-public
    c. social-private
    d. experiential

22. Joelin enjoys spending her free time visiting friends and going out to dinner. These kinds of activities would be classified in the _____ category.

    a. social-public
    b. social-private
    c. experiential
    d. developmental

23. During later middle age, less leisure time is spent in _____ activities.

    a. expensive
    b. intellectually demanding
    c. strenuous physical
    d. social

24. The leisure activities engaged in by an individual tend to

    a. change greatly over the years.
    b. be stable over long periods of time.
    c. become more physically intense with age.
    d. become less family-oriented upon entering middle-age.

ESSAY QUESTIONS

1. Your friend Pam recently started a job as a social worker. Pam has noticed that many of her coworkers who have been on the job for a few years seem to have no energy or motivation. They also seem to depersonalize their clients by referring to them as case numbers. Pam doesn't understand why these people chose a helping profession if they aren't interested in helping people. What can you tell Pam about burnout that might explain her coworkers' behavior and what she can do to avoid burnout herself?

2. Your friend Hilka has been with the same company for a number of years. She thinks that she works very hard. In fact, she feels that she has not received promotions that have gone to men who don't work as hard as she does. The other day, she found out that a man in a comparable position made quite a bit more money than she did last year. Hilka is beginning to wonder if there is something wrong with her and her job performance. What can you tell Hilka about the glass ceiling and pay equity?

3. Your friend Jelisa has told you that her boss compliments her appearance every day, calls her "honey" or "sweetie," and sometimes when they talk he will put his hand on her shoulder. Jelisa isn't sure if she is a victim of sexual harassment or if her boss is just being friendly. What can you tell Jelisa about the factors that are considered when determining if sexual harassment has occurred?

4. Your 49-year-old neighbor, Ira, just lost his job of 25 years when his company merged with another company. His wife, Marina, is worried about him. He feels ill much of the time and just sits around the house. What can you tell Marina about the effects of losing one's job, especially for people in Ira's position?

5. Your friends Fran and Jack are expecting their first baby soon. Both Fran and Jack intend to continue working after the baby is born but they are worried about the conflict between work, parenting, and running a household. What advice can you give Fran and Jack?

6. Your friend Jermaine went hang-gliding a few weeks ago, and he thought that it was a fantastic activity. Ever since, he has been bothering you to go with him the next time he goes. You don't really want to and don't think that you will enjoy hang-gliding. What can you tell Jermaine about the factors that influence which leisure activities one chooses to participate in and about the importance of satisfaction with leisure activities?

ANSWERS WITH PAGE REFERENCES

12.1 KNOW THE TERMS

1. Meaning-mission fit (421)
2. Social cognitive career theory (421)
3. vocational maturity (423)
4. Reality shock (425)
5. mentor (425)

6. job satisfaction (427)
7. alienation (428)
8. burnout (429)
9. passion (429)

12.1 KNOW THE DETAILS OF OCCUPATIONAL SELECTION AND DEVELOPMENT

1. T, 421	5. F, 422	9. F, 425	13. F, 429
2. T, 421	6. T, 423	10. T, 426	14. T, 430
3. T, 421	7. F, 423	11. T, 426	
4. T, 422	8. T, 424	12. F, 427	

12.2 KNOW THE TERMS

1. gender discrimination (434)
2. glass ceiling (434)

3. glass cliff (435)
4. age discrimination (438)

12.2 KNOW THE DETAILS OF GENDER, ETHNICITY, AND DISCRIMINATION ISSUES

1. T, 431	5. F, 433	9. T, 435
2. T, 432	6. F, 434	10. T, 437
3. T, 433	7. T, 434	11. T, 437
4. T, 433	8. F, 434	12. F, 438

12.3 KNOW THE DETAILS OF OCCUPATIONAL TRANSITIONS

1. T, 439	3. T, 440	5. F, 441	7. T, 441
2. T, 440	4. T, 441	6. F, 441	

12.4 KNOW THE TERMS

1. backup care (445)   3. work-family conflict (447)

12.4 KNOW THE DETAILS OF WORK AND FAMILY

1. F, 443	4. F, 445	7. T, 446	10. F, 448
2. T, 443	5. F, 445	8. F, 446	
3. F, 444	6. T, 446	9. T, 447	

12.5 KNOW THE DETAILS OF TIME TO RELAX: LEISURE ACTIVITIES

1. F, 449	3. F, 450	5. T, 450
2. T, 449	4. T, 450	6. T, 450

SUMMARY

12.1 OCCUPATIONAL SELECTION AND DEVELOPMENT

1. money (420)

2. interests (421); think (422); how well (422)

3. self-concept (423); establishment (423); retirement (423); Reality shock (425); occupational expectations (425); unwritten (425)

4. higher (427); self-selection (427); lower (427); Alienation (427); Obsessive (429); harmonious (429)

12.2 GENDER, ETHNICITY, AND DISCRIMINATION ISSUES

1. negatively (432)
2. family (433); adequate childcare (433); glass ceiling (434); successful (434)
3. satisfaction (434)
4. stops (434); Pay (435); reasonable person (437)

12.3 OCCUPATIONAL TRANSITIONS

1. obsolescence (439); global (439); aging (439); career plateauing (439)
2. anxiety (440)
3. every (441); financial (441); attachment (441)

12.4 WORK AND FAMILY

1. attached (443); sympathetic (445)
2. reduced (445); less (446); female (446); greater (447)

12.5 TIME TO RELAX: LEISURE ACTIVITIES

1. Leisure (449); ethnicity (450)
2. strenuous (450); family (450); earlier (450)
3. enhance well-being (450)

TEST YOURSELF

MULTIPLE-CHOICE QUESTIONS

1. c, 421	7. a, 427	13. b, 437	19. c, 446
2. a, 422	8. b, 428	14. a, 438	20. a, 447
3. d, 423	9. b, 432	15. c, 439	21. c, 449
4. b, 423	10. c, 433	16. a, 441	22. b, 449
5. a, 423	11. b, 433	17. b, 441	23. c, 450
6. d, 426	12. d, 434	18. c, 445	24. b, 450

ESSAY QUESTIONS

1.   People experience job burnout when the pressures of the job become too great to handle. Signs of burnout include physical, mental, and emotional exhaustion. People in the helping professions and the military are particularly prone to burnout. Pam is probably wrong about her coworkers; they entered social work because they wanted to help others. Unfortunately, people in helping professions are constantly confronted with people who have no easy solutions to their problems. They also spend a lot of time completing bureaucratic paperwork. Soon people in the helping professions become so frustrated, disillusioned, and exhausted that they suffer from burnout. Three things can help decrease the likelihood that Pam will experience burnout. First, Pam should lower other people's expectations. She cannot change the world all by herself. Second, restructure the work situation as best as she can. Third, Pam should find ways outside of her job to enhance personal growth. Fourth, she should also practice effective stress-reduction techniques. (429-430)

2.   The glass ceiling refers to the level to which women rise in an organization and then go no further. Studies have shown that many women rise to the upper levels of lower-tier jobs but rarely enter the upper tier of jobs. This glass ceiling keeps women in lower-level jobs in spite of their personal attributes and qualifications. Women are also often appointed to leadership positions when an organization is in crisis so her leadership position is precarious, which is known as the glass cliff. Women in the workplace also are victims of pay discrimination. In the United States, women earn 80% of the salary that men receive in comparable jobs. If Hilka thinks that she has been working hard but has not been rewarded for her work, she's probably right. Hilka should realize that this does not reflect upon her personally, but it is a problem in the workplace that affects many women. (434-436)

3.   Jelisa could be a victim of sexual harassment, which often occurs when there is a power differential between two people. The most frequent victims are single or divorced young women. People who experience sexual harassment on the job have negative job-related, psychological, and physical health outcomes. Even frequent low-level sexual harassment can have negative consequences. Jelisa should let her boss know that she finds his behavior offensive. If the behavior persists, she should pursue a complaint against him. (436-437)

4.   Poor subjective physical health, lower mental health, and decreased satisfaction with life, marriage, and family are common effects associated with the loss of one's job. Men who are Ira's age are particularly vulnerable to these effects because they have greater financial responsibilities than younger men. The more that one's job is viewed as an expected contribution to the family, as is often the case for men, the greater the negative effects of job loss. Ira's poor health and signs of depression are fairly typical of men in his position. If Ira does not improve, Marina should seek outside help for him. (441-442)

5. Yes, dual-earner couples do experience a lot of role conflict between their multiple roles, but these roles can be juggled successfully. First, women tend to be happier if their husbands not only do more around the house but also do traditionally female work like cooking, the dishes, etc. Second, dual-earner couples also experience the highest work-family conflict when they have at least two preschool children. Third, dual-earner couples who spend time together in shared activities tend to be happier (even simple activities like eating and conversing). In other words, Fran and Jack will be happier if Jack does more around the house, especially traditionally female tasks, when their children are no longer preschoolers, and if they spend time together in shared activities. (446-448)

6. Our choice of leisure activities is influenced by a number of factors. First, how well we think that we will perform at the activity (known as perceived competence) is important. Hang-gliding may be an activity that many people would perceive that they wouldn't do well. Second, how well our performance matches our goals for performance (known as psychological comfort) is important. You may be afraid that your goal of not making a fool of yourself or not hurting yourself may not be met if you go with Jermaine. Other factors include income (do you have the money for hang-gliding?), interest (you've already told Jermaine you aren't interested), physical health and ability (are you healthy enough and coordinated enough to hang-glide?), transportation, education, and social characteristics. Involvement in leisure activities also is important in promoting feelings of well-being and buffers the negative effects of stress. If one is forced to participate in a leisure activity, then little or no well-being and perhaps lots of stress will result from participation. In other words, leisure activities and satisfaction from them varies from person to person. One person's fantastic experience may be another person's nightmare. (449-450)

CHAPTER **13**

MAKING IT IN MIDLIFE

13.1 Physical Changes and Health

13.2 Cognitive Development

13.3 Personality

13.4 Family Dynamics and Middle Age

This chapter focuses on the changes that occur during middle age such as changes in physical well-being, cognition, personality, and family dynamics.

13.1 PHYSICAL CHANGES AND HEALTH

TO MASTER THE LEARNING OBJECTIVES:

How does appearance change in middle age?

- Explain the physical changes that cause wrinkles, gray hair, baldness, and middle-aged bulge.

What changes occur in bones and joints?

- Describe the causes and possible prevention of osteoporosis, and explain why it is more common in women than in men.

- Explain how dual-energy x-ray absorptiometry (DXA) tests, bisphosphonates, and selective estrogen receptor modulators (SERMS) are important in the detection and treatment of osteoporosis.

- Describe changes in the joints and problems such as osteoarthritis and rheumatoid arthritis.

What reproductive changes occur in men and women in middle age?

- Describe the physical changes that occur in women during the climacteric.

- Explain how ethnicity and culture are related to menopause.

- Describe how reproductive technology has changed the age of childbearing.

- Describe the risks and benefits associated with menopausal hormone therapy.

- Describe changes in men's fertility with age.

- Describe the changes that occur in men's sexual functioning with age.

What is stress? How does it affect physical and psychological health?

- Describe how control over one's job is related to stress.

- Describe how reported stress differs by age and gender.

- Describe the stress and coping paradigm.

- Describe how stress is related to one's physical health.

- Define Type A and Type B behavior patterns, and explain how both are related to cardiovascular disease.

- Describe how stress and psychological health are related.

What benefits are there to exercise?

- Describe the physiological effects of exercise.

13.1 KNOW THE TERMS

Aerobic exercise	Posttraumatic stress disorder
Climacteric	Rheumatoid arthritis
Coping	Selective estrogen receptor modulators
Dual-energy X-ray absorptiometry (DXA)	Skeletal maturity
Menopause	Stress and coping
Menopausal hormone	Type A
Osteoarthritis	Type B
Osteoporosis	Wear-and-tear
Perimenopause	

1. _____ occurs when bone mass is greatest and the skeleton is at peak development at the age of 19 years for women and 20 years for men.

2. The physical condition in which bones become porous like honeycombs and are extremely easy to break is called _____.

3. A _____ measures bone mineral density in the hip and spine.

4. Compounds that have estrogen-like effects on some tissues and estrogen-blocking effects on other tissues are called _____,

5. A disease marked by gradual onset and disability with minor signs of inflammation of the joints is called _____.

6. A degenerative disease caused by injury and overuse is known as a _____ disease.

7. A destructive disease of the joints that develops slowly and typically affects the joints in fingers, wrists, and ankles is called _____.

8. The physical and hormonal changes that are associated with passing from reproductive to nonreproductive years in women are called the _____.

9. The eventual end of menstruation is called _____.

10. The time of transition from regular menstruation to menopause is called _____.

11. _____ therapy involves women taking low doses of estrogen and progestin to alleviate symptoms associated with the climacteric.

12. The _____ paradigm is concerned with whether or not someone interprets a situation as stressful and how that person deals with the stress.

13. One's attempt to deal with stress is called _____.

14. People with the _____ behavior pattern tend to be intensely competitive, angry, hostile, impatient, aggressive, and restless

15. People with the _____ behavior pattern tend to be patient, relaxed, and laid back.

16. An anxiety disorder that can develop after exposure to a terrifying event or ordeal in which grave physical harm either occurred or was threatened is called _____.

17. _____ places a moderate stress on the heart and provides adults with many physiological benefits.

13.1 KNOW THE DETAILS OF PHYSICAL CHANGES AND HEALTH

1. Exposure to sunlight and smoking cigarettes can cause wrinkles.
   TRUE or FALSE

2. During middle adulthood, metabolism speeds up.
   TRUE or FALSE

3. Osteoporosis causes bones to become porous and to break more easily.
   TRUE or FALSE

4. Osteoporosis is more common in men than women.
   TRUE or FALSE

5. Estrogen replacement therapy reduces bone loss in women but has negative side effects.
   TRUE or FALSE

6. Osteoarthritis usually first becomes apparent in late middle age or early old age.
   TRUE or FALSE

7. Rheumatoid arthritis is not as destructive as osteoarthritis.
   TRUE or FALSE

8. During the climacteric, estrogen production increases.
   TRUE or FALSE

9. Symptoms of perimenopause and menopause include hot flashes, night sweats, headaches, mood changes, difficulty concentrating, and vaginal dryness.
   TRUE or FALSE

10. Cultural factors may influence the reporting of menopause symptoms.
    TRUE or FALSE

11. Reproductive technology has made it possible for postmenopausal women to have children.
    TRUE or FALSE

12. The decline in estrogen during the climacteric is related to an increased risk of osteoporosis, cardiovascular disease, and memory loss.
     TRUE or FALSE

13. At age 50 (prior to menopause), women have three times less risk of heart attacks than men, but 10 years after menopause, their risk is the same as men's.
     TRUE or FALSE

14. Hormone replacement therapy is associated with a decreased risk of breast cancer.
     TRUE or FALSE

15. Men are still capable of fathering a child when they are in their 80s.
     TRUE or FALSE

16. Prostate cancer becomes a significant risk for men during middle age.
     TRUE or FALSE

17. During middle adulthood, the effects of stress become most apparent.
     TRUE or FALSE

18   Workers in jobs where they have little control over their jobs tend to have higher levels of stress than do workers who have more direct control over their jobs.
     TRUE or FALSE

19. Men are more likely than women to rate their stressful experiences as more negative and uncontrollable.
     TRUE or FALSE

20. Stress tends to be highest in early adulthood.
     TRUE or FALSE

21. Stress results when you appraise a situation or event as taxing or exceeding your personal, social, or other resources and endangering your well-being.
     TRUE or FALSE

22. Experiencing stressful events results in lower immune system functioning.
     TRUE or FALSE

23. People with the Type B behavior pattern tend to be intensely competitive, angry, hostile, restless, aggressive, and impatient.
     TRUE or FALSE

24. Physical exercise slows the physiological aging process.
     TRUE or FALSE

25. People who exercise aerobically report lower levels of stress, better moods, and better cognitive functioning.

TRUE or FALSE

13.2 COGNITIVE DEVELOPMENT

TO MASTER THE LEARNING OBJECTIVES:

How does practical intelligence develop in adulthood?

- Define practical intelligence, and explain how it differs from traditional measures of intelligence.

- Describe the applications of practical intelligence.

- Explain the differences between the mechanics and pragmatics of intelligence.

How does a person become an expert?

- Describe the differences in the thinking of experts and novices, and describe the developmental course of expert performance.

- Define encapsulation, and explain how it is related to the ability to explain how one arrives at a particular answer.

What is meant by lifelong learning? What differences are there between adults and young people in how they learn?

- Explain why lifelong learning is becoming the norm.

- Describe the four ways in which adult learners differ from younger learners.

13.2 KNOW THE TERMS

Encapsulation	Practical intelligence
Mechanics	Pragmatics

1. _____ involves the skills and knowledge that people use to adapt to their physical and social environments.

2. The _____ of intelligence reflect the aspects of intelligence that comprise fluid intelligence.

3. The _____ of intelligence are the aspects of intelligence that reflect crystallized intelligence.

4. In expertise, the process of thinking becoming connected to the products of thinking is called _____.

13.2 KNOW THE DETAILS OF COGNITIVE DEVELOPMENT

1. Cognitive development goes through many rapid changes during middle adulthood.
   TRUE or FALSE

2. Traditional intelligence tests provide a good measure of practical intelligence.
   TRUE or FALSE

3. Practical intelligence decreases rapidly during middle adulthood.
   TRUE or FALSE

4. Late middle-aged adults most often take a passive-dependent or avoidant-denial approach to dealing with highly emotional problems.
   TRUE or FALSE

5. Middle-aged adults are less likely than adolescents or young adults to use problem-focused strategies in dealing with instrumental issues such as home management.
   TRUE or FALSE

6. People with a higher level of practical intelligence are less equipped to deal with rapid change.
   TRUE or FALSE

7. The mechanics of intelligence are comparable to fluid intelligence.
   TRUE or FALSE

8. The pragmatics of intelligence are more closely associated with neurophysiology than with sociocultural forces.
   TRUE or FALSE

9. Individuals who are experts in one area tend to be experts in most areas.
   TRUE or FALSE

10. Experts are more likely than beginners to skip steps when solving a problem.
    TRUE or FALSE

11. Encapsulation can hinder the ability to explain to others how to solve a problem.
    TRUE or FALSE

12. Adults are more willing to learn things about abstract, hypothetical situations than about things needed to solve real-world problems.

    TRUE or FALSE

13. The need for lifelong learning is increasing.

    TRUE or FALSE

13.3 PERSONALITY

TO MASTER THE LEARNING OBJECTIVES:

What is the five-factor model? What evidence is there for stability in personality traits?

- Describe Costa and McCrae's five dimensions of personality: neuroticism, agreeableness, openness to experience, conscientiousness, and extraversion.

- Describe the evidence that personality traits remain stable across adulthood.

- Describe the evidence for personality change during adulthood.

What changes occur in people's priorities and personal concerns? How does a person achieve generativity? How is midlife best described?

- Describe how priorities change over the course of one's lifetime.

- Explain generativity and stagnation and ethnic differences in generativity.

- Explain whether or not the midlife crisis is universal.

13.3 KNOW THE TERMS

Agreeableness	Narrative
Conscientiousness	Neuroticism
Ego resilience	Openness to experience
Extraversion	Stagnation
Generativity	

1. People who are high on the personality dimension of _____ tend to be anxious, hostile, self-conscious, depressed, vulnerable, and impulsive.

2. People who are high on the personality dimension of _____ love social interaction, like to talk, take charge easily, are very energetic, and prefer challenging and stimulating environments.

3. People who are high on the dimension of _____ tend to have a vivid imagination and dreams, appreciate art, and will try anything once.

4. People who are high on _____ are caring, accepting of others, and willing to work with others.

5. Those with high levels of _____ are hard working, ambitious, energetic, scrupulous, and persevering.

6. According to Erikson, _____ occurs when middle-aged adults try to help younger generations to ensure the continuation of society.

7. According to Erikson, _____ occurs when middle-aged adults cannot meet the needs of their children or cannot mentor younger adults.

8. A life story, or _____, helps create a person's identity.

9. A powerful personality resource that enables people to handle midlife is called _____.

13.3 KNOW THE DETAILS OF PERSONALITY

1. People who are high on the neuroticism dimension of personality thrive on social interaction, like to talk, take charge easily, like to keep busy, and have boundless energy.
TRUE or FALSE

2. Individuals who are high on the openness to experience dimension of personality tend to have a vivid imagination and dreams, an appreciation of art, and a strong desire to try anything once.
TRUE or FALSE

3. The five-factor model suggests that personality is stable over long periods of time.
TRUE or FALSE

4. According to Erikson, helping others in order to ensure the continuation of society by guiding the next generation becomes more important during middle adulthood.
TRUE or FALSE

5. Generative concern has not been found to be related to life satisfaction or overall happiness.
TRUE or FALSE

6. The majority of research evidence does not support the view of a universal stage, such as a midlife crisis, that everyone experiences at the same point in life.
   TRUE or FALSE

7. Individuals low in ego resilience are more likely to handle midlife successfully.
   TRUE or FALSE

13.4 FAMILY DYNAMICS AND MIDDLE AGE

TO MASTER THE LEARNING OBJECTIVES:

Who are the kinkeepers of families?

- Describe the role of kinkeeper that many middle-aged mothers assume.

- Define what is meant by the sandwich generation.

How does the relationship between middle-aged parents and their young adult children change?

- Describe how the relationship between parents and children changes as the children move from adolescence to young adulthood.

- Explain how most parents feel when they have an empty nest.

- Explain the reasons why adult children return home.

How do middle-aged adults deal with their aging parents?

- Describe the gender difference in caring for aging parents.

- Define filial obligation.

- Describe the two factors that contribute to negative feelings about caring for one's aging parents.

- Explain some of the psychological costs of caregiving.

- Describe ethnic differences in adult caregivers' stress.

What styles of grandparenthood do middle-aged adults experience? How do grandchildren and grandparents interact?

- Explain how personal and social dimensions of grandparenting influence grandparenting.

- Describe the different meanings of grandparenthood.

- Describe ethnic differences in grandparenthood.

- Describe how the role of grandparent has changed in recent years.

13.4 KNOW THE TERMS

Filial obligation   **Sandwich generation**

Kinkeeper

1. Middle-aged mothers often take on the role of _____ because they gather the family together for celebrations and keep family members in touch with each other.

2. Middle-aged adults are sometimes called the _____ because they must juggle the demands of their children and their aging parents.

3. The feeling of responsibility for caring for one's aging parents is called _____.

13.4 KNOW THE DETAILS OF FAMILY DYNAMICS AND MIDDLE AGE

1. Fathers are more likely than mothers to take on the role of kinkeeper.

   TRUE or FALSE

2. Parent-child relationships usually improve when children become adults.

   TRUE or FALSE

3. Female adult children are more likely than male adult children to move back in with their parents.

   TRUE or FALSE

4. Daughters and sons are equally likely to provide care for their aging parents.

   TRUE or FALSE

5. Becoming a caregiver to aging parents usually has no impact on a woman's employment situation.

   TRUE or FALSE

6. Caring for aging parents can bring parents and their adult children closer together.

   TRUE or FALSE

7. The social dimension of grandparenting includes societal needs and expectations of what grandparents are to do.

   TRUE or FALSE

8. The ways that grandparents and grandchildren interact varies in different ethnic groups.

   TRUE or FALSE

341

9. Fictive grandparenting is when grandparents request that their grandchildren be allowed to live with them to ensure that the grandchildren learn the native ways.

   TRUE or FALSE

10. Fewer grandparents today are serving as surrogate parents for their grandchildren than they did in years past.

    TRUE or FALSE

SUMMARY

13.1 PHYSICAL CHANGES AND HEALTH

1. **How does appearance change in middle adulthood?**

   Some of the signs of aging that appear in middle age include gray hair, _____, and _____.

2. **What changes occur in bones and joints?**

   An important change, especially in women, is loss of bone mass, which in severe form may result in the disease _____. Osteoarthritis generally becomes noticeable in late middle or early old age. Rheumatoid arthritis is a more common form affecting _____, wrists, and ankles.

3. **What reproductive changes occur in men and women in middle age?**

   The _____ (loss of the ability to bear children by natural means) and _____ (cessation of menstruation) occur in the 40s and 50s. Most women do not have severe physical symptoms associated with the hormonal changes. Menopausal hormone therapy is a _____ approach to treatment of menopausal symptoms. Reproductive changes in men are much less dramatic; even older men are typically still fertile. Physical changes do affect sexual response.

4. **What is stress? How does it affect physical and psychological health?**

   In the stress and coping paradigm, stress results from a person's _____ of an event as taxing his or her resources. Daily hassles are viewed as the primary source of stress. The types of situations people find stressful change across adulthood. Family and _____ issues are more important for young and middle-aged adults; _____ issues are more important for older adults.

   Type A behavior pattern is characterized by intense _____, anger, hostility, restlessness, aggression, and _____. It is linked with a person's first heart attack and

_____ disease. Type B behavior pattern is the opposite of Type A, and is associated with lower risk of first heart attack, but poorer prognosis afterward should one occur. Following an initial heart attack, Type A behavior pattern individuals have a _____ recovery rate. Although stress is unrelated to serious psychopathology, it is related to social isolation and distrust.

5. **What benefits are there to exercise?**

Aerobic exercise has numerous benefits, especially to cardiovascular health and fitness. Other physical benefits include lower _____, better strength, endurance, flexibility, and _____. Possible psychological benefits include lower levels of _____, better moods, and better _____ functioning. The best results are obtained through a _____ exercise program maintained throughout adulthood.

13.2 COGNITIVE DEVELOPMENT

1. **How does practical intelligence develop in adulthood?**

Practical intelligence does not appear to _____ appreciably until late life. The _____ of intelligence are related to the neurophysiology of the brain and the _____ of intelligence are associated more with bodies of knowledge that are available to someone.

2. **How does a person become an expert?**

People tend to become experts in some areas and not in others. Experts tend to think in more _____ ways than novices and are able to _____ steps in solving problems, which may make it difficult for them to explain solutions to novices. Expert performance tends to peak in middle age.

3. **What is meant by lifelong learning? What differences are there between adults and young people in how they learn?**

Adults learn differently than children and youth. Older students need practical _____ and rationale for learning and are more motivated to learn by _____ factors.

13.3 PERSONALITY

1. **What is the five-factor model? What evidence is there for stability in personality traits?**

    The five-factor model postulates five dimensions of personality: neuroticism, _____, openness to experience, _____, and conscientiousness. Several longitudinal studies indicate that personality traits show long-term _____, but increasing evidence shows that traits change across adulthood.

2. **What changes occur in people's priorities and personal concerns? How does a person achieve generativity? How is midlife best described?**

    Erikson believed that middle-aged adults become more concerned with doing for others and passing social values and skills to the _____, a set of behaviors and beliefs he labeled generativity. Those who do not achieve generativity are thought to experience _____. For the most part, there is little support for the theories based on the premise that all adults go through predictable life stages at specific points in time. Individuals may face similar stresses, but transitions may occur at any time in adulthood. Research evidence indicates that not everyone experiences a _____ at midlife.

13.4 FAMILY DYNAMICS AND MIDDLE AGE

1. **Who are the kinkeepers in families?**

    Middle-aged mothers tend to adopt the role of _____ in order to keep family traditions alive and as a way to _____ generations. Middle age is sometimes referred to as the sandwich generation due to its position between one's children and _____.

2. **How does the relationship between middle-aged parents and their young adult children change?**

    Parent-child relations _____ dramatically when children emerge from adolescence. Most parents _____ having an empty nest. Difficulties emerge to the extent that raising children has been a primary source of personal identity for parents. However, once children have left home, parents still provide considerable support. Children move back home primarily for _____ or child-rearing reasons. Neither parents nor children generally prefer this arrangement.

3.   **How do middle-aged adults deal with their aging parents?**

Caring for aging parents usually falls to a daughter or daughter-in-law. Caregiving creates a stressful situation due to conflicting feelings and roles; the potential for conflict is high as is _____ pressure. Caregiving stress is usually greater in women, who must deal with multiple roles. Older parents are often _____ with the situation as well.

4.   **What styles of grandparenthood do middle-aged adults experience? How do grandchildren and grandparents interact?**

Becoming a grandparent means assuming new roles. Styles of interaction vary across grandchildren and with the _____ of the grandchild. Also relevant are the personal and social dimensions of grandparenting. Grandparents derive several different types of meaning regardless of style. Most children and young adults report _____ relationships with grandparents, and young adults feel a responsibility to care for them if necessary. Ethnic differences exist in the degree to which grandparents take an active role in their grandchildren's lives. In an increasingly mobile society, grandparents are more frequently assuming a _____ relationship with their grandchildren. An increasing number of grandparents serve as the _____ parent. These arrangements are typically stressful.

TEST YOURSELF

MULTIPLE-CHOICE QUESTIONS

1.   Which of the following is associated with an increased risk of osteoporosis?

   a.   Eating foods high in calcium

   b.   Reducing alcohol intake

   c.   Exercising

   d.   Being postmenopausal

2.   The point at which menstruation stops during middle adulthood is called

   a.   the climacteric.

   b.   perimenopause.

   c.   menopause.

   d.   hormone replacement.

345

3. A decline in estrogen is related to

    a. a decreased risk of osteoporosis.

    b. a decreased risk of memory loss.

    c. an increased risk of extreme weight loss.

    d. an increased risk of cardiovascular disease.

4. Menopausal hormone therapy for women during the climacteric increases the risk of

    a. osteoporosis.

    b. colorectal cancer.

    c. breast cancer.

    d. hot flashes.

5. Men

    a. continue to produce sperm at a constant rate throughout adulthood.

    b. experience a gradual decline in sperm production but remain fertile throughout adulthood.

    c. experience a dramatic decline in sperm production in middle adulthood, comparable to the changes women go through during menopause, and lose fertility at that time.

    d. normally experience a complete loss of fertility during late adulthood.

6. Who is likely to have the highest level of stress?

    a. Dan, a 50-year-old male business executive

    b. Stella, a 45-year-old waitress

    c. Martha, a 70-year-old female community volunteer

    d. Raymond, a 75-year-old male retiree

7. The _____ paradigm emphasizes the interaction between a person and the environment and is the dominant framework used to study stress.

    a. five-factor

    b. encapsulation

    c. exercised-unexercised abilities

    d. stress and coping

8. _____ results when you appraise a situation or event as exceeding your personal, social, or other resources.

    a. Type A behavior

    b. Type B behavior

    c. Coping

    d. Stress

9. Harry hates to wait in lines, is very competitive, has a quick temper, and is often hostile toward others. Harry shows many symptoms of a _____ behavior pattern.

    a. Type A

    b. Type B

    c. Type C

    d. Type D

10. Rick has a Type B behavior pattern, whereas John has a Type A behavior pattern. John is

    a. more likely to have a heart attack and less likely to recover from one.

    b. less likely to have a heart attack and less likely to recover from one.

    c. more likely to have a heart attack and more likely to recover from one.

    d. less likely to have a heart attack but more likely to recover from one.

11. Aerobic exercise is associated with

    a. improved cardiovascular functioning.

    b. higher blood pressure.

    c. decreased flexibility.

    d. higher levels of stress.

12. The broad range of skills related to how individuals shape, select, or adapt to their physical and social environments is referred to as

    a. fluid intelligence.

    b. crystallized intelligence.

    c. practical intelligence.

    d. unexercised ability.

13. Which of the following tasks would be most appropriate to use as a measure of practical intelligence?

    a. Reconciling a sample bank statement with a checkbook register

    b. Memorizing a list of 50 unrelated words

    c. Naming as many words as one can think of that begin with the letter "t"

    d. Using blocks to reconstruct a pattern shown in a picture

14. Which of the following is NOT a way that practical intelligence problems differ from traditional intelligence test problems?

    a. People are more motivated to solve them.

    b. They rely more heavily on personal experience.

    c. They are less realistic.

    d. They usually have more than one correct answer.

15. When Margaret is faced with a practical problem, she tackles it head on and does something about it. What kind of approach does Margaret use to solve problems?

    a. Passive-dependent behavior

    b. Avoidant thinking and denial

    c. Cognitive-analysis

    d. Problem-focused action

16. When solving a problem in their areas of expertise, experts are more likely than novices to

    a. follow the rules.

    b. skip steps.

    c. be faster in terms of raw processing speed.

    d. be less flexible.

17. Encapsulation occurs when

    a. fluid intelligence increases and crystallized intelligence decreases.

    b. experts instruct novices in how to solve a problem.

    c. one withdraws from a situation in order to solve a problem.

    d. the processes of thinking become connected to the products of thinking.

18. Which of the following statements comparing learning during adulthood to learning during youth is true?

    a. Adults are more willing to learn to deal with abstract, hypothetical situations than with real-world problems.

    b. Most adults are more motivated to learn by external factors (e.g., job promotion) than by internal factors (e.g., self-esteem).

    c. Adults enter a learning situation with less varied experience on which to build.

    d. Adults have a higher need to know why they should learn something before undertaking it.

19. _____ and _____ are part of the five-factor model of personality.

    a. The Type A behavior pattern; the Type B behavior pattern

    b. Extraversion; conscientiousness

    c. Unexercised abilities; optimally exercised abilities

    d. Generativity; stagnation

20. Raymond is highly anxious, hostile, self-conscious, and impulsive. Raymond appears to be high on the _____ personality dimension.

    a. extraversion

    b. neuroticism

    c. openness to new experience

    d. conscientiousness

21. Costa and McCrae's research examining personality traits has found evidence suggesting that

    a. personality traits are generally stable across adulthood.

    b. personality traits change greatly across adulthood.

    c. personality is primarily due to environmental factors.

    d. personality is primarily due to age factors.

22. According to Erikson, _____ becomes of increased importance during middle adulthood.

    a. identity

    b. integrity

    c. intimacy

    d. generativity

23. In McAdams' multidimensional model of generativity, individuals derive personal meaning from being generative through

    a. generative action.

    b. generative concern.

    c. cultural demands.

    d. constructing a life story or narration.

24. Research evidence suggests that

    a. midlife is no more or less traumatic than other periods of life.

    b. midlife is slightly more likely to be a time of crisis than are other periods of life.

    c. midlife crisis is a universal stage.

    d. no fundamental changes of any kind occur during adulthood.

25. _____ appears to be a key factor in how well people negotiate the challenges and issues of midlife.

    a. Type A versus Type B personality

    b. Stress

    c. Ego resilience

    d. Encapsulation

26. _____ are most likely to take on the role of kinkeeper.

    a. Sons

    b. Young daughters

    c. Fathers

    d. Mothers

27. Who is a member of the sandwich generation?

    a. 66-year-old Mary, who has a husband, three daughters, and two sons

    b. 48-year-old Jan, who has two daughters in college and parents who live with her

    c. 28-year-old Shauna, who lives with her parents

    d. 54-year-old Sandy, who has an older brother and a younger sister

28. Adult children are more likely to move back in with their parents

    a. when the parents are in poor health.

    b. when adult children had high college GPAs.

    c. when adult children have a low sense of autonomy.

    d. when parents were verbally or physically abusive.

29. Who is most likely to provide care for aging parents?

    a. Sons and daughters

    b. Sons and daughters-in-law

    c. Daughters and sons-in-law

    d. Daughters and daughters-in-law

30. The sense of responsibility that adult children feel to care for their parent if necessary is called

    a. filial obligation.

    b. immortality through clan.

    c. cultural conservator.

    d. kinkeeper.

31. Adults who fill in for missing or deceased biological grandparents are engaged in the role of

    a. cultural conservator.

    b. fictive grandparenting.

    c. primary caregiver.

    d. story teller.

32. Grandparents who request that their grandchildren be allowed to live with them in order to ensure that the grandchildren learn the native ways have a _____ grandparenting style.

    a. fictive

    b. cultural conservator

    c. valued elder

    d. centrality

ESSAY QUESTIONS

1. In the past few months, your mother has had headaches frequently and often feels very hot when no one else in the room does. In fact, sometimes she wakes in the middle of the night drenched with perspiration. Your mother has heard about the use of hormone replacement therapy to relieve the symptoms during the climacteric, but she also has heard that this therapy causes cancer. What can you tell your mother about the benefits and risks of menopausal hormone therapy?

2. Your 40-year-old friend Inga recently commented on the fact that many of her same-age friends have begun to exercise regularly. Inga has never been overweight so she has never felt the need to exercise but now she is wondering if her friends know something that she doesn't. What can you tell Inga about the physical and psychological benefits associated with a program of regular exercise?

3. Your friend Lynn does not know how to cook so you send her to learn from your friend Bill who is an expert cook. After a few lessons, Lynn becomes frustrated and tells you that she could never learn to cook from Bill because he adds ingredients that aren't in the recipes, he doesn't measure things carefully, and he doesn't do a very good job of explaining what he is doing. What can you tell Lynn about the differences between thinking in experts and novices that might explain her frustration?

4. Your 55-year-old friend Hattie was wondering when she was going to experience her midlife crisis. She told you that she has been happy with being a teacher, has been happy with her children, and has been satisfied with her marriage, but she keeps hearing about the midlife crisis. What can you tell Hattie about the evidence for a universal midlife crisis?

5. Your friends Miriam and Jake had been living in an empty nest since their last child left home a year ago, but three months ago, their son Stan moved back home. Both Miriam and Jake think that Stan is very unusual. What can you tell Miriam and Jake about the frequency of young adults returning home and the factors related to it?

6.   Your friend Mona's mother recently moved in with her. Mona told you that she feels pulled in many directions because she needs to do things for her children, her mother, and her husband. She also wonders if they can afford to support her mother. Sometimes Mona feels angry and frustrated and wishes that her mother didn't live with her, and she feels guilty about those feelings. What can you tell Mona about the common effects of caregiving that might help alleviate some of her guilt?

ANSWERS WITH PAGE REFERENCES

13.1 KNOW THE TERMS

1. Skeletal maturity (457)

2. osteoporosis (457)

3. dual-energy x-ray absorptionmetry (459)

4. selective estrogen receptor modulator (460)

5. osteoarthritis (460)

6. wear-and-tear (460)

7. rheumatoid arthritis (460)

8. climacteric (462)

9. menopause (462)

10. Perimenopause (462)

11. Menopausal hormone (463)

12. stress and coping (466)

13. coping (467)

14. Type A (468)

15. Type B (468)

16. posttraumatic stress disorder (468)

17. Aerobic exercise (469)

13.1 KNOW THE DETAILS OF PHYSICAL CHANGES AND HEALTH

1. T, 456	8. F, 462	15. T, 465	22. T, 467
2. F, 457	9. F, 462	16. T, 465	23. F, 468
3. T, 457	10. T, 463	17. T, 465	24. T, 469
4. F, 457	11. T, 462	18. T, 465	25. T, 469
5. T, 458	12. T, 463	19. F, 466	
6. T, 460	13. T, 463	20. F, 466	
7. F, 460	14. F, 464	21. T, 466	

13.2 KNOW THE TERMS

1. Practical intelligence (471)

2. mechanics (472)

3. pragmatics (472)

4. encapsulation (474)

13.2 KNOW THE DETAILS OF COGNITIVE DEVELOPMENT

1. F, 470	5. F, 472	9. F, 474	13. T, 476
2. F, 471	6. F, 472	10. T, 474	
3. F, 472	7. T, 472	11. T, 474	
4. T, 472	8. F, 472	12. F, 476	

13.3 KNOW THE TERMS

1. neuroticism (477)

2. extraversion (477)

3. openness to experience (477)

4. agreeableness (477)

5. conscientiousness (477)

6. generativity (480)

7. stagnation (480)

8. narrative (480)

9. ego resilience (482)

13.3 KNOW THE DETAILS OF PERSONALITY

1. F, 477	4. T, 480	7. F, 482
2. T, 477	5. F, 481	
3. T, 478	6. T, 482	

13.4 KNOW THE TERMS

1. kinkeepers (483)

2. sandwich generation (483)

3. filial obligation (486)

353

13.4 KNOW THE DETAILS OF FAMILY DYNAMICS AND MIDDLE AGE

1. F, 483	4. F, 486	7. T, 489	10. F, 490
2. T, 484	5. F, 487	8. T, 490	
3. F, 485	6. T, 487	9. F, 490	

SUMMARY

13.1 PHYSICAL CHANGES AND HEALTH

1. wrinkles (456); weight gain (457).

2. osteoporosis (457); fingers (461)

3. climacteric (462); menopause (462); controversial (464)

4. appraisal (466); career (467); health (467); competitiveness (468); impatience (468); cardiovascular (468); faster (468)

5. blood pressure (469); coordination (469); stress (469); cognitive (469); moderate (470)

13.2 COGNITIVE DEVELOPMENT

1. decline (472); mechanics (472); pragmatics (472)

2. flexible (474); skip (474)

3. connections (476); internal (476)

13.3 PERSONALITY

1. extraversion (477); agreeableness (477); stability (478),

2. next generation (480); stagnation (480).; crisis (482)

13.4 FAMILY DYNAMICS AND MIDDLE AGE

1. kinkeepers (483); link (483); aging parents (483)

2. improve (484); look forward to (484); financial (485),

3. financial (487); dissatisfied (488)

4. age (489); positive (489); distant (490); custodial (490)

MULTIPLE CHOICE

1. d, 457	10. c, 468	19. b, 477	28. c, 485
2. c, 462	11. a, 469	20. b, 477	29. d, 485
3. d, 463	12. c, 471	21. a, 478	30. a, 486
4. c, 464	13. a, 471	22. d, 480	31. b, 490
5. b, 465	14. c, 471	23. d, 480	32. b, 490
6. b, 465	15. d, 472	24. a, 482	
7. d, 466	16. b, 474	25. c, 482	
8. d, 466	17. d, 474	26. d, 483	
9. a, 468	18. d, 475	27. b, 483	

ESSAY QUESTIONS

1. During the climacteric, there is a dramatic drop in the production of the female hormone estrogen. This drop in estrogen leads to many physical symptoms such as hot flashes, night sweats, vaginal dryness, changes in cholesterol levels, and the eventual end of menstruation. For most women, these symptoms are not severe, but your mother sounds like an exception to this rule. Menopausal hormone therapy involves giving women low doses of estrogen and progestin to alleviate the symptoms associated with the climacteric. Research has shown that women who are on MHT do show an increased risk of breast cancer, heart attack, stroke, and blood clots. However, women on MHT did have fewer bone fractures and a lowered risk of colorectal cancer. Your mother should discuss the various risks and benefits of MHT with her physician. (462-464)

2. Adults who engage in moderate aerobic exercise on a regular basis show better cardiovascular functioning, lower blood pressure, greater strength, greater endurance, better coordination, and better flexibility. People who exercise regularly report lower levels of stress, better moods, and better cognitive functioning. While Inga does not need to exercise for appearance reasons, she would benefit from exercise. (469-470)

3. Bill is not trying to frustrate Lynn; he is merely acting like an expert. Experts often skip steps that novices need to follow. Experts often don't follow the rules (or the recipes) like novices do. Experts are more flexible, creative, and curious and they have superior strategies for accomplishing a task. As experts' thinking becomes more encapsulated (the process of thinking becomes more connected to the products of thinking), experts become more efficient thinkers. Bill is merely using his expert cooking knowledge to be creative, skip unnecessary steps, etc. Bill's expertise also means that he doesn't need to think about each step, so he may not be very good at explaining what he is doing. Perhaps Lynn should take cooking lessons from someone who is not an expert or who is an experienced teacher. (473-475)

4. Erikson thought that people experience fundamental changes in priorities and personal concerns during middle adulthood, and Jung believed that adults may experience a midlife crisis. Theories such as these have led to a popular idea of a midlife crisis. In fact, most Americans believe that they have had or will have a midlife crisis, but most research evidence does not support age-related, major changes. For the vast majority of people, midlife is no more or less traumatic than any other period of life. Also, people who enter midlife with high ego resilience are more likely to see midlife as a time of opportunity for growth and change while people with low ego resilience see midlife as a time of stagnation or decline. So, Hattie should not feel unusual about not having had a midlife crisis because many people do not have them, and they do not occur at a specific age if they do occur. (481-482)

5. You can tell Miriam and Jake that Stan is not that unusual. In fact, approximately half of all young adults in the United States return to their parents' home to live at least once after leaving. "Boomerang kids" who are most likely to move back are male, have low college GPAs, have a low sense of autonomy, and expect that their parents would provide a large portion of their income following graduation. So, Miriam and Jake should realize that Stan is not unusual by moving back home. (484-485)

6. Mona's feelings are typical of many middle-aged adults who are caring for their children and their aging parents. Most aging adults and their children report that they would prefer not living together. In fact, when they do live together, there may be conflicts over daily routines and lifestyles. Feelings of depression, resentment, anger, and guilt are all common in caregivers. The feeling of financial burden also is typical. Mona may feel less stress if she can make arrangements so that caring for her mother is less confining and infringes less on the other aspects of her life. (488)

THE PERSONAL CONTEXT OF
LATER LIFE

14.1 What Are Older Adults Like?

14.2 Physical Changes and Health

14.3 Cognitive Processes

14.4 Mental Health and Intervention

This chapter focuses on the physical changes, cognitive changes, and mental health issues that are important to aging individuals.

14.1 WHAT ARE OLDER ADULTS LIKE?

TO MASTER THE LEARNING OBJECTIVES:

What are the characteristics of older adults in the population?

- Describe how the shape of the population pyramid has changed since 1900.

- Describe how the population of developing countries is changing.

- Describe the composition of the future older adult population in terms of gender, ethnicity, and education.

- Describe how prepared the United States is for the financial strain of increased numbers of elderly.

How long will most people live? What factors influence this?

- Define the average life expectancy, and describe the factors that have led to its increase.

- Define average life expectancy, useful life expectancy, and maximum life expectancy.

- Describe the genetic factors that are linked to longevity.

- Describe the environmental factors that are related to longevity.

- Describe ethnic differences in longevity.

- Describe the gender differences in longevity.

- Describe international differences in longevity.

What is the distinction between the third and fourth age?

- Define the third age and explain how it differs from the fourth age.

14.1 KNOW THE TERMS

Average	Maximum
Demographers	Population pyramid
Longevity	Useful

1. People who study population trends are called _____.

2. A _____ is a graphic technique that shows the distribution of people of various ages in a population.

3. The number of years that a person will live is influenced by both genetic and environmental factors; it is called _____.

4. The age at which half of the people born in a particular year will have died is called _____ life expectancy.

5. The number of years that a person lives that is free from debilitating chronic disease and impairment is called _____ life expectancy.

6. The oldest age to which any person lives is _____ life expectancy.

14.1 KNOW THE DETAILS OF WHAT ARE OLDER ADULTS LIKE?

1. There have never been as many older adults alive as there are now.

   TRUE or FALSE

2. By 2050, the number of older adults in developing countries will have increased dramatically.

   TRUE or FALSE

3. Older women outnumber older men in the U.S.

   TRUE or FALSE

4. The number of older adults is growing more rapidly among European Americans than among ethnic minority groups.

   TRUE or FALSE

5. In the future, older adults are expected to be better educated than older adults are today.

   TRUE or FALSE

6. Internationally, the number of older adults is growing slowly.

   TRUE or FALSE

7. Longevity is determined solely by genetic factors.

   TRUE or FALSE

8. Average life expectancy is the number of years that a person is free from debilitating chronic disease and impairment.

   TRUE or FALSE

9. The current maximum life expectancy is around 75 years of age.

   TRUE or FALSE

10. Social class is related to longevity.

    TRUE or FALSE

11. The average life expectancy is the same for all ethnic groups.

    TRUE or FALSE

12. African Americans who survive to age 85 tend to be healthier than their European-American counterparts.

    TRUE or FALSE

13. Women's average longevity is about five years more, on average, than men's at birth.

    TRUE or FALSE

359

14. Longevity is very similar in different countries around the world.

TRUE or FALSE

15. The term "the third age" is used to refer to the young-old (ages 60-80) population.

TRUE or FALSE

14.2 PHYSICAL CHANGES AND HEALTH

TO MASTER THE LEARNING OBJECTIVES:

What are the major biological theories of aging?

- Describe the wear-and-tear, cellular, and programmed cell death theories of aging.

What physiological changes normally occur in later life?

- Define neurofibrillary tangles, and describe why they are a problem.

- Describe the changes in the dendrites that occur with aging.

- Define neuritic plaques, and explain why they are a problem.

- Describe age changes in levels of neurotransmitters.

- Explain what imaging of the brain tells us about age-related declines in cognitive functioning.

- Describe the changes in the cardiovascular system with age.

- Explain the causes and effects of cerebral vascular accidents.

- Describe the cause and progression of vascular dementia.

- Describe how cerebral vascular accidents and vascular dementia are diagnosed.

- Describe how the respiratory system changes with age, and define chronic obstructive pulmonary disease.

- Describe the causes, symptoms, and treatments for Parkinson's disease.

- Describe the changes that occur in the eye with age, including presbyopia.

- Define presbycusis and its causes.

- Describe age-related changes in the sense of smell.

- Describe the consequences of age-related changes in balance.

- Describe the changes that one can make to one's home so that falls are less likely to occur.

What are the principal health issues for older adults?

- Describe the sleep disturbances that are common in older adults, and describe their possible causes.

- Describe the nutritional needs of older adults.

- Describe how the risk of getting cancer changes with age, and explain the importance of early detection and screening.

- Explain how immigrant status affects health.

14.2 KNOW THE TERMS

Cellular	Parkinson's
Cerebral vascular accidents	Presbycusis
Chronic obstructive pulmonary	Presbyopia
Circadian rhythm	Programmed
Cross-linking	Stroke
Free radicals	Telomeres
Neurofibrillary tangles	Transient ischemic attacks (TIAs)
Neuritic plaques	Vascular dementia
Neurotransmitters	Wear-and-tear

1. _____ theories of aging suggest that aging is genetically programmed.

2. The _____ theory of aging suggests that aging is a result of the body deteriorating and wearing out over time.

3. _____ are chemicals that are produced during normal cell metabolism that bind with other substances in cells, which cause cellular damage that impairs functioning.

4. _____ theories of aging assume that certain proteins interact randomly with body tissue such as muscles and arteries, causing them to be less flexible.

5. _____ theories of aging focus on processes that occur in individual cells that cause deterioration or the build-up of harmful substances over one's lifetime.

6. The tips of the chromosomes are called _____.

7. When fibers of the axon become twisted, the resulting spiral-shaped masses that are formed are called _____.

8. Damaged and dying neurons that collect around a core of protein produce _____.

9. Chemicals that allow communication between neurons are called _____.

10. _____ is another name for cerebral vascular accident.

11. _____ are caused by interruptions of blood flow to the brain due to a blockage or bleeding in a cerebral artery.

12. _____ involve interruption in blood flow to the brain and are often an early warning sign of stroke.

13. Numerous small cerebral vascular accidents can lead to _____.

14. The most common form of chronic respiratory disease in older adults is _____ disease.

15. _____ disease is caused by deterioration of the neurons in the midbrain, and it is characterized by very slow walking and hand tremors.

16. The difficulty in seeing close objects clearly is called _____.

17. A substantial loss in the ability to hear high-pitched tones is called _____.

18. The disruption of one's sleep-wake cycle, or _____, can lead to sleep disturbances.

14.2 KNOW THE DETAILS OF PHYSICAL CHANGES AND HEALTH

1. Programmed theories of aging state that aging is genetically programmed.
   TRUE or FALSE

2. Wear-and-tear theories explain most aspects of aging.
   TRUE or FALSE

3. Antioxidants prevent the formation of free radicals.
   TRUE or FALSE

4. Cellular theories explain aging by focusing on processes that occur within individual cells, leading to the buildup of harmful substances over a lifetime.
   TRUE or FALSE

5. Telomeres increase the number of cell divisions.
   TRUE or FALSE

6. Large numbers of neurofibrillary tangles are associated with Alzheimer's disease.
   TRUE or FALSE

7. With age, some dendrites shrivel up and die whereas others continue to grow.
   TRUE or FALSE

8. With age, the levels of neurotransmitters increase.
    TRUE or FALSE

9. Functional neuroimaging provides highly detailed images of anatomical features in the brain.
    TRUE or FALSE

10. The incidence of cardiovascular diseases increases significantly with age.
    TRUE or FALSE

11. Transient ischemic attacks (TIAs) are a form of incapacitating respiratory disease.
    TRUE or FALSE

12. Vascular dementia always has a gradual onset and progresses gradually.
    TRUE or FALSE

13. Chronic obstructive pulmonary disease is the most common incapacitating respiratory disease among older adults.
    TRUE or FALSE

14. Very slow walking, difficulty getting into and out of chairs, and a slow hand tremor are symptoms of Parkinson's disease.
    TRUE or FALSE

15. Hearing loss is one of the best-known normative changes with age.
    TRUE or FALSE

16. Presbycusis causes older adults' vision to become more susceptible to glare.
    TRUE or FALSE

17. Smell declines more than taste in late adulthood.
    TRUE or FALSE

18. Sensory changes may lead to accidents around the home.
    TRUE or FALSE

19. Older adults have more trouble sleeping than do younger adults.
    TRUE or FALSE

20. The incidence of cancer decreases with age.
    TRUE or FALSE

14.3 COGNITIVE PROCESSES

TO MASTER THE LEARNING OBJECTIVES:

What changes occur in information processing as people age? How do these changes relate to everyday life?

- Describe how practice and experience influence psychomotor speed.

- Describe the physical changes that affect driving.

What changes occur in memory with age? What can be done to remediate these changes?

- Describe what happens to working memory with age and how this affects cognitive performance.

- Define explicit, implicit, episodic, and semantic memory, and describe the typical age differences in each.

- Describe which autobiographical memories are most likely to be recalled.

- Describe the two steps that someone should take when trying to determine if one is suffering from abnormal memory problems.

- Explain the difference between internal and external memory aids, and describe how the E-I-E-I-O framework combines these types of memory and memory aids.

What are creativity and wisdom, and how do they relate to age?

- Explain how creative output varies across disciplines and across adulthood.

- Describe what neuroimaging tells us about the brains of creative people.

- Describe the four characteristics of wisdom that Baltes and his colleagues have described.

- Explain how life experiences are related to wisdom.

- Describe the three factors that seem to foster wisdom.

14.3 KNOW THE TERMS

Autobiographical	**Internal**
Episodic	**Psychomotor speed**
Explicit	**Semantic**
External	**Useful field of view**
Implicit	**Working memory**

1. The speed with which one can make a particular response is called _____.

2. The area from which one can extract visual information in a single glance without turning one's head or moving one's eyes is known as the _____.

3. The processes and structures involved in holding information in mind while simultaneously using it is called _____.

4. _____ memory involves the conscious and intentional recall of information that is learned and remembered at a specific time.

5. _____ memory involves the unconscious and effortless recall of information learned at an earlier time.

6. The type of explicit memory that has to do with the conscious recollection of information from a specific time or event is called _____ memory.

7. The type of explicit memory that involves remembering words or concepts not tied to a specific time or event is called _____ memory.

8. Memory for events that occur during one's lifetime is called _____ memory.

9. _____ memory aids rely on environmental resources such as calendars or notebooks.

10. _____ memory aids rely on mental processes such as mental imagery.

14.3 KNOW THE DETAILS OF COGNITIVE PROCESSES

1. Psychomotor speed increases with age.
   TRUE or FALSE

2. Reaction times slow down with age primarily because it takes older adults longer to decide that they need to respond.
   TRUE or FALSE

3. Working memory has an unlimited capacity.
   TRUE or FALSE

4.   Working memory does not decline with age.

       TRUE or FALSE

5.   Older adults perform equally to younger adults on episodic memory recall tasks.

       TRUE or FALSE

6.   Age differences are greater on recognition memory tests than on recall memory tests.

       TRUE or FALSE

7.   For both younger and older adults, vivid memories experienced after age 30 are reported more often than those occurring between ages 10 and 30.

       TRUE or FALSE

8.   Rote rehearsal is an example of an implicit-internal memory aid.

       TRUE or FALSE

9.   The most frequently used memory interventions are classified as explicit-external according to the E-I-E-I-O framework.

       TRUE or FALSE

10.   Creative output increases steadily throughout adulthood.

       TRUE or FALSE

11.   Wisdom is more dependent on having extensive life experience in a particular area than on age.

       TRUE or FALSE

14.4 MENTAL HEALTH AND INTERVENTION

TO MASTER THE LEARNING OBJECTIVES:

How does depression in older adults differ from depression in younger adults? How is it diagnosed and treated?

*   Describe how depression is diagnosed, particularly in older adults.

*   Describe the biological and psychosocial factors that may cause depression and how the influence of these factors may change with age.

*   Describe the effects and possible side effects of HCAs, MAO inhibitors, and SSRIs when treating depression.

*   Describe how behavior therapy and cognitive therapy can be used to treat depression.

How are anxiety disorders treated in older adults?

- Describe the symptoms associated with anxiety disorders.

- Describe how anxiety disorders are treated, particularly in older adults.

What is Alzheimer's disease? How is it diagnosed and managed? What causes it?

- Describe the symptoms and progression of Alzheimer's disease.

- Describe how Alzheimer's disease is diagnosed.

- Describe the possible causes of Alzheimer's disease.

- Describe what can be done to help Alzheimer's patients.

- Describe how spaced retrieval can be used to improve memory performance in Alzheimer's patients.

14.4 KNOW THE TERMS

Alzheimer's disease

Amyloid

Anxiety disorders

Autosomal dominance

Behavior

Cognitive

Dementia

Dysphoria

Heterocyclic

Incontinence

Internal belief system

MAO inhibitors

Risk genes

Selective serotonin reuptake inhibitors

Spaced retrieval

1. Feeling sad or down, which is the most prominent symptom of depression, is called
   _____.

2. What one tells oneself about why certain events happen, or _____, may be a cause of depression.

3. _____ antidepressants are drugs that are used to treat depression, but they cannot be used by people who take medication to control hypertension or who have certain metabolic disorders.

4. _____ are drugs that are used to treat depression, but they cause dangerous interactions with certain foods such as cheddar cheese, wine, and chicken liver.

5. Antidepressants that have the fewest side effects and work by boosting the level of serotonin are called _____.

6. The basic assumption of _____ therapy is that depressed people experience too few rewards from their environments.

7. _____ therapy is based on the assumption that beliefs about oneself are responsible for depression.

8. _____ are characterized by severe anxiety for no apparent reason, phobias, and obsessive-compulsive disorders.

9. _____ is a family of diseases involving serious impairment of behavioral and cognitive functioning.

10. _____ is characterized by gradual decline in memory, confusion, difficulties in communicating, and changes in personality.

11. The loss of bladder control is called _____.

12. _____ is a protein that is produced in abnormally high levels in Alzheimer's patients.

13. Early onset Alzheimer's disease has _____ inheritance, which means that there is 100% chance of getting the disease when certain genes are present.

14. Later onset Alzheimer's disease may be linked to _____ that increase one's risk of the getting the disease.

15. _____ involves teaching people with Alzheimer's to remember new information by gradually increasing the time between retrieval attempts.

14.4 KNOW THE DETAILS OF MENTAL HEALTH AND INTERVENTION

1. The rate of severe depression increases from young adulthood to old age.
   TRUE or FALSE

2. The most prominent symptom of depression is dysphoria.
   TRUE or FALSE

3. Imbalances in neurotransmitters may be related to depression later in life.
   TRUE or FALSE

4. Depression in late adulthood does not respond well to treatment.
   TRUE or FALSE

5. Behavior therapy for depressed individuals is based on the idea that depressed people experience too few rewards or reinforcements from their environment.
   TRUE or FALSE

6. Anxiety disorders in late adulthood can be effectively treated with medication and psychotherapy.

   TRUE or FALSE

7. The incidence of Alzheimer's disease increases with age.

   TRUE or FALSE

8. The earlier the onset of Alzheimer's disease, the slower the disease usually progresses.

   TRUE or FALSE

9. Definitive diagnosis of Alzheimer's disease is possible only by an autopsy of the brain after death.

   TRUE or FALSE

10. Some forms of Alzheimer's disease appear to be inherited.

    TRUE or FALSE

11. Alzheimer's disease can be permanently reversed with medication.

    TRUE or FALSE

SUMMARY

14.1 WHAT ARE OLDER ADULTS LIKE?

1. **What are the characteristics of older adults in the population?**

   The number of older adults is growing rapidly, especially the number of people over age _____. In the future, older adults will be more _____ diverse and _____ educated than they are now.

2. **How long will most people live? What factors influence this?**

   Average life expectancy has dramatically _____ in this century, which is due mainly to improvements in healthcare. Useful life expectancy refers to the number of years one has that are free from debilitating disease. _____ life expectancy is the longest time any human can live. Genetic factors that can influence longevity include familial longevity and family history of certain diseases. Environmental factors include acquired diseases, toxins, _____, and lifestyle. Women have a longer average life expectancy at birth than men. Ethnic group differences are complex; depending on how old people are, the patterns of differences change.

3.   **What is the distinction between the third and fourth age?**

The third age refers to changes in research that led to cultural, medical, and economic advances for older adults (e.g., longer average longevity, increased quality of life). In contrast, the fourth age reflects the fact that the oldest-old are at the limits of their _____, the rates of diseases such as cancer and dementia increase dramatically, and other aspects of psychological functioning (e.g., memory) also undergo significant and fairly _____ decline.

14.2 PHYSICAL CHANGES AND HEALTH

1.   **What are the major biological theories of aging?**

There are two main groups of theories of biological aging. First, _____ theories argue that aging is the result of a biological or genetic program. The damage or error theory approach includes _____ theories that postulate that aging is caused by body systems simply wearing out, and _____ theories focus on reactions within cells involving telomeres, free radicals, and cross-linking. No single theory is sufficient to explain aging.

2.   **What physiological changes normally occur in later life?**

Three important structural changes in the neuron are _____, dendritic changes, and neuritic plaques. Each of these has important consequences for functioning because they reduce the effectiveness with which neurons transmit information. The risk of cardiovascular disease increases with age. Normal changes in the cardiovascular system include a build-up of _____ deposits in the heart and arteries, a decrease in the amount of blood the heart can pump, a decline in heart _____ tissue, and a stiffening of the arteries. Most of these changes are affected by lifestyle. Stroke and vascular dementia cause cognitive impairment that depend on the location of the brain damage. Strictly age-related changes in the respiratory system are hard to identify due to the lifetime effects of pollution. However, older adults suffer _____ and the risk of chronic obstructive pulmonary disorder increases. Parkinson's disease is caused by insufficient levels of _____, but it can be effectively managed with the drug levodopa. In a minority of cases, dementia develops. Age-related declines in vision and hearing are well documented. The main changes in vision concern the structure of the eye and the retina.

Changes in hearing mainly involve presbycusis; loss of hearing, especially for _____ tones. However, similar changes in taste, smell, touch, pain, and temperature are not as clear.

3. **What are the principal health issues for older adults?**

    Older adults have more _____ disturbances than do younger adults. Nutritionally, most older adults do not need vitamin or mineral supplements. Cancer risk _____ sharply with age. The poorer health status of aging immigrants is largely due to _____ and barriers to care.

14.3 COGNITIVE PROCESSES

1. **What changes occur in information processing as people age? How do these changes relate to everyday life?**

    Older adults' psychomotor speed is _____ than younger adults'. However, the amount of slowing is lessened if older adults have _____ or expertise on the task. Sensory and information-processing changes create problems for older drivers. _____ is another powerful explanatory concept for changes in information processing with age.

2. **What changes occur in memory with age? What can be done to remediate these changes?**

    Older adults typically do worse on tests of _____; age differences are less on recognition tasks. Semantic memory and implicit memory are both largely _____ by aging. People tend to remember best those events that occurred between the ages of _____. Differentiating memory changes associated with aging from memory changes due to disease should be done through comprehensive evaluations. Memory training can be achieved in many ways. A useful framework is to combine _____ memory distinctions with external-internal types of memory aids.

3. **What are creativity and wisdom, and how do they relate to age?**

    Research indicates that creative output peaks in late _____ adulthood or early middle age and declines thereafter, but that the point of peak activity _____ across disciplines and occupations. Wisdom has more to do with being an _____ in living than with age *per se*. Three factors that help people become wise are general personal conditions, specific _____ conditions, and facilitative life contexts.

14.4 MENTAL HEALTH AND INTERVENTION

1. **How does depression in older adults differ from depression in younger adults? How is it diagnosed and treated?**

   The key symptom of depression is persistent sadness. Other psychological and physical symptoms also occur, but the importance of these depends on the _____ of the person reporting them. Major causes of depression include imbalances in _____ and psychosocial issues such as loss and internal belief systems. Depression can be treated with medications such as heterocyclic antidepressants, MAO inhibitors, selective serotonin reuptake inhibitors, and through psychotherapy such as behavioral or _____ therapy.

2. **How are anxiety disorders treated in older adults?**

   Many older adults are afflicted by a variety of anxiety disorders. All of these disorders can be effectively treated with either medications or _____.

3. **What is Alzheimer's disease? How is it diagnosed and managed? What causes it?**

   Dementia is a family of diseases that causes severe _____ impairment. Alzheimer's disease is the most common form of irreversible dementia. Symptoms of Alzheimer's disease include memory impairment, _____ changes, and behavioral changes. These symptoms usually worsen gradually, with rates varying considerably among individuals. Definitive diagnosis of Alzheimer's disease can only be made following a _____. Diagnosis of probable Alzheimer's disease in a living person involves a thorough process through which other potential causes are eliminated. Most researchers are focusing on a probable _____ cause of Alzheimer's disease. Although Alzheimer's disease is incurable, various therapeutic interventions can improve the quality of the patient's life.

TEST YOURSELF

MULTIPLE-CHOICE QUESTIONS

1. The fastest growing age group in the United States is
   a. 20 to 40 years.
   b. 40 to 60 years.
   c. 60 to 85 years.
   d. over 85 years

2. Which of the following ethnic groups has had the smallest increase in the relative number of older adults in recent years?

   a. Native Americans

   b. Asian Americans

   c. Hispanic Americans

   d. European Americans

3. The age at which half of the people born in a particular year will have died is referred to as

   a. longevity.

   b. useful life expectancy.

   c. average life expectancy.

   d. maximum life expectancy.

4. The maximum life expectancy for humans is about

   a. 80 years.

   b. 100 years.

   c. 120 years.

   d. 150 years.

5. Which of the following statements about life expectancy is true?

   a. At birth, the life expectancy of African Americans is longer than that of European Americans.

   b. At 85 years of age, the life expectancy of African Americans is longer than that of European Americans.

   c. At birth, the life expectancy for males is longer than for females.

   d. At 85 years of age, the life expectancy for males is longer than for females.

6. Which of the following descriptions accurately characterizes the fourth age?

   a. Substantial potential for physical and mental fitness, with improvement in each generation

   b. High levels of emotional and personal well-being

   c. Effective strategies to master the gains and losses of later life

   d. High prevalence of dementia

7. _____ adequately explains most aspects of aging.

   a. Wear-and-tear theory

   b. Cellular theory

   c. Programmed cell death theory

   d. No single theory

373

8. The _____ theory of aging compares the aging human body to an old, deteriorating machine.

    a. cellular

    b. cross-linking

    c. wear-and-tear

    d. programmed cell death

9. Theories of aging that focus on free radicals or cross-linking are categorized as _____ theories of aging.

    a. damage or error

    b. neurotransmitter

    c. wear-and-tear

    d. programmed cell death

10. When a neuron's axon fibers become twisted together, they form spiral-shaped masses called

    a. neuritic plaques.

    b. dendritic changes.

    c. neurofibrillary tangles.

    d. neurotransmitters.

11. Damaged and dying neurons sometimes collect around a core of protein, producing

    a. neurofibrillary tangles.

    b. neuritic plaques.

    c. neurotransmitters.

    d. transient ischemic attacks.

12. Which of the following is an example of functional neuroimaging?

    a. X-rays

    b. Computerized tomography (CT scans)

    c. Magnetic resonance imaging (MRI)

    d. Positron emission tomography (PET)

13. _____ is caused by interruptions in the blood flow in the brain.

    a. Cardiac arrest

    b. A stroke

    c. Hypertension

    d. Chronic obstructive pulmonary disease

14. Fred walks very slowly, has difficulty getting in and out of chairs, and has a hand tremor. Fred exhibits many of the symptoms of

    a. cardiovascular disease.

    b. Alzheimer's disease.

    c. Parkinson's disease.

    d. vascular dementia.

15. Older adults _____ than younger adults.

    a. are less bothered by glare

    b. take less time to adapt to changes in illumination

    c. have more difficulty seeing close objects clearly

    d. require less light to see

16. Henry is 75 years of age. He is most likely to have experienced a decline in

    a. smell.

    b. taste.

    c. temperature sensitivity.

    d. pain sensitivity.

17. Researchers agree that _____ is a universal behavioral change in aging.

    a. an increase in wisdom

    b. psychomotor slowing

    c. recognition memory decline

    d. intellectual decline

18. On episodic memory recall tasks,

    a. older adults tend to perform more poorly than younger adults.

    b. younger adults usually perform more poorly than older adults.

    c. younger and older adults usually perform similarly.

    d. age differences are eliminated when cues or reminders are given during recall.

19. In the E-I-E-I-O framework, memory aids that rely on mental processes such as imagery are referred to as

    a. internal.

    b. external.

    c. implicit.

    d. explicit.

20. Margaret always prepares a list before going shopping. Her shopping list is an example of an
    _____ memory aid.

    a. implicit-internal

    b. implicit-external

    c. explicit-external

    d. explicit-internal

21. Wisdom is

    a. the same thing as creativity.

    b. found exclusively in older adults.

    c. associated with life experience.

    d. unrelated to cognitive ability.

22. Which of the following is NOT a factor that would help one to become wise?

    a. General personal conditions

    b. Specific expertise conditions

    c. Facilitative life contexts

    d. Self-absorption

23. Trudy is suffering from dysphoria. In other words, Trudy

    a. has an anxiety disorder.

    b. has Alzheimer's disease.

    c. is unable to speak.

    d. is feeling sad and depressed.

24. Internal belief systems are of particular relevance for views of depression that focus on
    _____ factors.

    a. psychosocial

    b. biochemical

    c. neurological

    d. physiological

25. Lauren was diagnosed as depressed. To treat her depression, she was advised to increase the number of activities in which she was involved, so she joined a community service organization and started going out with friends at least once a week. This kind of treatment is associated with

    a. cognitive therapy.

    b. behavior therapy.

    c. psychoanalysis.

    d. a biochemical approach.

26. Anxiety disorders

    a. are more common in younger adults than in older adults.

    b. can be effectively treated with relaxation therapy.

    c. cannot be successfully treated with psychotherapy.

    d. require larger doses of medication to treat the disorder in late adulthood than in early adulthood.

27. Eighty-year-old Alfred is becoming very forgetful, is frequently confused about where he is, often can't think of words he wants to use, and sometimes fails to recognize members of his family. Alfred is displaying many of the symptoms of

    a. depression.

    b. an anxiety disorder.

    c. Alzheimer's disease.

    d. normal aging.

28. Definitive diagnosis of Alzheimer's disease can only be made based on

    a. blood tests.

    b. neurological tests.

    c. psychological tests.

    d. autopsy of the brain after the person has died.

29. _____ is a protein that is produced in abnormally high levels in Alzheimer's patients, perhaps causing the neurofibrillary tangles and neuritic plaques associated with the disease.

    a. Amyloid

    b. Monoamine oxidase inhibitor

    c. Serotonin

    d. Thioridazine

30. Spaced retrieval is a behavioral intervention that has been used to treat individuals with

    a. depression.

    b. anxiety disorders.

    c. Alzheimer's disease.

    d. presbycusis.

ESSAY QUESTIONS

1. Recently, your friend Mitchell visited an old cemetery while on vacation, and he was shocked at the number of young children, adolescents, and young adult children who died 100 years ago. One family had five children and only one lived to old age. Mitchell knows that people live longer now but had no idea that things had changed that much. What can you tell Mitchell about the reasons for increased average life expectancy?

2. Recently, you and a friend were talking about growing old and aging. Your friend said, "I think that you grow old because everything just wears out. The average television lasts 10 years, the average DVD player lasts five years, and the average person lasts about 75 years." What can you tell your friend about the adequacy of wear-and-tear theories of aging in explaining aging in general?

3. Another friend, who lives with his grandmother, commented on the fact that every time his grandmother walks into a room, she turns on some lights even if the room isn't dark. Your friend thinks that this is strange behavior particularly when his grandmother complains about the glare on bright, sunny days. What can you tell your friend about the age-related changes in the eye and their effects on vision that will explain his grandmother's behavior?

4. In the last few weeks, your grandmother forgot an item at the grocery store, misplaced her keys, and forgot about a dentist appointment. She is worried that these memory failures are a symptom of a more serious problem such as Alzheimer's disease. What can you tell your grandmother about age differences in memory and the incidence of abnormal memory problems that might relieve some of her worries?

5. Recently, a friend asked you for advice and then told you that you were "wise beyond your years." What can you tell your friend about the relation between age and wisdom, characteristics of wise people, and Baltes' three factors that facilitate becoming wise?

6. Lately, your grandfather has been staying in bed most of the day, seems to be apathetic and expressionless, and has lost his appetite. Your parents are worried about him because they think that there may be something physically wrong with him. What can you tell your parents about the signs of depression in older adults?

ANSWERS WITH PAGE REFERENCES

14.1 KNOW THE TERMS

1. demographers (498)
2. population pyramid (498)
3. longevity (501)
4. average (501)
5. useful (502)
6. maximum (502)

14.1 KNOW THE DETAILS OF WHAT ARE OLDER ADULTS LIKE?

1. T, 498	5. T, 500	9. F, 502	13. T, 503
2. T, 498	6. F, 500	10. T, 503	14. F, 504
3. T, 500	7. F, 501	11. F, 503	15. T, 504
4. F, 500	8. F, 501	12. T, 503	

14.2 KNOW THE TERMS

1. Programmed (507)
2. wear-and-tear (507)
3. Free radicals (507)
4. Cross-linking (508)
5. Cellular (508)
6. telomeres (508)
7. neurofibrillary tangles (509)
8. neuritic plaques (509)
9. neurotransmitters (510)
10. Stroke (511)
11. Cerebral vascular accidents (511)
12. Transient ischemic attacks (511)
13. vascular dementia (511)
14. chronic obstructive pulmonary (512)
15. Parkinson's (512)
16. presbyopia (513)
17. presbycusis (514)
18. circadian rhythm (517)

14.2 KNOW THE DETAILS OF PHYSICAL CHANGES AND HEALTH

1. T, 507	6. T, 509	11. F, 511	16. F, 514
2. F, 507	7. T, 510	12. F, 511	17. T, 515
3. T, 508	8. F, 510	13. T, 512	18. T, 516
4. T, 508	9. F, 510	14. T, 512	19. T, 516
5. F, 508	10. T, 510	15. T, 513	20. F, 517

14.3 KNOW THE TERMS

1. psychomotor speed (519)
2. Useful field of vision (520)
3. working memory (522)
4. Explicit (522)
5. Implicit (522)
6. episodic (522)
7. semantic (522)
8. autobiographical (523)
9. External (525)
10. Internal (525)

14.3 KNOW THE DETAILS OF COGNITIVE PROCESSES

1. F, 519	4. F, 522	7. F, 523	10. F, 526
2. T, 519	5. F, 522	8. F, 525	11. T, 528
3. F, 522	6. F, 523	9. T, 526	

14.4 KNOW THE TERMS

1. dysphoria (530)
2. internal belief systems (531)
3. Heterocyclic (531)
4. MAO inhibitors (531)
5. selective serotonin reuptake inhibitors (531)
6. behavior (531)
7. Cognitive (531)
8. Anxiety disorders (532)
9. Dementia (532)
10. Alzheimer's disease (532)
11. incontinence (533)
12. Amyloid (534)
13. autosomal dominance (535)
14. risk genes (535)
15. Spaced retrieval (535)

14.4 KNOW THE DETAILS OF MENTAL HEALTH AND INTERVENTION

1. F, 530	4. F, 531	7. T, 532	10. T, 535
2. T, 530	5. T, 537	8. F, 532	11. F, 535
3. T, 531	6. T, 538	9. T, 533	

SUMMARY

14.1 WHAT ARE OLDER ADULTS LIKE?

1. 85 (500); ethnically (500); better (500)

2. increased (501); Maximum (502); pollutants (502)

3. functional capacity (504); rapid (504)

14.2 PHYSICAL CHANGES AND HEALTH

1. programmed (507); wear-and-tear (507); cellular (508)

2. neurofibrillary tangles (509); fat (511); muscle (511); shortness of breath (511); dopamine (512); high-pitched (513)

3. sleep (516); increases (517); communication problems (518)

14.3 COGNITIVE PROCESSES

1. slower (519); practice (520); Working memory (522)

2. episodic recall (522); unaffected (523); 10 and 30 (523); implicit-explicit (525)

3. young (526); varies (526); expert (528); expertise (528)

14.4 MENTAL HEALTH AND INTERVENTION

1. age (530); neurotransmitters (531); cognitive (531)

2. psychotherapy (532)

3. cognitive (532); personality (533); brain autopsy (533); genetic (535)

TEST YOURSELF

MULTIPLE-CHOICE QUESTIONS

1. d, 500	9. a, 507	17. b, 519	25. b, 531
2. d, 500	10. c, 509	18. a, 522	26. b, 532
3. c, 501	11. b, 510	19. a, 525	27. c, 532
4. c, 502	12. d, 510	20. c, 525	28. d, 533
5. b, 503	13. b, 511	21. c, 528	29. a, 534
6. d, 506	14. c, 512	22. d, 528	30. c, 535
7. d, 507	15. c, 513	23. d, 530	
8. c, 507	16. a, 515	24. a, 530	

ESSAY QUESTIONS

1. The average life expectancy is the age at which half of the people born in a particular year will have died. Average life expectancy has increased dramatically since the early 1900s. Many people used to die during childhood from diseases or died as young adults from infections or complications of pregnancy and childbirth. Life expectancy increased when diseases such as polio and small pox were eliminated and drugs such as antibiotics were developed. One's life expectancy is determined by genetic factors and environmental factors. Even though many aspects of the environment have improved since the turn of the century, diseases, pollution, and lifestyle factors continue to influence life expectancy. Genes also may influence one's risk for certain disease. In other words, average life expectancy is much greater for people now, but there are still many factors that work to decrease one's life expectancy. (501-504)

2. Your friend has just explained the wear-and-tear theory of aging, which suggests that people are like machines, and with age, their bodies don't work as well and eventually wear out. This wear-and-tear view is good at explaining some things such as the deterioration of cartilage in joints after years of use. While this theory of aging may explain some aspects of aging, it does not adequately explain aging in general. (507)

3. With age, less light passes through the eye, which means that older adults need more illumination to see. Older adults also are more sensitive to glare and take longer to adapt to changes in illumination. A young person like your friend may find that there is adequate illumination in a room, but an older adult may need to turn on lights to see. Even though older adults need more light, the increased sensitivity to glare means that they are more likely to be uncomfortable in bright sunlight. In other words, the behavior of your friend's grandmother is not unusual for someone her age. (512-513)

4. It is true that older adults don't do as well as younger adults on tests of episodic recall. These age differences are well documented and large. On recognition tests, age differences are smaller but are not eliminated. On semantic memory and implicit memory tasks, age differences are typically absent. Your grandmother should realize that Alzheimer's is not a normal part of aging and that most older adults are not affected by it. If your grandmother is really concerned, she could be tested to see if her memory shows patterns of decline that are associated with more serious memory problems. If the memory problems are interfering with everyday functioning, then a complete battery of physical, neurological, and neuropsychological tests should be completed. These help identify the nature and extent of the problem and may suggest a course of treatment. (522-525)

5. Contrary to popular opinion, research does not find an association between age and wisdom. Being wise seems to be associated more with extensive life experiences with the type of problem given. Wise people also are more likely to integrate thinking and feeling to come up with a solution to a problem. Baltes identified three factors that facilitate the development of wisdom: 1) general personal condition such as mental ability, 2) specific expertise conditions such as mentoring or practice, and 3) facilitative life contexts such as education or life experiences. So, you can tell your friend that you are wise because you are an intelligent person who knows how to interpret life events who also has many life experiences in the area in which he needed advice. (528)

6. Your grandfather may have a physical problem, but he may also be suffering from depression. In older adults, depression is characterized not only by feelings of dysphoria but also by apathy, expressionless behavior, confining oneself to bed, neglecting oneself, and making derogatory comments about oneself. Loss of appetite, insomnia, and trouble breathing can also be signs of depression. Your grandfather should be evaluated to rule out any physical problems and to consider the possibility of depression. (530)

SOCIAL ASPECTS OF LATER LIFE

15.1 Theories of Psychosocial Aging

15.2 Personality, Social Cognition, and Spirituality

15.3 I Used to Work at...: Living in Retirement

15.4 Friends and Family in Late Life

15.5 Social Issues and Aging

This chapter focuses on the social aspects of later life such as theories of psychosocial aging, personality, retirement, social relationships with family and friends, and the social issues of aging.

15.1 THEORIES OF PSYCHOSOCIAL AGING

TO MASTER THE LEARNING OBJECTIVES:

What is continuity theory?

• Define continuity theory, and describe the difference between internal and external continuity.

What is the competence and environmental press model, and how do docility and proactivity relate to the model?

• Define competence and environmental press, and explain how they are related.

• Define adaptation level, zone of maximum performance potential, and zone of maximum comfort.

- Define proactivity and docility and describe how they are related to competence and environmental press.

15.1 KNOW THE TERMS

Adaptation level	**Environmental press**
Competence	**Maximum performance potential**
Continuity	**Proactivity**
Docility	**Zone of maximum comfort**

1. According to _____ theory, people tend to cope with daily life in later adulthood in the same ways that they coped during earlier periods of life.

2. _____ is the upper limit of a person's functioning in the domains of physical health, sensory-perceptual skills, motor skills, cognitive skills, and ego strength.

3. _____ is the number and types of physical, interpersonal, or social demands that the environment puts on people.

4. _____ is the area where the press level is average for a particular level of competence, and behavior and affect are normal.

5. Press levels that are slightly higher than average tend to improve performance, which is in the zone of _____.

6. Press levels that are slightly below average create the _____, where people are able to live happily without having to worry about environmental demands.

7. When people exert control over their lives and choose new behaviors to meet new needs, they are exhibiting _____.

8. When people have little control over their lives and allow situations to dictate their options, they are exhibiting _____.

15.1 KNOW THE DETAILS OF THEORIES OF PSYCHOSOCIAL AGING

1. According to continuity theory, people cope best with aging if there is as much change as possible in their lives.
   TRUE or FALSE

2. Maintaining internal, but not external, continuity is important for adaptation in later life.
   TRUE or FALSE

3. According to the competence and environmental press model, people tend to cope with daily life in later adulthood by applying familiar strategies based on past experience.
TRUE or FALSE

4. Competence is defined as the upper limit of a person's ability to function in five domains.
TRUE or FALSE

5. The zone of maximum comfort occurs when the environmental press is slightly higher than average for a particular level of competence.
TRUE or FALSE

6. Few demands on a person with high competence tend to result in maladaptive behavior and negative affect.
TRUE or FALSE

7. Proactivity occurs when people allow the situation to dictate the options they have.
TRUE or FALSE

15.2 PERSONALITY, SOCIAL COGNITION, AND SPIRITUALITY

TO MASTER THE LEARNING OBJECTIVES:

What is integrity in late life? How do people achieve it?

- Describe Erikson's crisis of integrity versus despair, and explain how the life review process is related to this crisis.

- Describe the results of research on the relations between the life review process and achieving integrity.

How is well-being defined in adulthood? How do people view themselves differently as they age?

- Define subjective well-being and the factors related to it.

- Describe gender differences in subjective well-being.

- Explain how age-related changes in the amygdala may explain changes in emotional changes in older adults.

What role does spirituality play in late life?

- Describe how religion is used to cope with stress.

- Describe the relationship between spirituality and physical and mental health.

- Explain the three steps involved in using spirituality to cope with problems.

- Describe ethnic differences in the importance of religion and the church.

15.2 KNOW THE TERMS

Integrity versus despair	Spiritual support
Life review	Subjective well-being

1. According to Erikson, the crisis of later life involves _____, the process by which people try to make sense of their lives.

2. The process by which people reflect over the events and experiences they have had over their lives is called _____.

3. The positive evaluation of one's life associated with positive feelings is called _____.

4. _____ includes seeking pastoral care, participation in organized and nonorganized religious activities, and expressing faith in a God who cares for people.

15.2 KNOW THE DETAILS OF PERSONALITY, SOCIAL COGNITION, AND SPIRITUALITY

1. According to Erikson, people begin struggling with the issue of intimacy versus isolation during late adulthood.
   TRUE or FALSE

2. To achieve integrity, a person must come to terms with the choices and events that made his or her life unique.
   TRUE or FALSE

3. Engaging in a life review is associated with achieving integrity.
   TRUE or FALSE

4. Subjective well-being refers to a positive evaluation of one's life associated with positive feelings.

TRUE or FALSE

5. Subjective well-being is related to hardiness, chronic illness, marital status, social network, and stress.

TRUE or FALSE

6. Subjective well-being tends to increase with age.

TRUE or FALSE

7. Age-related changes in how the amygdala functions may play a key role in understanding emotional regulation in older adults.

TRUE or FALSE

8. Older adults use religion more than they use family or friends to help themselves cope.

TRUE or FALSE

9. When under high levels of stress, individuals who rely on spiritual support report better personal well-being than do people who do not rely on spiritual support.

TRUE or FALSE

10. Regular church attendance is a predictor of life satisfaction among African Americans.

TRUE or FALSE

11. Neurological evidence indicates that there may be changes in brain activity associated with spiritual practices that help people cope.

TRUE or FALSE

15.3 I USED TO WORK AT....: LIVING IN RETIREMENT

TO MASTER THE LEARNING OBJECTIVES:

What does being retired mean?

- Explain the differences between "crisp" and "blurred" retirement processes.
- Define *bridge job*.

Why do people retire?

- Describe how health is related to the decision to retire.

- Describe the main factors that influence a woman's decision to retire.

- Describe ethnic differences in the decision to retire.

How satisfied are retired people?

- Describe the factors that are related to a successful adjustment to retirement.

- Explain how retirement is related to health.

How do retirees keep busy?

- Give examples of the activities that cater to retired adults.

- Explain the reasons why retirees volunteer in the community.

- Explain the reasons for high rates of volunteerism by retirees.

15.3 KNOW THE DETAILS OF I USED TO WORK AT…: LIVING IN RETIREMENT

1. Retirement is best defined as a complete withdrawal from the workforce.
   TRUE or FALSE

2. Retirement is a complex process by which people withdraw from full-time participation in an occupation.
   TRUE or FALSE

3. A "blurred" retirement involves making a clean break from employment by stopping work entirely.
   TRUE or FALSE

4. A bridge job is the job one holds between one's exit from the career job and final retirement.
   TRUE or FALSE

5. If their health is good, more people retire by choice than for any other reason.
   TRUE or FALSE

6. Both women and men have a strong influence on a partner's decision to retire.
   TRUE or FALSE

7. Retirement is an important life transition.
   TRUE or FALSE

8. If either the husband or wife in a couple is satisfied with retirement, then the couple is likely to be jointly satisfied.

   TRUE or FALSE

9. When retirement is forced, not voluntary, a decline in physical and mental health is likely to result.

   TRUE or FALSE

10. In cases of voluntary retirement, health begins to decline as soon as people stop working.

    TRUE or FALSE

11. Leisure activities provide retirees with many sources of satisfaction.

    TRUE or FALSE

12. Healthy, active retired adults maintain can maintain community ties by volunteering.

    TRUE or FALSE

15.4 FRIENDS AND FAMILY IN LATE LIFE

TO MASTER THE LEARNING OBJECTIVES:

What role do friends and family play in late life?

- Define social convoy and describe how the size and amount of support from it are related to different generations.

- Describe the importance of online friendships to older adults.

- Describe the key factors that predict sibling closeness.

What are older adults' marriages and same-sex partnerships like?

- Describe marital satisfaction in older couples.

- Describe the characteristics of older married couples.

- Describe the benefits of being married late in life.

- Describe long-term gay and lesbian partnerships and the possible effects of aging.

What is it like to provide basic care for one's partner?

- Explain how spousal caregiving is related to marital satisfaction and the caregiver's emotional state.

- Describe how feelings of competence affect spousal caregivers.

391

How do people cope with widowhood? How do men and women differ?

- Describe who is most likely to be widowed, and describe the typical length of widowhood.

- Describe how widowhood affects other social relationships.

- Describe the similarities and differences in how men and women react to widowhood.

What special issues are involved in being a great-grandparent?

- Describe how great-grandparents differ from grandparents.

- Describe the three important aspects of great-grandparenthood.

15.4 KNOW THE TERMS

Social convoy   **Socioemotional selectivity**

1. The group of people who provides support during good and bad times throughout one's life is called a _____.

2. _____ implies that social contact is motivated by many goals, including information seeking, self-concept, and emotional regulation.

15.4 KNOW THE DETAILS OF FRIENDS AND FAMILY IN LATE LIFE

1. The size of the social convoy gets larger with age.
    TRUE or FALSE

2. Older adults' life satisfaction is more strongly related to the quality of relationships with younger family members than with the quality of relationships with friends.
    TRUE or FALSE

3. Older adults develop fewer new relationships than do younger or middle-aged adults.
    TRUE or FALSE

4. The importance of sibling relationships is typically less in late life than earlier in adulthood.
    TRUE or FALSE

5. Older couples are more likely to report positive behaviors in their spouse than are middle-aged couples.
    TRUE or FALSE

6. Studies of spousal caregivers of persons with Alzheimer's disease show that satisfaction is higher than for healthy couples.
    TRUE or FALSE

7. European-American widowed adults have an increased likelihood of dying themselves for at least 10 years after the death of their spouse.
    TRUE or FALSE

8. Men are more likely than women to experience the death of a spouse.
    TRUE or FALSE

9. Men are usually older than women when they are widowed.
    TRUE or FALSE

10. Older widowers are less likely to form new, close friendships than are widows.
    TRUE or FALSE

11. Great-grandparents are usually less involved with the children than are grandparents.
    TRUE or FALSE

15.5 SOCIAL ISSUES AND AGING

TO MASTER THE LEARNING OBJECTIVES:

Who are frail older adults? How common is frailty?

- Define frail older adults, and describe how the proportion of these older adults changes with increasing age.

- Define activities of daily living and instrumental activities of daily living.

- Describe the prevalence of frailty.

What housing options are there for older adults?

- Describe the different housing options of older adults.

- Explain how a sense of place is related to independent living.

- Describe the resident of assisted living facilities.

- Describe the typical nursing home resident, and explain why these people are more likely to be in nursing homes.

- Describe the characteristics of good nursing homes.

- Describe the Eden Alternative, Green House Project, and Cohousing Initiatives.

How do you know if an older adult is abused or neglected? Which people are most likely to be abused and to be abusers?

- Describe the problems associated with defining elder abuse and neglect.
- Describe the prevalence of elder abuse and neglect.
- Describe the factors that put someone at risk for elder abuse.

What are the key social policy issues affecting older adults?

- Describe how the aging of baby boomers will affect Social Security.
- Describe the various options to save Social Security.
- Describe how the aging of baby boomers will affect Medicare.

15.5 KNOW THE TERMS

Activities of daily living	Household
Assisted living facilities	Instrumental activities of daily living
Frail older adults	Sense of place
Functional health	

1. People over the age of 65 who have physical disabilities, are very ill, and may have some cognitive or psychological disorders are considered _____.

2. Basic self-care tasks that include bathing, eating, toileting, walking, and dressing are called _____.

3. Activities that require intellectual competence and planning such as paying bills, shopping, and taking medications properly are called _____.

4. An individual who lives alone or a group of individuals who live together is called a _____.

5. The ability to perform activities of daily living and instrumental activities of daily living is known as _____.

6. The cognitive and emotional attachment that a person puts on his or her place of residence is known as a _____.

7. _____ provide a supportive living arrangement for people who need help with ADLs or IADLs, but who are not so impaired physically or cognitively that they need 24-hour care.

15.5 KNOW THE DETAILS OF SOCIAL ISSUES AND AGING

1. Frail older adults constitute a majority of the population over 65.

   TRUE or FALSE

2. Bathing and dressing are examples of activities of daily living.

   TRUE or FALSE

3. Instrumental activities of daily living are actions that require some intellectual competence and planning.

   TRUE or FALSE

4. The number of people needing help with activities of daily living decreases with age.

   TRUE or FALSE

5. Most older adults do whatever they can to adapt their homes and activities to accommodate the changes that occur with age.

   TRUE or FALSE

6. Functional health refers to the ability to perform the activities of daily living (ADLs) and instrumental activities of daily living (IADLs).

   TRUE or FALSE

7. Aging in place in one's own home is not very important to older adults.

   TRUE or FALSE

8. Assisted living facilities provide 24-hour care.

   TRUE or FALSE

9. The majority of older adults do not want to live in a nursing home.

   TRUE or FALSE

10. The majority of older adults live in nursing homes.

    TRUE or FALSE

11. The most common form of elder abuse is neglect.

    TRUE or FALSE

12. Telemarketing and Internet fraud against older adults is a growing problem.

    TRUE or FALSE

13. The number of older adults below the federal poverty limit is higher now than it was in the 1950s.

    TRUE or FALSE

14. Social Security was originally designed to provide complete financial support for older adults.

TRUE or FALSE

15. U.S. citizens over 65 are eligible to receive Medicare for their medical insurance.

TRUE or FALSE

SUMMARY

15.1 THEORIES OF PSYCHOSOCIAL AGING

1. **What is continuity theory?**

   Continuity theory is based on the view that people respond to daily life in later adulthood by applying _____ strategies based on past experience to maintain and preserve both internal and external structures.

2. **What is competence-environmental press theory model, and do docility and proactivity relate to the model?**

   According to competence-environmental press theory, people's optimal adaptation occurs when there is a balance between their ability to cope and the level of environmental _____ placed on them. When balance is not achieved, behavior becomes maladaptive. When people choose behaviors, they exert proactive control over their lives. When people allow the situation to dictate their options they demonstrate _____. Several studies indicate that competence-environmental press theory can be applied to a variety of real-world situations.

15.2 PERSONALITY DEVELOPMENT IN LATER LIFE

1. **What is integrity in late life? How can people achieve it?**

   Older adults face the Eriksonian struggle of _____ versus despair, primarily through a life review. Integrity involves _____ one's life for what it is; despair involves _____ about one's past. People who reach integrity become self-affirming and self-accepting, and judge their lives to have been worthwhile and good.

2. **How is well-being defined in adulthood? How do people view themselves differently as they age?**

   Subjective well-being is a positive evaluation of _____ that is associated with positive feelings. In life-span developmental psychology, subjective well-being is usually assessed with measures of life satisfaction, _____, and self-esteem. Neuroscience research shows a developmental connection with brain _____ in the prefrontal cortex and the amygdala.

3. **What role does spirituality play in late life?**

   Older adults use religion and spiritual support more often than any other strategy to help them _____ with problems of life. This is especially true for _____, but all ethnic groups use spiritual-based coping to some degree.

15.3 I USED TO WORK AT...: LIVING IN RETIREMENT

1. **What Does Being Retired Mean?**

   Retirement is a complex _____ by which people withdraw from _____ employment. No single definition is adequate for all ethnic groups; self-definition involves several factors including eligibility for _____.

2. **Why Do People Retire?**

   People generally retire because they _____, although some people are forced to retire or they retire because of serious _____ problems such as cardiovascular disease or cancer. However, there are important _____ and ethnic differences in reasons people retire and how they label themselves after retirement. Most of the research is based on European-American men from traditional marriages.

3. **How satisfied are retired people?**

   Retirement is an important life transition. Most people are _____ with retirement. Most retired people typically maintain their _____, friendship networks, and _____ levels, at least in the years immediately following retirement. For men, personal life priorities are all-important; little is known about women's retirement satisfaction.

4. **How do retirees keep busy?**

   Most retired people stay busy in activities such as volunteer work and helping others. From a life-course perspective, it is important to maintain social integration in retirement. Participation in community organizations and _____ are primary ways of achieving this.

15.4 FRIENDS AND FAMILY IN LATER LIFE

1. **What role do friends and family play in late life?**

   A person's _____ is an important source of satisfaction in late life. Patterns of friendships among older adults are very similar to those of young adults, but older adults are more _____. Sibling relationships are especially important in old age. Because people cannot choose their siblings like they do their friends, these relationships often take more _____ than friendships.

2. **What are older adults' marriages and same-sex partnerships like?**

   Long-term marriages tend to be happy until one partner develops serious _____ problems. Older married couples show a lower potential for _____ and greater potential for pleasure. Long-term gay and lesbian relationships tend to be very _____ in characteristics to long-term heterosexual marriages, but issues pertaining to legal rights are challenging.

3. **What is it like to provide basic care for one's partner?**

   Caring for a spouse puts considerable strain on the relationship. The degree of marital _____ strongly affects how spousal caregivers perceive stress. Although caught off guard initially, most spousal caregivers are able to provide _____ care. Perceptions of _____ among spousal caregivers at the outset of caregiving may be especially important.

4. **How do people cope with widowhood? How do men and women differ?**

   Widowhood is a difficult transition for most people. Feelings of _____ are hard to cope with, especially during the first few months following bereavement. Men generally have problems in social relationships and in _____ tasks; women tend to have more severe _____ problems. Some widowed people remarry, partly to solve loneliness and financial problems.

5. **What special issues are involved in being a great-grandparent?**

   Becoming a great-grandparent is an important source of personal _____ for many older adults. Great-grandparents as a group are more _____ to each other than grandparents are. Three aspects of great-grandparenthood are most important: sense of personal and family renewal; new _____ in life; and a major life milestone.

15.5 SOCIAL ISSUES AND AGING

1. **Who are frail older adults? How common is frailty?**

   The number of frail older adults is growing. Frailty is defined in terms of impairment in activities of daily living (basic _____ skills) and instrumental activities of daily living (actions that require _____ or planning). As many as half of those over age 85 may need assistance with ADLs or IADLs. Supportive environments are useful in optimizing the balance between competence and environmental press.

2. **What housing options are there for older adults?**

   Most older adults prefer to stay in place in their community; home modification offers one option to achieve that. Assisted living facilities offer support for _____ and IADLs while providing a significant degree of independence. Nursing homes provide 24/7 _____ for those who need continual assistance. Newer alternatives include the Eden Alternative, the Green House Project, and cohousing options that focus on providing greater _____ for people to remain in the community.

3. **How do you know whether an older adult is abused or neglected? Which people are most likely to be abused and to be abusers?**

   Abuse and neglect of older adults is an increasing problem. However, abuse and neglect are difficult to define precisely. Several categories are used, including _____, psychological or emotional, sexual, abandonment, _____ exploitation, neglect, and _____. Most perpetrators are _____, usually partners or adult children of the victims. Research indicates that abuse results from a complex interaction of characteristics of the caregiver and care recipient.

4. **What are the key social policy issues affecting older adults?**

   Although, initially designed as an income _____, Social Security has become the primary source of retirement income for most U.S. citizens. The aging of the baby boom generation will place considerable stress on the system's financing. Medicare is the principal health insurance program for adult in the United States over age 65. _____ is a major concern, and there are no easy answers for ensuring the system's future viability.

TEST YOURSELF

MULTIPLE-CHOICE QUESTIONS

1. _____ states that people tend to cope with daily life in later adulthood by applying familiar strategies based on past experience to maintain and preserve both internal and external structures.

   a. The competence and environmental press model

   b. Continuity theory

   c. The zone of maximum comfort

   d. The zone of maximum performance potential

2. Internal continuity concerns one's

   a. physical and social environments.

   b. role relationships.

   c. activities.

   d. personal identity.

3. _____ refers to the number and types of physical, interpersonal, or social demands that environments put on people.

   a. Competence

   b. Environmental press

   c. Adaptation level

   d. Zone of maximum performance

4. When the demands put on individuals by the environment are slightly lower than their competence level, they are in the

   a. adaptation level.

   b. zone of maximum performance potential.

   c. zone of maximum comfort.

   d. environmental press.

5. When people show control over their lives by choosing new behaviors to meet new needs or desires in their lives, they are displaying

   a. docility.

   b. continuity.

   c. environmental press.

   d. proactivity.

6. Proactivity is more likely to occur in highly competent people, whereas _____ is more likely to occur in people with relatively low competence.

    a. docility

    b. continuity

    c. adaptation

    d. integrity

7. Erikson proposed that during late adulthood, the issue of _____ is of central importance.

    a. generativity versus stagnation

    b. intimacy versus isolation

    c. identity versus role confusion

    d. integrity versus despair

8. In order to achieve integrity, older adults engage in

    a. life review.

    b. despair.

    c. a fear of death.

    d. blaming others for their troubles.

9. Which of the following factors is most strongly associated with the achievement of integrity?

    a. Socioeconomic status

    b. Cultural background

    c. Self-acceptance

    d. Self-criticism

10. Subjective well-being tends to be highest in

    a. adolescence.

    b. early adulthood.

    c. middle adulthood.

    d. late adulthood.

11. Older adults rely on _____ more than anything or anyone else to help them cope with problems.

    a. spouses

    b. children

    c. friends

    d. religious faith

12. Using "the faith of the people" is a coping strategy most strongly associated with older adults of what ethnic background?

    a. European

    b. African

    c. Native American

    d. Mexican

13. Who would be best described as having a "crisp" retirement?

    a. Suzanne, who retired from her engineering job when she was 65 and started her own consulting business

    b. John, who worked full-time as a financial consultant until age 70 at which time he began working part-time

    c. Olive, who taught high school math until she was 65 and then retired completely

    d. Steve, who retired from nursing at age 65, didn't work for several years, then began working part-time at a hospice

14. Ken retired from his position as a research scientist but now works in a state park gift shop on weekends. Ken would be best described as having a

    a. crisp retirement.

    b. bridge job.

    c. social convoy.

    d. volunteer position.

15. The majority of workers retire

    a. by choice.

    b. because they turned 65.

    c. because they lost their jobs.

    d. because of health reasons.

16. Older adults' life satisfaction is strongly related to

    a. the number of relationships with younger family members.

    b. the quality of relationships with younger family members.

    c. the number and quality of their friendships.

    d. neither relationships with younger family members nor friendships.

17. Which factor would NOT be positively related to the likelihood of sibling closeness?

    a. Living nearby

    b. Being twins

    c. Being unmarried

    d. Being rivals

18. Older married couples

    a. exhibit selective memory regarding the occurrence of negative events.

    b. usually had higher marital satisfaction when their children were at home.

    c. have increased potential for marital conflict.

    d. show more gender differences in sources of pleasure.

19. Which of the following statements about widowhood is true?

    a. Most widowed older adults manage to cope reasonably well.

    b. Widows usually suffer less financial loss than widowers after the death of their spouses.

    c. Widowers are more likely than widows to form new, close friendships.

    d. Women are usually older than men when they are widowed.

20. Which of the following is NOT true about great-grandparenthood?

    a. It provides a sense of personal and family renewal.

    b. Great-grandchildren provide new diversions in great-grandparents' lives.

    c. Great-grandparents are usually as involved with the great-grandchildren as grandparents are with grandchildren.

    d. Becoming a great-grandparent is usually perceived positively because it is a mark of longevity that most people don't reach.

21. Edna needs help with eating, bathing, and dressing. These tasks are called

    a. instrumental activities of daily living (IADLs).

    b. activities of daily living (ADLs).

    c. social tasks.

    d. cognitive tasks.

22. The percentage of adults over age 80 needing assistance with tasks of daily living is about

    a. 9%.

    b. 29%.

    c. 49%.

    d. 69%.

23. Which of the following living situations provides a supportive living situation for people who need assistance with ADLs or IADLs but who are not so impaired that they need 24-hour care?

    a. Sense of place

    b. Assisted living facility

    c. Nursing home

    d. Independent living

24. _____ are most likely to abuse older adults.

    a. Nursing home caregivers

    b. Family members

    c. Attorneys

    d. Clergy

ESSAY QUESTIONS

1. Your 78-year-old grandmother is relatively healthy and competent, but recently she told the family that she wants to sell the house that she has lived in for 35 years and move into an apartment that has an emergency call system, 24-hour security, and housecleaning services. Everyone in your family is puzzled by this decision. How would you explain your grandmother's situation using the competence-environmental press framework?

2. Your sister told you that she doesn't like to visit your grandmother because she is tired of hearing your grandmother talk about the past and the decisions that she made earlier in life. What can you tell your sister about Erikson's crisis of integrity versus despair and the importance of life review in achieving integrity?

3. Recently you were talking to two friends, one whose grandmother is widowed and the other whose grandfather is widowed. Your friends were discussing whether or not widowhood is harder on men or women. What can you tell your friends about the gender differences in the effects of widowhood?

4. Recently your sister had a baby, which made your grandmother a great-grandmother. Your sister told you that your grandmother seems to be very proud of being a great-grandmother, and your sister is surprised that being a great-grandmother doesn't make your grandmother feel very old. What can you tell your sister about the importance of great-grandparenthood to great-grandparents?

5. One of your friends is looking for a nursing home for his father. He is concerned about finding a good one, but he isn't sure what he should consider when making the decision. What can you tell your friend about some other factors that are important to consider when choosing a nursing home?

ANSWERS WITH PAGE REFERENCES

15.1 KNOW THE TERMS

1. continuity (542)
2. Competence (543)
3. Environmental press (543)
4. Adaptation level (543)

5. maximum performance potential (543)
6. zone of maximum comfort (543)
7. proactivity (544)
8. docility (544)

15.1 KNOW THE DETAILS OF THEORIES OF PSYCHOSOCIAL AGING

1. F, 542
2. F, 543

3. F, 543
4. T, 543

5. F, 543
6. T, 544

7. F, 544

15.2 KNOW THE TERMS

1. integrity versus despair (546)
2. life review (547)

3. subjective well-being (547)
4. Spiritual support (551)

15.2 KNOW THE DETAILS OF PERSONALITY, SOCIAL COGNITION, AND SPIRITUALITY

1. F, 546
2. T, 547
3. T, 547

4. T, 547
5. T, 547
6. T, 548

7. T, 548
8. T, 550
9. T, 551

10. T, 551
11. T, 552

15.3 KNOW THE DETAILS OF I USED TO WORK AT...: LIVING IN RETIREMENT

1. F, 553	4. T, 554	7. T, 555	10. F, 556
2. T, 554	5. T, 554	8. F, 555	11. T, 556
3. F, 554	6. F, 555	9. T, 556	12. T, 556

15.4 KNOW THE TERMS

1. social convoy (558)

2. Socioemotional selectivity (559)

15.4 KNOW THE DETAILS OF FRIENDS AND FAMILY IN LATE LIFE

1. F, 558	4. F, 559	7. T, 562	10. T, 563
2. F, 558	5. T, 560	8. F, 563	11. T, 564
3. T, 559	6. F, 561	9. T, 563	

15.5 KNOW THE TERMS

1. frail older adults (565)

2. activities of daily living (566)

3. instrumental activities of daily living (566)

4. household (568)

5. functional health (568)

6. sense of place (569)

7. Assisted living facilities (569)

15.5 KNOW THE DETAILS OF SOCIAL ISSUES AND AGING

1. F, 565	5. T, 568	9. T, 570	13. F, 573
2. T, 566	6. T, 568	10. F, 570	14. F, 573
3. T, 566	7. F, 569	11. T, 572	15. T, 575
4. F, 566	8. F, 569	12. T, 572	

SUMMARY

15.1 THEORIES OF PSYCHOSOCIAL AGING

1. familiar (542)
2. demands (543); docility (544)

15.2 PERSONALITY DEVELOPMENT IN LATER LIFE

1. integrity (546); accepting (547); bitterness (547)
2. one's life (547); happiness (547); activity (548)
3. cope (550); African Americans (550)

15.3 I USED TO WORK AT...: LIVING IN RETIREMENT

1. process (554); full-time (554); social programs (554)
2. choose to (554); health (554); gender (555)
3. satisfied (555); health (555); activity (555)
4. volunteering (556)

15.4 FRIENDS AND FAMILY IN LATER LIFE

1. social convoy (558); selective (559).; work (559)
2. health (560); marital conflict (560); similar (561)
3. satisfaction (561); adequate (562); competence (562)
4. loneliness (563); household (563); financial (563)
5. satisfaction (564); similar (564); diversions (564)

15.5 SOCIAL ISSUES AND AGING

1. self-care (566); intellectual competence (566)
2. ADLs (569); medical care (569); support (571)
3. physical (571); material or financial (572); self-neglect (572); family members (572)
4. supplement (573); Cost containment (575)

TEST YOURSELF

MULTIPLE-CHOICE QUESTIONS

1. b, 542	8. a, 547	15. a, 554	22. b, 566
2. d, 542	9. c, 547	16. c, 558	23. b, 569
3. b, 543	10. d, 548	17. d, 560	24. b, 572
4. c, 543	11. d, 550	18. a, 560	
5. d, 544	12. d, 551	19. a, 563	
6. a, 544	13. c, 554	20. c, 564	
7. d, 546	14. b, 554	21. b, 566	

ESSAY QUESTIONS

1. According to the competence-environmental press framework, competence is defined as a person's upper-limit of functioning in the domains of physical health, sensory-perceptual skills, motor skills, cognitive skills, and ego strength. Environmental press refers to the number and types of physical, social, and interpersonal demands that the environment puts on a person. Both competence and environmental press change throughout the life-span. The adaptation level is the area where press is average for a particular level of competence. If press is increased slightly, performance tends to improve. This is the zone of maximum performance potential. The zone of maximum comfort occurs when press is decreased slightly, and people are able to live happily without worrying about environmental demands. Even though your grandmother is relatively healthy, she may find that living in a house puts slightly higher than average demands on her, so that she is living in the zone of maximum performance potential. Living in a house has increased her performance because she has cleaned it, changed storm windows, maintained the yard, dealt with security issues, etc. As she sees her physical competence decreasing, she may feel that these demands from the environment are too great. A move to an apartment where she doesn't have to worry about maintenance, housecleaning, and security means that she can live in an environment with fewer demands and greater comfort (zone of maximum comfort). Your grandmother's behavior is a good example of proactive behavior. (543-545)

2. According to Erik Erikson, the crisis of later life is one of integrity versus despair. Older adults who can look back on their lives and feel a sense of satisfaction and contentment have achieved integrity. However, older adults who are bitter about their earlier choices and feel that their lives are meaningless will feel despair. Reviewing one's life, or life review, seems to be important in achieving integrity. In one study, older adults who participated in life review activities showed an increased quality of life. This positive effect was still apparent three months later. Also, older women who accepted the past were less likely to show signs of depression. It appears as if life review is an important step in achieving integrity. (546-547)

3. Both older widows and widowers may become more socially isolated because others may feel uncomfortable around their grief, or friends who are still couples may not include them anymore. Widowers may recover more slowly than widows unless they have strong social support systems. Also, older men are ill-equipped to do many of routine tasks such as laundry, cooking, cleaning, and shopping. Older widowers are also less likely to form new friendships than widows. Some of these effects experienced by widowers may be due to the fact that widowers are generally older than widows when they lose their spouses. Widows usually suffer more financially when they lose their spouses, but they may have more friendships to provide social support. Overall, widowers may have a harder time adjusting to the death of a spouse than do widows. (562-563)

4. In general, great-grandparents are not as involved with children as are grandparents, but they do view the role of great-grandparent as an important role. Three aspects of great-grandparenthood seem particularly important. First, being a great-grandparent provides a sense of personal and family renewal. The many generations make it clear that the family line will continue for many years into the future. Second, great-grandchildren provide new diversions in the great-grandparents' lives. Third, becoming a great-grandparent provides a sense of achievement and longevity that most people view positively. In other words, your grandmother's attitude about being a great-grandparent is not unusual. (563-564)

5.   First, your friend should evaluate the quality of life of the residents of any nursing home he considers. Are the residents well-groomed, does the food taste good, are the rooms pleasant? Second, quality of care should be considered. Does the staff respond quickly to calls or do residents have to wait a long time? Are family members involved in care decisions? Third, is the safety of the nursing home. Are there enough staff? Are the halls free of clutter? In addition to these considerations are things such as outdoor areas, activities, pleasantness of public spaces, etc. Your friend may want to talk to both residents and staff at the nursing homes that he is considering for his father. (569-570)

THE FINAL PASSAGE

This chapter focuses on defining death, ethical issues surrounding death, people's personal feelings about death, dealing with grief, and coping with different types of loss.

16.1 DEFINITIONS AND ETHICAL ISSUES

TO MASTER THE LEARNING OBJECTIVES:

How is death defined?

- Describe the sociocultural definitions of death.

- Explain how culture influences mourning rituals and states of bereavement.

- Describe the different views of death.

What legal and medical criteria are used to determine when death occurs?

- Define clinical death, whole-brain death, and persistent vegetative state.

411

What are the ethical dilemmas surrounding euthanasia?

- Define bioethics, euthanasia, active euthanasia, and passive euthanasia, and explain how they are related to each other.

- Describe the laws in the Netherlands, Oregon, and Washington that deal with physician-assisted suicide.

- Describe the importance of living wills, durable power of attorney, and DNR orders.

16.1 KNOW THE TERMS

Active euthanasia	Living will
Bioethics	Passive euthanasia
Clinical death	Persistent vegetative state
Do not resuscitate (DNR)	Physician-assisted suicide
Durable power of attorney for healthcare	Thanatology
Euthanasia	Whole-brain death

1. The study of death, dying, grief, bereavement, and social attitudes toward these issues is called _____.

2. The lack of respiration and heartbeat is termed _____.

3. The lack of spontaneous movement, respiration, reflexes, and a flat EEG for a specified period of time is called _____.

4. The lack of cortical functioning accompanied by brain-stem activity is called a _____ from which people do not recover.

5. The area of study that examines the interface between human values and technological advances in health and life sciences is called _____.

6. The practice of ending life for merciful reasons is called _____.

7. _____ involves deliberately ending someone's life based on a statement of the person's wishes or a decision made by someone with the legal authority to make such a decision.

8. _____ involves letting someone die by withholding an available treatment.

9. _____ occurs when a physician provides a dying patient with a fatal dose of medication that the patient self-administers.

10. In a _____, a person states his or her wishes about life support and other treatments.

11. In a _____, an individual appoints someone to act as his or her agent for healthcare decisions.

12. A _____ order means that cardiopulmonary resuscitation is not started should one's heart and breathing stop.

16.1 KNOW THE DETAILS OF DEFINITIONS AND ETHICAL ISSUES

1. Mourning rituals and bereavement are very similar across cultures.
   TRUE or FALSE

2. Clinical death is defined as a lack of heartbeat and respiration.
   TRUE or FALSE

3. When a person is declared whole-brain dead, there is no cortical functioning, but there may be some brain-stem activity.
   TRUE or FALSE

4. Euthanasia refers to the practice of ending life for reasons of mercy.
   TRUE or FALSE

5. Allowing someone to die by withholding available treatment is a form of active euthanasia.
   TRUE or FALSE

6. A living will enables people to state their wishes about the use of life support and other treatments in the event they are unconscious and decisions need to be made.
   TRUE or FALSE

7. A durable power of attorney names an individual who has the legal authority to speak for a person if necessary.
   TRUE or FALSE

16.2 THINKING ABOUT DEATH: PERSONAL ASPECTS

TO MASTER THE LEARNING OBJECTIVES:

How do feelings about death change over adulthood?

- Describe young adults' feelings about death.
- Explain how middle-aged people feel about death.
- Describe middle-aged adults' perceptions of time.
- Describe older adults' feelings about death.

How do people deal with their own death?

- Describe Kübler-Ross's five stages of dying: denial, anger, bargaining, depression, and acceptance.
- Describe contextual theories of dying.

What is death anxiety, and how do people show it?

- Define death anxiety and terror management theory, and how they are related.
- Describe age, gender, and cultural differences in death anxiety.
- Describe the ways in which people can cope with death anxiety.

How do people deal with end-of-life issues and create a final scenario?

- Define end-of-life issues and creating a final scenario.

What is hospice?

- Define hospice and palliative care.
- Describe the differences between in-patient hospices and the hospital model of care.
- Explain the seven considerations people should use to determine if hospice care is appropriate for them.

16.2 KNOW THE TERMS

Death anxiety	Hospice
End-of-life issues	Palliative care
Final scenario	Terror management theory

1. People's anxiety or fear of death and dying is called _____.

2. _____ proposes that people engage in certain behaviors to reach a particular psychological state based on their concerns about mortality.

3. Management of the final phase of life, after-death disposition of the body, memorial services, and distribution of assets are known as _____.

4. Making choices about how one wants one's life to end is known as a _____.

5. _____ is an approach to care for dying individuals that emphasizes pain management and death with dignity.

6. _____ is focused on providing relief from pain and the other symptoms of diseases at any point during the disease process.

16.2 KNOW THE DETAILS OF THINKING ABOUT DEATH: PERSONAL ASPECTS

1. During middle adulthood, thinking about time tends to change from thinking about how long you have lived to how long you have left to live.
    TRUE or FALSE

2. Older adults tend to be less anxious about death than any other age group.
    TRUE or FALSE

3. According to Kübler-Ross, people's first reaction to finding out that they are dying is typically depression.
    TRUE or FALSE

4. All terminally ill patients progress through Kübler-Ross's stages in the same order.
    TRUE or FALSE

5. Corr identified bodily needs, psychological security, interpersonal attachments, and spiritual energy and hope as four dimensions of the tasks of dying.
    TRUE or FALSE

6. Older adults tend to have lower death anxiety than younger adults.
    TRUE or FALSE

7. Taking part in an experiential workshop about death can significantly lower death anxiety.
    TRUE or FALSE

8. A final scenario involves making choices known about how one does or does not want one's life to end.
    TRUE or FALSE

9.   The emphasis in a hospice is on quality of life.

      TRUE or FALSE

10. Hospice patients are less mobile, more anxious, and more depressed than hospital patients.

      TRUE or FALSE

16.3 SURVIVING THE LOSS: THE GRIEVING PROCESS

TO MASTER THE LEARNING OBJECTIVES:

How do people experience the grief process?

*   Define bereavement, grief, and mourning.

*   Describe the four activities that need to occur during the grief process.

*   Describe the three misconceptions that people have concerning the grief process.

*   Describe the risk factors that may make bereavement more difficult.

What feelings do grieving people have?

*   Describe the feelings that are typical of normal grief reactions.

*   Define grief work and anniversary reaction.

*   Describe the five concerns that are related to grieving.

*   Describe ethnic differences in grieving.

*   Describe physiological grief reactions.

*   Describe the four-component model for understanding grief.

*   Describe the dual-process model of coping.

What is the difference between normal and complicated or prolonged grief disorder?

*   Define complicated or prolonged grief disorder, separation distress, and traumatic distress.

16.3 KNOW THE TERMS

Anniversary reaction	Grief work
Anticipatory grief	Grief work as rumination
Bereavement	Mourning
Dual process	Prolonged
Four-component	Separation
Grief	Traumatic

1. The state or condition caused by loss through death is known as _____.

2. The sorrow, hurt, anger, guilt, confusion, and other feelings that arise after suffering a loss is known as _____.

3. The ways in which we express our grief is known as _____.

4. When death is anticipated, many of the feelings of grief occur before the death, which might buffer the impact of the loss when it actually comes. This is known as _____.

5. The psychological side of coming to terms with bereavement is called _____.

6. Changes in behavior and feelings of sadness associated with the date of death are known as _____.

7. The _____ model proposes that understanding grief is based on the context of the loss, subjective meaning of the loss, changing representations of the lost relationship over time, and the role of coping and emotional regulation.

8. The _____ hypothesis rejects the necessity of grief work for recovery and views extensive grief processing as a form of rumination that may increase distress.

9. The _____ model of coping with bereavement integrates existing ideas regarding stressors.

10. Grief that continues to interfere indefinitely with one's ability to function is a sign of _____ grief disorder.

11. Symptoms of _____ distress include preoccupation with the deceased to the point where it interferes with everyday functioning.

12. Symptoms of _____ distress include feeling disbelief about the death and mistrust, anger, and detachment from others as a result of the death.

16.3 KNOW THE DETAILS OF SURVIVING THE LOSS: THE GRIEVING PROCESS

1. Bereavement is the sorrow, hurt, anger, guilt, confusion, and other feelings that arise after suffering a loss.
    TRUE or FALSE

2. All people go through the process of grieving in the same way.
    TRUE or FALSE

3. Grief is a process over which we have no control.
    TRUE or FALSE

4. Researchers and therapists suggest that a person needs at least one year following a loss to begin recovery.
    TRUE or FALSE

5. When death is expected, people go through a period of anticipatory grieving that helps buffer the impact of the loss when it does come.
    TRUE or FALSE

6. Women have higher rates of depression than men following bereavement.
    TRUE or FALSE

7. The psychological side of coming to terms with bereavement is referred to as grief work.
    TRUE or FALSE

8. Muller's themes of grief are mourning and bereavement.
    TRUE or FALSE

9. Holidays and the anniversary of the death of a loved one may reintroduce feelings of grief for individuals who suffered a loss years ago.
    TRUE or FALSE

10. According to the four-component model of grieving, dealing with grief is a complex process that can only be understood as a complex outcome that unfolds over time.
    TRUE or FALSE

11. In the dual-process model of coping with bereavement, loss-oriented stressors are those relating to adapting to the survivor's new life situation.
    TRUE or FALSE

12. The distinguishing features between normal and prolonged grief are related to symptoms of separation distress and traumatic distress.
    TRUE or FALSE

16.4 DYING AND BEREAVEMENT EXPERIENCES ACROSS THE LIFE-SPAN

TO MASTER THE LEARNING OBJECTIVES:

What do children understand about death? How should adults help them deal with it?

- Explain the differences in the ways that young children and older children view death.
- Describe how death should be explained to children.

How do adolescents deal with death?

- Describe the effects of bereavement on adolescents.
- Describe how adolescents may react to the death of a sibling, a parent, or a friend.

How do adults deal with death? What are the special issues they face concerning the death of a child or parent?

- Describe the reactions of young adults to death.
- Describe the effects of loss of a partner in young adulthood.
- Describe the effects of the death of a child during young and middle adulthood.
- Describe the effects of the death of a parent during adulthood.

How do older adults face the loss of a child, grandchild, or partner?

- Describe the effects of the death of a child or grandchild on older adults.
- Explain the effects of the death of a partner.
- Describe the sanctification that occurs in some widows.
- Describe the reactions that occur in gay and lesbian couples when the loss of a partner occurs.

16.4 KNOW THE DETAILS OF DYING AND BEREAVEMENT EXPERIENCES ACROSS THE LIFE-SPAN

1. American society tends to distance itself from death.
    TRUE or FALSE

2. Preschool children usually believe that death is temporary.

TRUE or FALSE

3. Children in Piaget's concrete operational stage understand that death is final and permanent.

TRUE or FALSE

4. In early childhood, it's not unusual for children to react to the death of someone close to them by feeling guilt for causing the death.

TRUE or FALSE

5. Using euphemisms such as "Grandma is just sleeping" to explain death to children will help them understand death better.

TRUE or FALSE

6. When teenagers experience the death of someone close to them, they are usually able to make sense of the event.

TRUE or FALSE

7. When adolescents lose a sibling or parent due to death, their friends are often uncomfortable talking to them about it.

TRUE or FALSE

8. Young adults feel strongly that those who die at this point in their lives would be cheated out of their future.

TRUE or FALSE

9. Young adult widows typically continue grieving for 5 to 10 years after the loss.

TRUE or FALSE

10. The loss of a child is one of the worst, if not the worst, type of loss.

TRUE or FALSE

11. There is pressure from society to mourn the loss of one's partner for a period of time and then to "move on."

TRUE or FALSE

12. The number of friends is more important than the quality of the support system in determining how well one adjusts to the loss of a spouse.

TRUE or FALSE

13. Some widows tend to describe their late husbands in idealized ways.

TRUE or FALSE

SUMMARY

16.1 DEFINITIONS AND ETHICAL ISSUES

1. **How is death defined?**

   Death is a very difficult concept to define precisely. Different cultures have different _____ for death. Among the meanings in Western culture are images, statistics, events, states of being, _____, mystery, boundary, thief of meaning, basis for anxiety, and reward or punishment.

2. **What legal and medical criteria are used to determine when death occurs?**

   For many centuries, a _____ definition of death based on the absence of a heartbeat and _____ was used. Currently, _____ brain death is the most widely used definition and is based on several highly specific criteria such as brain _____ and responses to specific stimuli.

3. **What are the ethical dilemmas surrounding euthanasia?**

   Two types of euthanasia are distinguished. Active euthanasia consists of _____ ending someone's life based on the patient's wishes by taking some action, such as turning off a life-support system. Physician-assisted suicide is a controversial issue and form of active euthanasia. Passive euthanasia is ending someone's life by _____ some type of intervention or treatment, such as stopping nutrition. It is essential that people make their wishes known, either through a durable power of attorney or a _____.

16.2 THINKING ABOUT DEATH: PERSONAL ASPECTS

1. **How do feelings about death change over adulthood?**

   Young adults report a lessened sense of _____. Cognitive developmental level is important for understanding how young adults view death. Middle-aged adults begin to confront their own mortality and undergo a change in their sense of time _____ and time until death. Older adults are more _____ of death.

2. **How do people deal with their own death?**

   Kübler-Ross's theory includes five stages: denial, anger, _____, depression, and acceptance. Some people do not progress through all these stages, and some people move through them at different _____. People may be in more than one stage of dying at a time and do not necessarily go through all of them or go through them in order. A

421

contextual theory of dying emphasizes the _____ a dying person must face. Four dimensions of these tasks have been identified: bodily needs, psychological security, _____, and spiritual energy and hope. A contextual theory would be able to incorporate differences in reasons people die and the places people die.

3. **What is death anxiety, and how do people show it?**

   Most people exhibit some degree of anxiety about death, even though it is difficult to define and measure. Individual difference variables include gender, religiosity, age, ethnicity, and _____. Death anxiety may have some benefits. The main ways death anxiety is shown are by _____ death (e.g., refusing to attend funerals) and deliberately challenging it (e.g., engaging in dangerous sports). Several ways to deal with anxiety exist: living life to the fullest, personal reflection, and education. Death education has been shown to be extremely _____.

4. **How do people deal with end-of-life issues and create a final scenario?**

   Managing the final aspects of life, after-death disposition of the body and memorial services, and _____ of assets are important end-of-life issues. Making choices about what people do and do not want done constitutes a _____.

5. **What is hospice?**

   The goal of a hospice is to maintain the _____ and to manage the pain of terminally ill patients. Hospice clients typically have cancer, AIDS, or a progressive neurological disorder. Family members tend to stay involved in the care of hospice clients.

16.3 SURVIVING THE LOSS: THE GRIEVING PROCESS

1. **How do people experience the grief process?**

   Grief is an active process of coping with loss. Four aspects of grieving must be confronted: the _____ of the loss, the emotional turmoil, adjusting to the environment, and _____ with the deceased. When death is expected, survivors may go through _____ grief; unexpected death is usually more difficult for people to handle.

2. **What feelings do grieving people have?**

   Grief is equally intense for expected and unexpected death, but it may begin before the actual death when the patient has a terminal illness. This is known as _____. Normal grief reactions include sorrow, sadness, denial, disbelief, _____, and _____ reactions. In terms of dealing with normal grief, middle-aged adults have the _____ time. Two interpersonal risk factors are lack of _____ and kinship.

3. **What is the difference between normal and prolonged grieving?**

The four-component model proposes that the context of the loss, continuation of subjective meaning associated with the loss, _____ of the lost relationship over time, and the role of coping and emotion-regulation processes describe the grief process. The dual-process model of coping with bereavement focuses on loss-oriented stressors and restoration-oriented stressors. Prolonged grief involves symptoms of separation distress and symptoms of _____. Excessive guilt and _____ are common manifestations of traumatic grief.

16.4 DYING AND BEREAVEMENT EXPERIENCES ACROSS THE LIFE-SPAN

1. **What do children understand about death? How should adults help them deal with it?**

The cognitive and psychosocial developmental levels of children determine their understanding of and ability to cope with death. This is especially evident in the behaviors children use to display their grief. Research indicates that there are few _____ effects of bereavement in childhood.

2. **How do adolescents deal with death?**

Adolescents may have difficulty making sense of death and are often _____ affected by bereavement. Adolescents may be _____ to discuss their feelings of loss, and peers often provide little support.

3. **How do adults deal with death? What are the special issues they face concerning the death of a child or parent?**

Young and middle-aged adults usually have _____ feelings about death. Attachment theory provides a useful framework to understand these feelings. Midlife is a time when people usually deal with the death of their parents and confront their own _____. The death of one's child is especially difficult to cope with. The death of one's parent deprives an adult of many important things, and the feelings accompanying it are often complex.

4. **How do older adults face the loss of a child, grandchild, or partner?**

Older adults are usually _____ anxious about death and deal with it better than any other age group. The death of a grandchild may be very traumatic for older adults. The death of one's partner represents a deep personal loss, especially when the couple had a long and close relationship.

TEST YOURSELF

MULTIPLE-CHOICE QUESTIONS

1. A person who asks, "How many years do I have left?" is viewing death as an(n)

   a. analogy.

   b. thief of meaning.

   c. boundary.

   d. image or object.

2. _____ is now the most widely accepted criteria for determining when death has occurred.

   a. Clinical death

   b. Whole-brain death

   c. A persistent vegetative state

   d. Bioethics

3. After an automobile accident, Lynn was left with brain-stem activity but no cortical functioning. Lynn would be classified as

   a. clinically dead.

   b. brain dead.

   c. in a persistent vegetative state.

   d. euthanized.

4. _____ is defined as allowing a person to die by withholding an available treatment.

   a. A living will

   b. Durable power of attorney

   c. Active euthanasia

   d. Passive euthanasia

5. The case of Terry Schiavo, which involved the withdrawal of forced feeding, was an example of

   a. active euthanasia.

   b. passive euthanasia.

   c. suicide.

   d. a universally accepted act.

6. A shift from thinking about time in terms of how long one has lived to thinking about how long one has left to live usually occurs during
   a. adolescence.
   b. early adulthood.
   c. middle adulthood.
   d. late adulthood.

7. _____ tend to be more accepting and less anxious about death than any other age group.
   a. Adolescents
   b. Young adults
   c. Middle-aged adults
   d. Older adults

8. The initial sequence of Kübler-Ross's stages of dying was
   a. anger, denial, depression, acceptance, bargaining.
   b. acceptance, depression, denial, anger, bargaining.
   c. denial, anger, bargaining, depression, acceptance.
   d. denial, depression, anger, bargaining, acceptance.

9. When Helen's physician informed her that she had an incurable disease and only six months to live, Helen promptly made an appointment at a major medical center for a second opinion and expected a more favorable diagnosis. Helen appears to be in Kübler-Ross's _____ stage of dying.
   a. anger
   b. bargaining
   c. depression
   d. denial

10. Roger is terminally ill. His family is concerned because he seems to be emotionally withdrawing from them, but they are glad that he seems to be at peace with the fact of his imminent death. Ralph is most likely in Kübler-Ross's _____ stage of dying.
    a. acceptance
    b. bargaining
    c. depression
    d. denial

11. In hospices,

    a. the emphasis is on prolonging life.

    b. families are discouraged from visiting.

    c. a goal of medical care is to control pain.

    d. there is no medical care available.

12. The state or condition caused by loss through death is called _____, whereas the ways in which we express our grief are called _____.

    a. mourning; grieving

    b. bereavement; mourning

    c. grieving; mourning

    d. mourning; bereavement

13. Elaine's husband died several weeks ago. In Elaine's grief process, she should

    a. expect to be "back to normal" soon.

    b. expect to make a full recovery in about two years.

    c. expect to begin recovery in a year or two.

    d. expect that she may never be able to move on from her loss.

14. The psychological side of coming to terms with bereavement is called

    a. an anniversary reaction.

    b. grief work.

    c. mourning.

    d. traumatic grief.

15. The theme related to the experience of grief that refers to what people do to deal with their loss, in terms of what helps them, is called

    a. affect.

    b. narrative.

    c. change.

    d. coping.

16. According to the four-component model, grief is based on the context of the loss, continuation of subjective meaning associated with loss, changing representations of the lost relationship over time, and

    a. the role of coping and emotion-regulation processes

    b. the rumination hypothesis

    c. loss-oriented stressors.

    d. restoration-oriented stressors.

17. Loss- and restoration-oriented stressors are part of

    a. the four-component model of grieving.

    b. the dual-process model of coping with bereavement.

    c. traumatic grief reactions.

    d. the anniversary reaction.

18. After Sarah's husband died, she was preoccupied with her late husband to the point that it interfered with her everyday functioning, she continued to feel disbelief about his death, and she became detached from others as a result of the death. Sarah appears to be experiencing

    a. an anniversary reaction.

    b. restoration-oriented stressors.

    c. a normal grief reaction.

    d. a prolonged grief reaction.

19. By about _____ years of age, most children begin to realize that death is permanent, that everyone dies eventually, and that all biological functions stop when a person dies.

    a. 2 to 3

    b. 5 to 7

    c. 9 to 12

    d. 13 to 15

20. When their child is faced with the death of someone close to them, parents should

    a. explain death as being similar to sleeping.

    b. not allow the child to attend the funeral.

    c. keep explanations simple but truthful.

    d. avoid talking about the death.

21. Which one of the following statements regarding death and adolescence is true?

    a. Only a very small minority of adolescents have experienced the loss of a family member or friend.

    b. Grief during adolescence has been linked to depression, chronic illness, and low self-esteem.

    c. Adolescents are usually very willing to discuss their grief.

    d. Adolescents tend to recover from the death of a sibling fairly quickly.

22. When older adults lose a grandchild,

    a. they may try to control and hide their grief behavior to shield their child.

    b. they are unlikely to feel survivor guilt.

    c. they usually have no regrets about their relationship with the deceased grandchild.

    d. they usually experience only slight emotional upset.

23. Which of the following statements concerning spousal bereavement and ratings of the marital relationship is true?

    a. Bereaved widows and widowers rate their marriage more positively than nonbereaved spouses.

    b. Bereaved widows and widowers rate their marriage less positively than nonbereaved spouses.

    c. There are no differences between bereaved and nonbereaved adults in the way they rate their marriages.

    d. The more depressed the bereaved spouse, the less positively the marriage is rated.

ESSAY QUESTIONS

1. Recently a friend of yours said that if he had a terminal illness, he would not like to receive life-prolonging treatments. What can you tell your friend about the legal issues that surround euthanasia?

2. You have a friend whose father was just told that he has cancer of the liver. Your friend was wondering what changes he should anticipate in his father's feelings and behavior. What can you tell your friend about Kübler-Ross's stages of dying?

3. The wife of one of your coworkers, Brandon, died 18 months ago. Brandon seems to be preoccupied with his wife and he has cut off contact with family and friends. Recently, Brandon has not been coming to work. You have heard that he just spends the day lying in bed watching TV and drinking. Everyone at work is beginning to wonder if Brandon's grief is normal. What can you tell everyone about the differences between normal and prolonged grieving?

4. Last month, while you and your sister were crying over the death of a close friend, your three-year-old son came into the room and asked why you were crying. You tried to explain that you were crying because you missed your friend who had died. Your son responded that you shouldn't cry because your friend would come back. Your sister thought that this was an inappropriate remark. What can you tell your sister about young children's conceptions of death?

5.   Recently, your teenage daughter told you that her best friend's dad died, but her friend doesn't want to talk about her feelings. Your daughter is wondering if this is normal. What can you tell your daughter about grief in adolescents?

6.   Your friend Liz's first husband, Jack, died in an accident when she was 23 years old. She is now 38 years old, has remarried, and has a family with her new husband. Jack's mother continues to call Liz every year on the anniversary of Jack's death. Liz grieved greatly when Jack died, but has since moved forward in her life and can't understand why her former mother-in-law doesn't seem to be able to do the same thing. She feels guilty about this but wishes that her former mother-in-law would stop dragging up the past by calling her every year. What can you tell Liz that might help her understand her mother-in-law's feelings compared to her own?

ANSWERS WITH PAGE REFERENCES

16.1 KNOW THE TERMS

1. Thanatology (582)
2. clinical death (584)
3. whole-brain death (584)
4. persistent vegetative state (585)
5. bioethics (585)
6. euthanasia (585)

7. Active euthanasia (585)
8. Passive euthanasia (586)
9. Physician-assisted suicide (587)
10. living will (589)
11. durable power of attorney for healthcare (589)
12. do not resuscitate (589)

16.1 KNOW THE DETAILS OF DEFINITIONS AND ETHICAL ISSUES

1. F, 583	3. F, 584	5. F, 585	7. T, 589
2. T, 584	4. T, 585	6. T, 589	

16.2 KNOW THE TERMS

1. death anxiety (595)
2. Terror management theory (595)
3. end-of-life issues (596)
4. final scenario (597)
5. Hospice (598)
6. Palliative care (598)

16.2 KNOW THE DETAILS OF THINKING ABOUT DEATH: PERSONAL ASPECTS

1. T, 592	4. F, 593	7. T, 596	10. F, 599
2. T, 592	5. T, 594	8. T, 597	
3. F, 593	6. T, 595	9. T, 598	

16.3 KNOW THE TERMS

1. bereavement (601)
2. grief (601)
3. mourning (601)
4. anticipatory grief (602)
5. grief work (603)
6. anniversary reaction (604)
7. four-component (605)
8. grief work as rumination (605)
9. dual-process (606)
10. complicated or prolonged (607)
11. separation (607)
12. traumatic (607)

16.3 KNOW THE DETAILS OF SURVIVING THE LOSS: THE GRIEVING PROCESS

1. F, 601	4. T, 602	7. T, 603	10. T, 605
2. F, 601	5. T, 602	8. F, 603	11. F, 606
3. F, 601	6. T, 603	9. T, 604	12. T, 607

16.4 KNOW THE DETAILS OF DYING AND BEREAVEMENT EXPERIENCES ACROSS THE LIFE-SPAN

1. T, 608	5. F, 609	9. T, 611	13. T, 614
2. T, 608	6. F, 610	10. T, 611	
3. T, 608	7. T, 610	11. T, 613	
4. T, 609	8. T, 611	12. F, 613	

SUMMARY

16.1 DEFINITIONS AND ETHICAL ISSUES

1. meanings (582); analogy (584)
2. clinical (584); respiration (584); whole-brain (584); activity (584)
3. deliberately (585); withholding (586); living will (589)

16.2 THINKING ABOUT DEATH: PERSONAL ASPECTS

1. immortality (591); lived (592); accepting (592)
2. bargaining (593); rates (594); tasks (594); interpersonal attachments (594)
3. occupation (595); avoiding (595); effective (596)
4. distribution (596); final scenario (597).
5. quality of life (598)

16.3 SURVIVING THE LOSS: THE GRIEVING PROCESS

1. reality (601); loosening ties (602); anticipatory (602)
2. guilt (603); anniversary (604)
3. changing representations (605); traumatic distress (607); self-blame (607)

16.4 DYING AND BEREAVEMENT EXPERIENCES ACROSS THE LIFE-SPAN

1. long-lasting (609)
2. severely (610); reluctant (610)
3. intense (611); mortality (611).
4. less (613)

TEST YOURSELF

MULTIPLE-CHOICE QUESTIONS

1. c, 584	7. d, 592	13. d, 602	19. b, 608
2. b, 584	8. c, 593	14. b, 603	20. c, 610
3. c, 585	9. d, 593	15. d, 603	21. b, 610
4. d, 586	10. a, 594	16. a, 605	22. a, 613
5. b, 586	11. c, 598	17. b, 606	23. a, 613
6. c, 592	12. b, 601	18. d, 607	

ESSAY QUESTIONS

1. Deliberately ending someone's life by withholding treatment is known as passive euthanasia. In most jurisdictions in the United States, euthanasia is illegal unless patients have made their wishes known. If your friend feels strongly about this issue, there are two things that he should do to make his wishes known. First, he should have a living will that states his wishes regarding life support and other medical interventions in case he cannot state them when the time comes. Second, he should have a durable power of attorney for healthcare that names someone else to speak for him if he is unconscious or otherwise incapable of speaking for himself. Both of these documents can be used as the basis for a "Do Not Resuscitate" medical order. He should make sure that family members or friends know where these papers are kept so that they can act as his advocate if the need arises in the future. (585-589)

2. According to Elisabeth Kübler-Ross, a Chicago physician, terminally ill people experience five stages as they approach death. The first stage, denial, can be seen when people are told that they are terminally ill. They may ask for second opinions or may want labs to rerun diagnostic tests. Anger occurs during the second stage. This anger may be directed at healthcare workers, family, and friends. People may be angry at the unfairness of an early death. The third stage, bargaining, can be seen when people try to find a way out of dying. People may promise to do a good deed if they don't die. Depression is characteristic of the fourth stage. During this stage people may mourn the losses that have occurred (e.g., loss of a limb, loss of strength) and the losses that will occur in the future. In the final stage, people accept and come to terms with death. People may be in more than one stage at a time, and they may not experience every stage, but this is a guide for your friend to use. (593-594)

3. Both normal and prolonged grieving are characterized by guilt and sadness, but normal and prolonged grieving differ in the degree and intensity of those feelings. Prolonged grief involves both symptoms of separation distress such as preoccupation with the deceased that interferes with daily living, and symptoms of traumatic distress such as feelings of mistrust, anger, and detachment from others. People suffering from prolonged grieving may have increased morbidity, diminished sense of self, increased smoking and substance abuse, and difficulties with family and other social relationships. Brandon may be experiencing prolonged grieving because his grief is interfering with his daily functioning and he seems to be showing separation distress and traumatic distress. Brandon's grief doesn't' seem normal and he should seek professional help. (606-607)

4. Your child's remark was typical of statements made by young children. Most young children do not realize that death is a permanent, irreversible state. Instead, they believe that death is magical and temporary like going away on a magical trip from which one will return. Most children don't understand the permanent, biological nature of death until 5 to 7 years of age. So, your child's attempt to comfort you was not inappropriate but was instead consistent with his conception of death as being temporary. (608)

5. Most adolescents are particularly reluctant to talk about their grief, mainly because they do not want to appear different from their peers. This reluctance to discuss their grief may lead to psychosomatic symptoms like headaches and stomach pains. Even when adolescents want to talk about their grief, their friends often do not want to listen. In general, nonbereaved peers do not want to talk with bereaved students and they may even feel uncomfortable just being around a grieving peer. So, you can tell your daughter that her friend's behavior is not unusual, but she should let her friend know that she is willing to talk to her about her grief. (610)

6. Liz's former mother-in-law experienced what is generally thought to be the most traumatic type of loss there is: the death of a child. Mourning for a child is always intense, and some parents never recover or reconcile themselves to the loss. Even many years after the death of a child, most parents still feel a keen sense of loss and continued difficulty in coming to terms with it. Most parents expect their children to outlive them, so it is very difficult to accept when a child dies first. So, Liz should realize that it's not uncommon for her former mother-in-law to want to remember her lost child, especially on the anniversary of his death, but at the same time, Liz should not feel guilty about not wanting to dwell on the past herself. Maybe now that she has children of her own she can better empathize with her former mother-in-law's feelings. (611-612)

433